Virtual Heaven, redux

by,

Taylor Kole

To Gregory Kompes, a teacher
who helped me with more
than prose alone

Chapter One

Like most of his adult life, Alex Cutler was bent over the latest computer monitor. His black hair swayed against his smooth jawline as he rocked in sync with the keyboard's rhythmic clicks, entering commands for the latest program.

His coworker, Sean, knocked on the open door to Alex's office. With long thinning hair, a happy-stoner personality, and an inflated belly, he reminded Alex of an alcoholic skate-boarder from the early two thousands.

Alex read the prominent white font of Sean's shirt: *99.9% CHIMPANZEE.* He laughed to himself and thought, if Sean ever wanted to be famous, all he had to do was post a daily shot of his eclectic T-shirts. He'd have millions of followers in no time.

And, if Alex ever got rich, he would hire Sean as a wardrobe consultant, or at least bribe him for his T-shirt source. Until then, he would dress similar to today: slim jeans, a snug V-neck under a loose fitting flannel, and shoes with fat laces.

"Today's the big day?" Sean said from the doorway.

Sean's presence always comforted Alex. Even more so today. "I guess we'll see. Come in." He hadn't seen much of Sean the past few days and had worried his decision to leave Vision Tech bothered Sean. Despite never meeting outside of the office, he was Alex's closest friend.

"Stop typing, man. You don't work here anymore," Sean said.

"I do for another…" He looked at the digital wall clock and furrowed his brow. He was supposed to have left the office twenty minutes ago.

"Even being our rock star, I'm surprised you have system access on your final day."

"What's that supposed to mean?"

"It means, when a max-level sorcerer leaves the guild, you don't give him the ability to nuke the kingdom on his way out."

Alex harrumphed and increased his lightning fast typing.

Sean plopped in the chair across from him, set a few stapled pages on the desk, and grabbed the lone knickknack—two metallic stick figures on a seesaw—before leaning back.

"…Aanndd there," Alex said. A few clicks, followed by a series of musical notes, and he shut down his computer for the final time as a Vision Tech employee. Remembering that he was deserting his coworker; his eyes darted from Sean's as he gathered the random flash drives left in his desk and placed them in a box on the floor.

"You can keep that," Alex gestured toward the knickknack. Once tapped, the seesaw rocked for an exorbitant length. Every time someone activated it, he thought of his childhood—of happy times gone forever. "Something to remember me by if I'm never seen again." He spoke in jest, but the words stung as they slipped out. Perhaps his subconscious was sending him warning signals. Beyond "somewhere in the northwestern United States," the exact geographic location for his new employer, the Broumgard Group, remained a mystery. His grasp of Broumgard's business model could be surmised in one line: Broumgard provides solace for the suffering and leisure for the affluent.

"Thanks, bro." Sean inspected the knick-knack. "Now, if you save the world or something, I'll auction this off on eBay for a couple thou." Apparently satisfied, he placed it on the desk and set it in motion. "I've done some digging on the Broumgard Group." His voice grew somber as he nodded to the stapled pages. The change in demeanor ignited fire under Alex's skin, until he noticed Sean's mouth twitch, struggling to suppress a smile. "You're not going to like what I found."

5

Even with the knowledge of some impending gag, Alex hesitated. He had scoured the Internet, yet still knew little. "What did you find?"

Sean placed his fingers on the stapled pages and rotated them for Alex's viewing. "The Devil, my man. You're going to be working for Satan. Like you always have."

Alex chuckled, relieving tension. "Is that so."

His friend motioned for him to look at the document. "I'm serious. It's total mind-fellatio. You're going to be working on a computer, right?" He pointed at the printout. "And computers are here to usher in the Antichrist."

Alex focused on the apparent farewell joke. A simple bar graph constructed the black header, *Youplaywiththedevil.com*, accentuated with orange flames. He appreciated the gesture, but…

"It starts with them breaking down the book of Revelation." Sean scooted to the edge of his chair. "How the first communication between artificial life is a sign of the end times, known as the abomination of desolation. That was accomplished in 1969, when computers from Cal and UCLA spoke to one another. And how their mascots, the bear and the tiger, match the Bible's prophecy."

"That is pretty strange."

"I mean, you're into computers, but I bet you didn't know that the first Macintosh personal computer, the Apple 1, retailed for six hundred sixty-six dollars?"

Alex located that notation and frowned. He wasn't ready to bathe in holy water, but six hundred sixty-six dollars seemed an odd price point, and he thought it would've been a terrible marketing strategy, but Apple thrived. Alex read a recent article claiming that Apple teetered on the brink of becoming the first trillion-dollar company.

Noticing his consternation, Sean hummed a satisfied, "Mmm-hmm."

Despite the strange subject matter, Alex warmed with nostalgia. Part of him wanted to stay at Vision Tech. Keep life simple. He knew this world and would miss Sean's antics, but something else pulled him forward, toward a grander fate.

6

Broumgard's impressive salary held little sway. He had been headhunted before, especially after the success of his program, *Plow Straight*, which had become universally adopted software for code writers. The secrecy of Broumgard meant less. During his freshman year of college, the NSA extended him an offer to apply. He tossed their information packet in the trash. Nothing could induce him to disregard the masses in favor of politicians. No, he chose medium pay in the private sector at a firm close to his vexing mother. But the Broumgard Group offered riches, secrecy, and the promise to work on a project of benevolence—who could resist that?

"That's not all," Sean leaned forward and flattened the stapled edge before tapping halfway down the paper. "If you take the word computer, and assign each letter a numerical value based on its alphabetical positioning, like A equals one, B equals two, C equals three, etc, add up the letters, then multiply that by six, the word computer totals six hundred sixty-six." He paused for effect. "The Devil is rubbing it in our faces, my man."

Concluding that in the Internet era, a person could find data to support any argument, Alex relinquished his interest and said, "Pretty compelling stuff." He then resumed his packing, knowing, that despite the absurdity of computers as the chariot for Satan's son, he would check the math at a later time.

Grabbing the cardboard top to his box, he slowed at the sight of a plastic-protected copy of *Computer World* magazine sitting atop the items. A younger version of him adorned its cover—an eighteen-year-old misfit wanting nothing more than to escape the madness of Roger's Park, his lower-class neighborhood.

The photographer had given him a Vision Tech sweatshirt for the photo shoot. Recalling the ratty condition of the gray, coffee stained V-neck underneath, he grinned.

In the six years since that photograph, Alex's ability to visually encompass an idea, take all of the many possibilities, and transform them into lines of codes, sequences, and commands, had grown exponentially. His hair hung farther down, too. But Alex knew, behind that smiling young man's eyes lay an inner confusion, an uncertainty regarding the point of life.

His job had taken away most of that angst, for a time. His returning bouts of anxiety argued he was regressing. He started having that same old thought: that he busied himself each day to avoid thinking about the final one. Perhaps needing a change was the main reason he accepted Broumgard's offer. Maybe, if their definition of benevolence aligned with his, he would once again find salvation in his work.

Sean stretched his neck to see what held Alex's attention. "I kept a copy of that too." His sincerity caught Alex off-guard. When their eyes met, Sean bobbed his head. "Always knew you were special, bro. For real."

Alex shimmied the box lid on tight, leaned over, and stopped the seesawing stick figures.

"So, what's next?" Sean lifted the knick-knack as he rose.

"Well, I'm all packed and my household items have been picked up. I'm gonna stop by the condo for a final inspection and then that's it for me and Chi-town."

"Wow."

"Wow is right," Alex said, and breathed deeply. The banter had soothed his nerves, but, as he approached the point of no return, the trill crept back in. Hefting the box, he rounded the desk, where Sean stood stiffly, chewing his bottom lip, his face crumpled in concentration.

Unfamiliar with seeing his friend ill at ease, Alex said, "I'll stay in touch."

"That's fine," Sean said with a wave, "But I want to ask a favor." He locked eyes with Alex. "No, I want a pledge from you."

"Sure, man—whatever."

"It might be unethical or whatnot, but I don't care. You have to promise me: if you find out the world's about to end, and you're working on some Noah's-Ark-type deal, you'll get me a ticket."

Over the weeks, Alex had spent a lot of time thinking about Broumgard, and what they would want him to program. He had considered bionic prostitutes, text messaging God, or aliens, or the dead. One of his favorites involved programming robotic dolphins that could spin at tremendous velocities, allowing them to sink multiple enemy vessels. He hadn't considered any doomsday scenarios.

Seeing Sean's expectant face watching his, Alex nodded.

Sean's gaze lingered, possibly gauging Alex's sincerity. Once accepted, Sean cracked a sly smile, they bumped fists, and he left.

Alex's soon-to-be ex-boss, Vision Tech founder Robert Stetson, waited halfway down the center aisle that split the cubicles. He was the only person on the floor who dressed formally. The sight of the dapper man saddened Alex.

Alex's queasiness mounted with each step. Reaching Robert, Alex balanced the box on his hip, and they shook hands.

"We're going to miss you something fierce here at VT," Robert said.

A few employees gathered around to share in the farewell speech.

"We all wish you the best of luck wherever…"

As Robert spoke about Alex having a job here if his new employment didn't work out, and them being family, things Alex appreciated and agreed with, he retreated internally. Before completely cocooning himself, he glimpsed a screensaver behind Robert. The green mask from Jim Carrey's movie *The Mask* floated across a black monitor: dominating eyes, oversize teeth, a demonic bone structure. The periodic animation of the green face bursting into a cackle recalled his earlier conversation about computers being tools of the devil.

A thought chilled Alex enough to make him shiver. If he somehow discovered that computers were harbingers of the end times, would that be enough for him, or anyone else, to forsake the beloved device?

Chapter Two

"Am I coming through, sir?" Victor, Alex's electronic assistant asked him through an earpiece.

"Loud and clear," Alex said.

Two-and-a-half days later, Alex was still adjusting to the helpful voice that came from speakers in his home, and from an earpiece when venturing into Eridu, Broumgard's compact city nestled in the mountains of Montana.

His weekend passed in a hum of shock and amazement. Stepping from a private jet at a private airport in a private city and experiencing ultimate luxury—touring a towering glass hotel packed with amenities, riding a magnetic rail, visiting recreational parks and trails, moving into one of many stone residential buildings more appropriate to Park Avenue—had been like stepping into a futuristic backdrop for the chosen.

Alex's two-story, six-thousand-square-foot condo blew away all notions of fancy, starting with a glass-encased leather trench coat in the foyer. The coat was actually worn in the movie, *The Matrix*. The rest of the place was equally badass.

His lone neighbor on the top floor, Brad Finder, worked as a biomedical engineer. How smart does someone have to be to do that? Learning Brad helped found Broumgard and design their hidden oasis amplified Alex's respect for the man, and this opportunity.

Exiting building A, the easternmost structure of Eridu, he scanned the high-tech compound. It stretched roughly two miles from end to end. At the early hour, the morning sun chased shadows from the long road. A person could be seen here and there, crossing the street to one of many tram towers, riding a bike toward the center of town, or walking in pairs.

His breath plumed from the morning chill, making him thankful he had worn a green flannel over his maroon dragon T-shirt. He saw a pair of young men enter a cylindrical tram tower near him. The tower rose three stories. It's shape, along with a shimmering chrome surface, made it look like a recently buffed spacecraft set to launch.

Feeling motivated by a building eagerness, he ignored the elevator at the tower's base, found a set of zigzagging stairs, and attacked them two at a time.

Near the top, he heard voices and slowed. He didn't want to be the guy who ran to his first day of work, despite its truth.

He stepped onto the concourse and winced that there were already over a dozen people gathered. It must be close to a dozen. He'd wake up earlier tomorrow. The boss—which was soon to be him—had to be the first to arrive, to make sure people knew he didn't think he was better than anyone else.

There was a group of people wearing white button up shirts and black pants, as if waiters; a mismatched crop of slackers he assumed were the programmers; two men and a woman in business attire; a dash of lab coats; a sprinkle of hospital scrubs. His gaze lingered on a woman in hospital scrubs.

She waited with crossed arms between the programmers and medical professionals. The world around her lost focus.

She had shoulder-length black hair, which was currently tied behind her. Her loose fitting scrubs accentuated shapely hips and an ample chest. Her casual morning countenance sparked to life, as if a profound thought surfaced. The sudden change made her large brown eyes more attractive. She turned in Alex's direction and met his stare. Caught peeping, he pressed his lips together, raised his right hand flush, and waved.

She lifted her four fingers from the grip they previously had on her opposite arm, rolled them in a wave, and then looked away.

Alex felt stupid. He was super far from being a ladies man, but psychotic staring was a common sense no-no. Even at twenty-seven years old, he'd never had a true girlfriend, but instincts told him he'd piqued this woman's interest.

A minute later, he spotted the tram. It arrived and stopped in a near silence.

As employees boarded the tram, the woman added evidence to his suspicions by looking at him a final time before entering a car three ahead of his. He considered racing to join her, but quickly found himself alone on the platform, so he dashed into the rear car.

Well-spaced, sanguine-colored booths lined the interior. A television between the windows displayed the morning news, which recounted yet another strain of avian flu, one that scientists feared would soon mutate and decimate the human race. He wanted to turn off the program, but an acrylic screen guard denied access to the controls.

He avoided the news as if *it* were the contagion. If ever a day arrived when he found himself one of the throngs salivating for the national news—which had become mouthpieces for powerful bastards—he would fill a bath and pull the television in with him.

Before he could query Victor about changing the channel, a stainless steel cart grabbed his attention. Trays were filled with fruits, yogurts, and protein bars. Considering the cost of these in Chicago, them appearing free was a nice perk. He selected a bottle of Evian water.

Like George Carlin and a thousand others, Alex found it interesting that one of the first major water companies chose to invert the word naïve, and market a previously free product to consumers. Bottled waters continued success was more quizzical. The highest selling companies openly admitted to using city tap-water, yet we still paid them absurd millions.

Finally, and only in the Land of Oz, a quaint condiment section offered bins of pills representing every color, size, and shape.

Alex peered closer. Cognitex/cognitive function, Glucosamine sulfate/joint health, Kyolic/improved artery efficacy.

"What's up with the pills, Victor?" he asked as he traced his fingers over a pile of fish oil tablets.

"Vitamins and minerals, sir."

Alex grabbed two for brain function and one for intestinal integrity, then said, "When in Rome," before washing them down with water whose name mocked its customers.

Not a screech sounded as the tram glided to its first stop at the second tower. Judging from the employee uniforms, this tram was near the security housing. A half-dozen men in gray and black police-like uniforms entered the cars ahead of his. None joined his cabin, which brought a little relief. Commoners knew to avoid Roman soldiers. It also added to his disappointment. This was his big day. He wanted to acclimate. He wanted to chat with someone, but it was like his maroon dragon T-shirt was an Eridu scarlet *A*.

At the next stop, Hotel La Berce, passengers exited and a few boarded. Alex's mystery woman waved goodbye to someone staying on the tram and sought out the back car before she followed the group inside.

As the doors to Alex's car started to shut, an obese man with greasy hair barged in and past Alex. Almost as round as he was tall, the man wore a white lab coat over a dangerously tight TCU football jersey. The baffling contrast stifled Alex's normally automated greeting.

The man carried a briefcase with both hands, shuffled to one of the booths, and sat. He situated the case on his lap, unclasped the locks, retrieved *Doctor Sleep* by Stephen King, opened it to his bookmarked page, and, while keeping his eyes on his book, said, "You're one of the new guys?"

Alex considered sitting across from him, but instead stepped closer. "I am. My name's Alex."

"I'm Jason." He flipped a page. "You're the one taking over the CSD?"

Comprehensive Software Design. People who worked with computers were always altering their titles, as if the glamour of what they did increased with each new moniker. Programmers referred to themselves as software engineers, network specialists were DevOps engineers, and animators were graphic designers. Presumably, Alex would be heavily involved in programming and overseeing the others. Maybe he should ask to be called a technological maestro?

"Are you a programmer?" Alex asked.

"Software engineer."

"I mean, obviously."

Jason's hand went to his lab coat side pocket and removed a king-size Snickers. With two fingers, a thumb, and deft precision, he opened the wrapper and bit into the chocolate bar.

Alex wondered if this guy knew how tightly his faded TCU jersey fit. It confined his torso like a girdle and had to be obstructing circulation, definitely respiration. Packing even one extra bite into his body might cause the jersey to spontaneously Hulk Hogan.

Flashing colors drew Alex's eyes to the muted television. Breaking news. Some guy shot people. He turned away, disgusted. Evidence abounded that airing these stories perpetuated them—if you start with Columbine, it could be argued the media was responsible for all the mass shootings to follow. Yet in America, ratings trumped morality.

Beyond the screen, the mountain scenery captivated him. A beauty behind man's beast. Even in June, snow still coated the mountaintops. Alex wondered what temperature it was at those elevations. It looked sunny and comfortable? Could he wear shorts as he forged through snow? He'd never been near a mountain, but if the opportunity presented itself, he intended to find out.

Inertia gently pitched him forward as the tram arrived at its final stop, and Alex's destination A beautiful glass building dubbed, the Atrium, sat before an empty parking lot.

Alex waited by the door as the tram crawled to a stop. He adjusted his hair and posture. Today he would learn exactly what Broumgard considered a technology unrivaled by anything on the planet.

He wasn't much of a reader, but bookshelves lined his new home office, and surprisingly, the previous night he'd finished the majority of a fiction novel. Some sci-fi bender about wormhole travel. The possibility that he'd be gate-hopping to other worlds kept him awake past midnight.

"Need my help getting anywhere?" Jason asked from behind him.

Alex could use the guidance, but it was day one at ground zero, and he wanted to take it in.

"No thanks. I've got Victor with me." He tapped his ear as he exited.

"Who? Oh, yeah. Alright." When the doors opened, Jason stepped past Alex and joined the back of the crowd.

Like an oversize hamster tunnel, the tram tower connected to the Atrium with a three-hundred-and-sixty-degree glass skywalk. He waited for the employees to pass through the two sets of double-doors and then, once alone, asked, "Victor, which way?"

"Your destination is Work Area One. Once you enter the Atrium, you will have the option of taking the elevators to your left or the stairs directly in front of you. When you arrive at the main floor, speak with one of the front desk clerks."

Alex pushed through the double-doors and paused. A glass rail encompassed the third floor. He eased to its edge and peered over the main lobby.

Morning sunlight slanted through the glass front and reflected off the emerald-colored floor tiles, illuminating the open entrance. Two vertical chrome letters, *B* and *G*, dominated the west wall. Two arching reception desks waited beneath them with generous halls on either side. A half-dozen security officers busied themselves behind the desks, some watching monitors, a few jotting notations, others conversing. Eridu's security officers resembled NFL linebackers in their prime. Because of poorly-done tattoos and numerous scars, some looked more like weight-pit champions from Riker's Island.

Spotting Broumgard's director of personnel, Tara Capaldi, brought some relief, and memories of their first meeting at Eridu's airport. She wore a tan business skirt that hugged athletic thighs and hips, designer watch and pumps, blond hair streaked with brown and styled in a ponytail. She was the prettiest woman Alex had ever touched, even if it was just a hand shake. Though in her late twenties, something in her hazel eyes seemed aged and cold. The feeling he got when near her repelled any notion of attraction. She was a professional, destined for bigger things. Alex respected her knowledge and organizational skills. Beyond that, he appreciated her ability to detect and then disarm his tension with banter.

She was working behind the closest counter, bent at the waist, observing a monitor with one of the security officers (Victor's idea of front desk clerks). The elevator chimed its arrival behind him. Turning, he saw the final stragglers from the tram boarding, and he hurried to join them.

As the glass elevator descended, he stared at the only familiar face in the crowd. Tara laughed at something a security officer said. Everyone near her turned to glimpse the act.

He placed his ear piece in his flannel pocket before exiting.

Making eye contact with Alex, she beamed, and waved him over.

"Good morning, Mr. Cutler," Tara said as they shook hands. "Is everything going well so far?"

"Yeah. I can't imagine things going any better."

A coy smile. "Don't be so sure about that," she said as she passed him and motioned for him to follow her down one of the two main hallways.

A mammoth security guard watched Alex trailing her. His gaze stayed firm, but non threatening. "Good morning, Mr. Cutler," the guard said.

"Morning," Alex said as he scratched his neck, unsettled that a man of those dimensions knew his name prior to introduction.

"I'll take you to meet your team," Tara said. "We have twenty-six full-time programmers here. Without guidance, they lack the type of synergy you instilled at Vision Tech."

He wasn't sure if he'd instilled anything more than *Plow Straight*. Camaraderie was probably the by-product of the superiority complex they shared at knowing the useful software started with them.

She stopped in front of a door marked "Work Area One" and grabbed the knob. "Are you ready to have your life fulfilled?"

He nodded. Who wasn't ready to have their life fulfilled.

Tara opened the door before he could speak.

Casually dressed people occupied the average-size room. Desks were in rows and given space. The pin-up posters were of comic books and sci-fi movies. A section of the floor was elevated. A dominant desk faced the rest of the room. Alex saw his name on that desk.

A few women dotted the room of predominantly male, middle-aged, computer-geek types. Two men wore VR headsets. By the way their fingers strummed the air, they were interacting with private worlds. He loved the concept of VR. He'd bought all the best gear on day one. Unfortunately, he was one of the many who experience EXTREME motion sickness. Alex's first VR lasted less than five minutes. He became ill afterwards. He had to go home from work, but couldn't drive. He needed three days to fully recover. Stupid him tried one more time, only for one minute, to try and acclimate. He was sick and disoriented the rest of the day. He'd never touched VR again.

A foursome of Asians had their desks pushed together near the far wall. They focused on a small man with bright orange hair who stood atop a chair, engaged in an animated tale in a foreign dialect. Alex felt like this would be a fun place to work.

Alex spotted his rotund tram companion, Jason, in the rear, feet propped on a desk. His back faced the rest of the room as he read his novel and mined Whoppers from a spilled pile.

"The annual hiring day is a big one for us," Tara said. "A day when we open our lives and allow special individuals, like you, to become part of the family.

"Here at Broumgard, we offer a multitude of entertaining events for our clients. I'm sure you've heard about many amenities offered at Hotel La Berce, but I want to introduce you to our real attraction: the Lobby."

Alex peered toward the lobby, wondering if he'd missed something, then back to Tara, who watched him with a conspicuous smile.

"Do you like football, Alex? We play a game each year: security personnel versus programmers."

Football's basic rules eluded Alex. He wasn't sure if a touchdown meant six, seven, or eight points; but as her words settled, he surveyed the room. Most of the men and women were either small, overweight, or brittle.

He recalled the security officers mulling behind the service counters, took in his teammates, and felt the first bite of disappointment. If football was involved along with programmers, this whole hyped event must revolve around a video game. Secretly, he'd been hoping for alien technology or maybe the Noah's Ark thing—God knew the world needed another cleansing.

Video gaming bummed him out. He didn't play video games as much as his peers, and despite having a knack for them, enjoyed them less. He could spend an afternoon behind a controller, but after finishing, he always wondered where the time had gone, and regretted the waste. One hour into his first day and he was thinking he might buck Tara's claim and become the first programmer to quit the Broumgard Group.

Tara raised her voice. "Everyone, quiet please." Tara's voice silenced the rowdy room and brought order. Even the orange-haired man quieted, hopped down, and sat.

"This is Alex Cutler. He will be leading you nomads once he completes orientation. If anyone has any questions before we head over, now is the time."

Alex raised his hand and noticed another man—a thin albino with white hair, reddish eyes and large freckles—doing the same.

Tara sighed. "Does anyone who has worked here more than a few days have any questions?" She stared playfully at Alex until he lowered his arm. "You two can learn names from security tags, so I'll skip the introductions."

The other newb's security tag read "Carl W." The ghost-like man didn't appear old enough to drink alcohol. His full lips and wide nose made him look African. Alex wondered if an African would look this light-skinned? Regardless, Carl's bewildered features comforted Alex, for they exceeded his own.

"Okay, everyone, let's go to the elevators," Tara announced.

As if a school bell had sounded, the chatter resumed and everyone stood. A few employees gathered around Alex.

"What position are you looking to play?" a man named Kole asked. His dimensions matched Alex's. However, in a society that demanded perfection, Kole's quarter of an inch off the forehead, eyes two millimeters larger, and slightly longer nose increased Alex's average seven to Kole's handsome nine.

Alex shrugged. He would play whatever, once he figured out the controls.

"How about this: are you a hot shot or a team player?" Kole said.

"Team player," Alex answered honestly.

"That's good. We have too many hot shots on this team," said Denise, a dark-skinned, five-foot-one, bulldozer of a woman. The plastic beads on the ends of her braids rattled against her shoulders as she moved. The *E* at the end of her nametag traveled around the tag, providing a border, complete with thorns and leaves.

"If you need anything," she placed her hand on Alex's forearm, "anything at all, you come see me." She glided her fingers across his arm as she turned to leave. Near the door, she high-fived another female on her way out.

Kole patted Alex's shoulder. "What's it gonna be then, bud—offense or defense?"

"I haven't played football since I was eight," he said groggily, as he recovered from Denise's come-on, which might be his first. "But I can hold my own at Madden."

The orange-haired Asian jumped on a chair and flexed his arms into various poses. "I hold down the Dee!"

His display earned numerous chuckles, applause, and supportive cheers from the exiting programmers.

"The thing is," Kole said, drawing Alex's attention, "this is no video game. It's full-contact, take-no-prisoners football."

"Well, I hope the guards play touch," Alex said with a dry laugh.

"I play left tackle," a wiry woman in her early twenties said, "so don't try and snake it."

19

A female left tackle that weighed a hundred and thirty pounds? That seemed off to Alex.

No VR. He had made his sickness known to Tara. So, if not a video game, maybe they wore robotic suits and this would be some future ball where gravity didn't matter and propulsion amplified their movements. High-velocity contacts would create jarring sounds as loud as head-on collisions. If so, the technology might be safe enough for everyone present, but Alex would pass. Well, more likely, he would *want* to pass, but suit up and play, the entire time spent in discomfort, wishing he'd had the balls to say no thank you..

The two newbies, Alex and Carl, were the last to enter the hallway. A congestion of more than two-dozen security officers and programmers shuffled as one, all hooting and trash-talking.

"Carl, Alex, you guys stay with the group," Tara said. "They'll get you where you need to go." She made sure they heard her and then knifed toward the front of the crowd.

Most of the security officers wore gray police-like uniforms, while a few wore college jerseys. The two-way heckling frothed—a bass versus tenor showdown.

The programmers' confident demeanor did little to soothe Carl, who maintained a bewildered half-snarl as they moved down the hall. Alex knew they were going to a massive X-Box showdown, or something like that movie *Surrogates*, where you controlled an avatar.

Now that would be awesome.

Alex trailed the man who'd spoke to him earlier. He was six-foot six, with a XXXXL University of Michigan jersey that might as well have been made of spandex, and whose biceps were so thick, they could have stored Alex's thighs. As if sensing Alex's inspection, he turned to face him. His smile appeared normal enough.

The giant pointed at his own nametag to communicate above the ruckus: Dalton.

Alex checked himself for his nametag, found the security tag, intending to lift it, but Dalton waved away his effort, non-verbally saying he knew all about Alex Cutler. Dalton gave two dual thumbs up and faced forward.

Employees gathered around a set of ivory-accented chrome elevators. The more time he spent loitering around the excited combatants, the more his tension abated.

The third time the elevator went up and down, he boarded.

A mix of security jocks and programming nerds filled the car. Alex's anticipation climbed with each centimeter rise in elevation. He found himself wishing months had already passed, and he was integrated into the amiable atmosphere. The conversations inside the elevator carried an air of diplomacy and a pinch of jest.

"Who are you guys starting at quarterback?"

"This year *we* win."

"I'M A BEAST!"

"Seriously, how are you going to stop Jason?"

Jason? thought Alex. If they meant the guy in the skin tight TCU jersey from the tram, they only needed to toss a couple Baby Ruths on the ground. Boom, stopped.

The elevator opened into a spacious, white room. Rows of chairs, delineated with heavy green curtains stretched as far as he could see. A few curtains were pulled shut.

Staff members in lab coats interacted with holographic charts floating two feet in front of them, a pea-size lens was clipped to each of their shoulders. He marveled at the design's simplistic efficiency. The nurses shouted names. Individuals stepped forward, received terse directions, then merged into the rows of chairs. He watched a man enter the fifth row and walk down five stations, to where a nurse waited for him. As the man sat, the nurse guided the army green privacy curtain around them.

"Alex." Tara clutched his arm, her eyes excited. "Are you ready for the greatest experience on the planet?"

"What is it? Are we playing football on a VR screen or something?"

"Alex Cutler!" a worker shouted.

"Something like that. Words can't describe it. Just remember that you will be totally safe." Tara pulled him toward the female worker who'd shouted his name.

"Alex Cutler?" The worker inspected him.

He nodded.

"Two-eighteen."

Alex allowed himself to be led deep into the second row. His mind processed the possibilities, a new type of virtual reality, deep hypnosis, sensory deprivation, toxin-induced hallucinations. All of these had appealed to him, some more than others. He simply wished for some back-story.

On his approach, he spotted Carl nestling into a chair. Two security officers stood businesslike to either side of him. Carl did nothing to hide his anxiety. Before he could notice Alex, who waited to give him a comforting nod, an officer shucked the durable curtain closed.

"Here we are," Tara placed her hand on the back of a chair. "Take a seat, please." The area was eight feet square. A control panel that resembled an electronic lectern rested in the corner. Alex eased into the comfortable, black leather seat. Underneath him, a block-shaped apparatus flickered with lights. Once settled, he detected the slight vibrations of hardware. With hardware present, he could eliminate toxin-induced hallucinations, but not much else.

"Sit back, Alex. Relax," Tara coaxed as she gently assisted him.

The chair reminded him of a top-of-the-line dental seat. Flat and strong at the shoulders, curved to hug his lower back. Alex tingled with his first bite of excitement. The chair inflated near his ankles, the space behind his knees, and near his armpits, effectively reducing the feel of contact all over his body.

Two uniformed guards entered and stood sentry, replacing Alex's excitement with angst.

"It's okay," Tara said. "The officers are here for first-time jitters." She removed a compact plastic case from her pocket and withdrew a small metallic pistol with a glass vial, its fluid splashed about.

Toxin-induced hallucinations were back on!

One look at the pair of beefcakes helped him understand his current options.

"I'm going to give you a mild sedative." She held the device, waiting for his redundant approval. "Trust me."

"I guess I have to, huh?" he said with a half-smile and a bit of spite. This was life in a nutshell. Limitless possibilities around you, but only one actual choice, usually decided by another person.

"It's a very small needle," she said as she reached for his arm.

He closed his eyes and braced for the puncture, but it never came.

Tara was right, a ssmmaall…

His world went black.

Chapter Three

Alex first heard muffled voices in the distance. They continued to clarify until he recognized them as the playful banter of the security officers and programmers. After a few hard blinks, the grogginess left as abruptly as if from a full night's sleep.

He sat on a woven cloth loveseat in an all white room. White as if the entire world had been erased. Carl shared the sofa with him, staring into the distance. His back was stiff, his white hair neared camouflaged, his hands clasped between his legs as if he were awaiting a bus.

A man with a CrossFit body and shaved head sat on another love seat to their left. His physique indicated security officer. Everyone seated wore Broumgard shirts, blue jeans, and low-top sneakers. Fear striked through Alex as he realized they been stripped and re-dressed.

Next to him, the officer's right knee bounced. He smeared his palms across the tops of his thighs, and his head swiveled as if he expected an ambush.

The rest of the employees were gathered in the center of the whiteness. Lacking objects to provide perspective—trees, cars, desks—the distance was difficult to judge. They could be twenty yards, or two hundred yards away from him.

Tara stood in front of the three men, with her hands behind her back. She wore a snug skirt and a light pink business blazer with black piping. Her shirt, unbuttoned to mid-breast, exposed more cleavage then he would have thought her capable of gathering.

"Welcome, gentlemen." She spread her arms as if about to start an open house, then paused, and peered at Carl. "Are you okay, Mr. Wright?"

Carl lifted his head, his red eyes glossy, as if medicated.

"Are you with us?" Tara stepped toward him.

"Umm..." Carl cleared his throat. "Err... I think so."

"What kind of shit is this?" the man with the shaved head barked and stood. "Where the hell did you take me? And what kind of freaky drugs were in that needle?"

"Calm down, Mr. Robertson. You are in the Lobby, our main attraction here at Eridu. If you would please take your seat, I will lay out a brief explanation and then answer any questions you may have."

"I ain't sittin' shit, lady." He horse-kicked the love seat, knocking it a few inches across the indefinable white.

Alex inhaled sharply and looked at Carl, who stared straight ahead.

"I didn't sign up for no freaky shit. Wherever the hell you took me, it was against my will and I want to leave. Now." He stepped closer to her.

The crowd's volume decreased; heads turned toward them.

Alex stared at the employees, expecting one of them to come to Tara's aid? If this muscular man got physical Carl would probably just sit there? Which left Alex. Perhaps Alex could muster the courage to stand, maybe ask the guy to take it easy. That would probably end with Alex getting grabbed in an expert judo move and feeling his arm break. Maybe he would just stay quiet?

"Mr. Robertson, you need to calm down and let me explain."

"Explain my ass." He stepped closer to her and pointed. "I fought for this country. Did shit for you you'll never know—"

In the midst of his rant, Tara casually said, "Employee command, Tara Capaldi. Halt Mr. Robertson, lower volume thirty percent."

The man's voice quieted.

Noticing the change, he hesitated before he continued. "Halt? I don't think so. In fact, I'm outta here." He pivoted to leave, but as his foot extended, it hit an invisible barrier and went back to the ground. He shoved out his arms in a pushing motion. They encountered some sort of wall.

Tara paced around the angry man as he kicked and pushed in all directions, finding himself encased. Meanwhile, she scooted the love seat back to its original position.

"Look, lady, if you—"

"No. You look," Tara snapped. Then to the air, she said, "Manual move, Mr. Robertson." She placed her hands on the invisible cage and effortlessly guided it until it butted against the love seat.

"You can either sit down and take some deep breaths or you can stand here for the next four hours and yell yourself hoarse. Those are your options."

Mr. Robertson tested his new surroundings and, discovering his mobility limited, swallowed, and swiped his palms across his face. With a clearer demeanor he said, "I mean, I just feel I'm entitled to know where I am." He kicked at the invisible barrier one more time, much of his venom dissipated. That last one appeared to be a verification kick. "How is this happening?"

"All I need is your word that you'll relax, have a seat, and let me explain."

Mr. Robertson licked his lips.

"Remove halt of Mr. Robertson." Tara motioned for him to sit.

He slid his hands across his wide thighs as he eased onto the cushion's edge.

Tara allowed a few seconds to pass. The crowd's chatter resumed, and then she spoke. "Monitor, orientation video." On her right side, a rectangle, the size of a playing card, manifested. With one swift movement, it expanded to a seventy-inch monitor and displayed the company logo.

"Adisah Boomul assembled the Broumgard Group," Tara began. "A Rwandan born American considered by many to be the first true hacker. Adisah wrote the first program for ghost bots, commonly known as botnets, inadvertently spawning a class of cyber rebels."

Alex had heard rumors of a godfather of hacking, but he didn't involve himself in hacking. That was a destructive tool, black

26

hatter stuff. Alex liked to build, expand, create. Nevertheless, he knew that botnets were the most popular method for crashing the servers that allowed websites to function. A hacker would send a slew of e-mails or instant messages to normal, unsuspecting citizens. When the recipient opened the e-mail or replied to the instant message, the ghost haunted their system.

To be an effective hacker, a person must be able to take websites offline. To do that, they need thousands of botnets, often tens of thousands of different IP addresses bombarding the URL simultaneously.

A few infamous hackers claimed to have hundreds of thousands of botnets at their disposal, and whispers rumored of an Internet megalodon who controlled millions.

Alex had written his own software to detect botnet activity and learned that hackers tried to capture his IP address five to twenty times per year. When friends asked for copies of his program, they would call minutes after installation and confirm they had unwillingly been hacker slaves.

To Alex, most of the hackers were modern day Robin Hoods. Anonymous, the global hacker group, represented the people and targeted the power hungry, *most* of the time. They were Davids fighting the ever dominant Goliaths. That was why his botnet program not only collected dust, but also had been wiped from his personal computer. *¡Viva la revolucion!*

Tara continued, "After a six-year stint helping the Federal Bureau of Investigation secure their sensitive data, Mr. Boomul moved to his beautiful Lake Tahoe estate, where he began working on his dream child," Tara gestured with her arms, "The Lobby."

"Using his notoriety, Mr. Boomul pooled specialists from varying fields and different parts of the globe. With funding from Roy Guillen, Broumgard's controlling partner, a coalition was created with one purpose: to create a virtual reality simulator capable of transporting a person's consciousness to the limits of the human imagination." She paused. "And today, decades later, you will experience our newest world." The screen next to Tara changed to a

27

football field. Players emptied out of a locker-room tunnel onto a field of green striped with white.

Behind the monitor, off in the distance, the crowd of employees grew restless. The occasional, "Let's go" and even "Hurry up, you dumb bitches," was overheard.

"In this particular world, Big Hitters' Ball, players are assigned positions and given improved physical attributes equal to their counterparts: concentration, execution, and teamwork decide victory." She made a fist in front of her face. "Full contact, heavy hitting football is played here, gentlemen. So be ready for it."

The screen showed a football player in full accouterments. The guy ran to the linebacker position and practiced a series of drills. In one, the linebacker charged at a runner and smashed into him. The collision dislodged the runner's helmet.

Virtual reality or not, Alex could not be involved in a hit like that—giving or receiving. His head would fly off. His spine would snap. He'd crumple into a pile of mush.

"Not to worry," Tara added as the runner got up and trotted in the opposite direction. "In this world, nothing can cause actual injury. The Lobby removes your ailments. It imbues you with confidence; it connects you, on equal terms, with people of all ages and geographies. With each new world, it brings you closer to many of the dreams we all share."

Mr. Robertson's attitude seemed to have improved. He teetered on his seat's edge, looking eager. Finally, he stood, hands raised in surrender. "So right now, I'm in a machine? The only one like it in the world?" He motioned to Alex, Carl, and himself. "And if we go down there with them, we will enter a football stadium?"
Tara waited a beat. "Yes."

"And my knee?" Mr. Robertson lifted his right knee and clasped it with both hands. "My military injury will be totally healed?"

"Yes, all physical ailments are removed as soon as you enter the Lobby. In Big Hitters' Ball, your entire physical makeup will be altered even further."

Mr. Robertson stepped closer to Tara, still holding his hands up in a submissive gesture. "Well," he clapped them together, "that's all I need to hear, Ms. Capaldi." He crept toward the group of people. As he neared Tara he asked, "That's okay, right? I can be done here?"

"Yes, that's fine. Go ahead."

Joining the rest of the employees, he hopped on his right leg as he went, as if testing its durability.

At Mr. Robertson's approach, the crowd broke into applause and catcalls.

Tara turned her attention back to Alex and Carl, "Any questions?" The screen next to her flashed a purple question mark.

Carl's hand rose slowly, as if being inflated with helium. "Where are we, physically, right now?"

"Physically, you are sitting in your access station on the upper level of the Atrium."

"What about... has anyone ever died or gone crazy after entering? Are there other worlds? And how are we connected?"

"Great set of questions, Carl. The answer to the first is no. No one has ever died. I am happy to tell you we have not had so much as a headache reported. Second, creating worlds is a debilitating task. All of your work as programmers will be to that end. Currently, we offer three worlds: Big Hitters' Ball, which we will visit today, Pleasure House 101, and our most interactive world, San Francisco 1968, where clients can spend eight hours each day enjoying the sunshine and atmosphere of the Bay area, as it was in 1968."

Alex considered the implications. The particulars aside, the software to operate complex machines, like an F-22 Raptor fighter jet, required millions of lines of code. What exactly would it take to create and populate a world? Especially one that appeals to the five senses? Even something as trivial as the physics and texture of a blade of grass could devour terabytes of RAM.

"And as to your question of how we connect..." Tara said to Carl. Then to the air she added, "Monitor, run AD-11 intro."

The screen flipped through classroom images: employees in lab coats, posters of the brain, anatomical replicas on countertops.

"Initially, the Broumgard Group's entire staff focused on connectivity. Since our inception, a team of biologists, physiologists, and many others, headed by Dr. Bradley Finder, worked around the clock, postulating and testing a multitude of theories. After forty-two months, the team designed the AD-11, which is commonly referred to as 'the Marker.'"

The shape of the object on the screen reminded Alex of an anvil. He edged forward, his face creased in concentration.

"The Marker is two millimeters in diameter and almost paper thin. Once a client is anesthetized, the Marker is attached to the back of the scalp."

The screen showed a 3-D model of a human head. A transparent hand placed the Marker onto a shaved section on the back of the model's cranium. The Marker rocked a little from side to side, coming to life. Once activated, it stood on six legs. Then a robotic arm extended from its body, cut and lifted flesh, and burrowed into the exposed wound.

When sufficiently embedded, a slight puff of smoke billowed out, as if the Marker had sutured itself inside.

"Once situated, the Marker's feelers deploy and lodge themselves throughout the brain, allowing it to interact with the electrical impulses and chemicals in the mind."

The screen angled the transparent model's head to a profile view. All at once, a dozen mechanical arms extended from the Marker, some drilling all the way to the frontal lobe.

"Don't let this alarm you," Tara said. "These probes are microscopic," she displayed her finger and thumb and squeezed them together in emphasis, "and can be instantly liquefied."

"So we have these in us now?" Alex asked as he searched the back of his scalp, finding nothing out of the ordinary.

"Yes, you do. Again, it is a simple, pain-free, needle-free experience to have the Markers removed."

Alex pondered everything she said. It wouldn't matter to him if this was a toxin-induced hallucination or if some robotic implant lived in his brain. He felt great. Clean. He realized the lightness in his chest was the absence of worry.

Looking over at Carl, who scratched the back of his head, Alex weighed the advantages of visiting a bona fide virtual reality world versus a device being forced into his head. He wanted to be offended and upset, but to him, the trade-off was a no-brainer.

A calming acceptance passed through him as his smile stretched into a grin. "Are there any more surprises?"

"None you'll disapprove of."

"Well," Alex said, "I'm ready to go."

Tara clapped with her hands near her face, "Let's get to it."

He stood and walked toward the other employees.

"Hurry up down there, would ya?" Someone yelled as Alex passed Tara. He kept eye contact with her in case she wanted to add something. Seeing that she didn't, he increased his pace.

The cheers down the hall amplified with his approach.

Behind Alex, Carl asked if he could do the kickoff.

"Sure can," Tara assured him. "Unless you want to wait out here?"

Alex looked back and saw them standing together. "I'll sit with you. We can talk politics. I can explain the Defend Trade Secrets Act to you."

Carl smiled and said, "No thanks." He then jogged next to Alex.

The crowd jeered for them to hurry.

When Tara joined the group, everyone huddled together. Anticipation pulsed through the air. She moved to the front and the chatter stopped. Facing away from them, Tara said, "Big Hitters' Ball, group entry, updated player modifications."

An ephemeral wave shimmered fifteen feet to her right. It continued to delineate until a visible object appeared. It was a tunnel, ten-feet wide, fifteen high, that resembled the dark concrete corridor at Soldier Field stadium. The doorway looked solid, but it wavered, like a high-definition television viewed from beneath still water. Peering around the portal's side, its depth ended two feet back.

A security officer yelled, "Hook 'em Horns!" and ran at the tunnel. His large frame hit the portal, froze in motion, and faded to nothing.

This set off a chain reaction. Everyone tumbled into the tunnel, most yelling and clapping.

"Go Trojans!"

"Raider Nation!"

Another hummed the Florida State Seminoles fight song.

Alex waited near the back. Each cheer amplified his charge. The shouts from all around him juiced an electric current in him until he finally chimed in with terse encouragement. "Let's go team!" He shouted, then jumped in place and ran at the tunnel.

Meeting the entrance seemed to pause time. A tugging sensation, reminiscent of a panic attack, emanated from his core. He felt a clenching in his stomach, a wrenching of his intestines, as if two hands had torn through the flesh and were squeezing his organs to the point of bursting. He tried to move his arms to fight away the pain, but found himself paralyzed.

He opened his mouth to scream, yet at that exact moment, he rocketed forward at light speed.

The pulverizing of his body, followed by the grinding of his entire essence, lasted three to four seconds; leaving him panting and sweating. Clamping his eyes shut, he assessed himself to make sure he was still alive.

He was alive, but felt totally different. This reality forced him to close his eyes and gather himself. His second deep breath alerted him that the new feeling was better. A healthy density, which boosted his confidence, weighted him from head to heel. Eyes open, his field of vision encompassed more, as if he were inches taller. He stood in a professional locker room. There were now rows of doorless mahogany lockers with golden name plates and hooks, stained benches, carpeted floors, and various offices along the outer walls.

His heart thumped in knocks powerful enough to pump torrents of water from a sinking ship. His neck remained proportionate, but a roll of his head revealed its added girth. Without looking, he sensed the enlarged circumference of his thighs and calves.

His teammates stood around him, wearing orange and navy blue football uniforms, augmented by the full pads underneath, and matching cleats and gloves. A few players wore helmets; others held them. A room of athletes, that were previously out-of-shape programmers, bobbed in rhythmic jigs all around him. A palpable energy filled the room, melted into his skin, and coalesced in his chest.

A broad man with orange hair hanging down to his shoulders noticed Alex observing him, and nodded. Alex recognized Song from their first encounter, the Asian who orated from chairs. Except this version of Song had gained a hundred and twenty-five pounds and fifteen inches in height. His face and his bright orange hair were the only two clues that this was the same guy.

The players focused on a coach who yelled about pride and concentration, about never giving up, about keeping a level head.

Through the locker room's concrete exterior, the stadium crowd's collective voices produced a susurration of energy, a cadence willing him to perform in a game he'd never before considered playing.

Like a boxer before a bout, Alex swayed his shoulders to the crowd's hum. A powerful hand clasped his shoulder and turned him. The hand belonged to Jason from the tram, who wore the number twenty—a number assigned to running backs. This Jason stood at the same height and with much the same countenance as the previously rotund one; nothing else remained. Black dreadlocks hung to his shoulders. His face had transformed from a round, greasy pie-eater to that of a square-jawed Marine.

"So, what do you think?" Jason asked, his wide smile revealing a mouthful of diamond encrusted teeth. "You're gonna be fine, my dude." He laughed. "You should see the dumb smile on your face."

Was Alex smiling? Had he arrived that way? After testing his facial muscles, Alex relaxed his perma-grin.

The coach yelled and waved his arms, directing everyone out of the locker room. "Let's go! Come on, men! Let's go, let's go!"

"Dude, let's go have some fun," Jason said as he affixed his helmet, banged on Alex's shoulder pads, and joined the mass exodus.

Alex had difficulty fitting his head into his helmet, but once finished, he fell in line with the group.

"One play at a time!"

"Don't let Stevens get hot!"

"Aaaagggghhhh!"

Alex's first movement unveiled the totality of the virtual reality tune-up. His legs were as thick as fire logs yet light as air, almost pulling themselves forward. He held his hands in front of his helmet as he jogged. Through the opening of his mask he saw two gloved crushers attached to arms etched with veins and subterranean muscle.

Someone next to him asked if he had ever played wide receiver or if he even knew what that meant. The words sounded distant and irrelevant. He was too busy withholding the urge to sprint, leap, lunge, dive, grab, tumble. Had any human ever been as powerful as he was right then?

The steel double-doors crashed open, drawing in thunderous vibrations that rattled every bone and strummed every artery in Alex.

Once through the door, he hooted with all his might and loved that the frenzy of the crowd snuffed out his voice. The open, outdoor stadium allowed the sun's rays to blanket the eighty-thousand screaming fans with warmth. A steady breeze carried the smell of fresh cut grass.

The realism of the game's attendees amazed Alex. He considered the possibility that these people were really here, logged in somewhere, but there were too many for that to be true. As he took in the tumult, he spotted a section of fans wearing jerseys with the number eighty-seven, waving signs with his name on them. He double-checked himself, and sure enough, he wore number eighty-seven. Jogging to the sideline, he wondered if anyone had ever died from elation overdose.

"Everyone take your spot on the bench," the coach said through his helmet. Alex's transformed co-workers obeyed and he followed. Industrial water-spritzing fans oscillated behind the benches, tables of Gatorade in between, chanting cheerleaders beyond.

Three players from his team trotted to midfield and met three of the security players, whose uniforms were similar to the Dallas Cowboys: navy blue and white.

Jason, Song, and Denise (who now wore a flat top and resembled an Olympic sprinter), were the programmers' team captains.

The security officers won the coin toss. After Carl's booming kickoff, the defense took the field.

Fans bellowed their approval at every snap. The spirit of camaraderie between the teams never deviated—as opponents helped each other up and congratulated one another on well-executed plays. The crowd, along with Alex, loved every minute of it.

The security team drove the ball from the twenty, past the fifty, and punted. Then the coach's voice returned inside his helmet. "Okay, offense. Let's get out there."

Alex watched the offensive half of his team run onto the field. He had never been so eager to see a game played.

"Alex, that's you bud," Denise's voice came through his helmet.

Yeah, I guess that is, he thought as he rose and jogged to join them. The crowd's thunderous bawl refreshed his anticipation. He stepped into the team's huddle.

"Alex?"

"Can you hear me?" Alex asked.

"Sure can," Denise replied. "We want to open with a sneak play. The last thing they'll expect is us getting your sweet buns involved right away. You run straight. Keep your eyes on the distance marker to your right. At twenty-five yards down the field, angle toward the center and look for the ball. If things go as planned, I'll put it right in your hands."

He'd played catch, but he'd never run a route and been targeted for a reception.

Starting in elementary school, he always landed in the bottom three chosen for contact sports. Kids tended to think his silent nature meant he was stupid, but it actually stemmed from intense consideration and deep interest.

Clenching his fist, he watched as his forearm muscles bulged and reshaped the flesh. Lifting himself onto his toes, he felt a power and dexterity he'd only fantasized about.

"Yeah, I'm ready."

"That's my boy," Kole encouraged.

"Give 'em hell," chimed another.

The huddle dispersed with a ritualistic, "Break!" and a simultaneous clap.

A green circle of light showed Alex where to line up. He jogged to it and checked his fan section. Finding them glued to him, he imparted a salute. They jumped about hysterically, waving their signs of support.

The green circle disappeared while he stood inside of it. He focused his mind and assumed what he hoped was a proper stance: elbows clutched to his sides, hands at right angles, knees bent, body tilted forward, supported by the balls of his feet.

His defender lined up five yards in front of him. The man talked trash, but Alex blotted out the words. He focused on the yard markers and visualized his route.

"Set. Hut, hut!"

Alex exploded out of his stance.

Utilizing his new body's strength, he blew past his defender. The G-force of his strides quaked his cheeks. Wind whistled past the helmet's ear holes. He heard the muffled contact of his cleats on the ground, felt the propulsion of his modified form.

Only one man remained in front of him as he slanted. Two more steps and he would turn and search for the ball.

His defensive counterpart seemed to intuit what approached; the player ran toward Alex at the perfect time to intercept.

Worry wormed into his mind. What if this plan was a setup to hurt the new guy? A conspiratorial hazing where they would snap his legs or shatter his ribs, and then heckle him about it not being real?

He thrust the speculation aside, focusing on what he knew: his teammates had placed trust in him. Looking over his shoulder, he found the ball in flight.

Alex's calculations were inconclusive as to what would connect first—the ball to his hands or the defender's body to one of his kneecaps.

The rotating pigskin glided within reach, and he stretched out his arms. Every man, woman, and child in the stadium stood. The volume muffled. Time slowed. Only him and that chunk of spinning leather remained. It connected against his hands with an audible thump. His strong fingers secured it like a fly dive-bombing a sticky-strip.

Instead of the roar he expected, the stadium fell silent.

Remembering the diving defender, the fans presumably held their breath in anticipation of an impending collision.

On a subconscious level, Alex pictured his opponent in flight, aimed at his knees. Using that blueprint, he hurdled the air. His drag foot's toes scraped over the diving defender's helmet. His opponent's hand connected with his thigh and tried to wrestle him down, but Alex's momentum powered him through.

Alex extended his arm out and achieved balance. He hopped twice on one foot, regained his form, and ran like Usain Bolt.

The crowd erupted.

After Alex crossed the goal line, half of his teammates met him in the end zone to celebrate the perfectly executed play.

His eyes bloated as if pumped with air; his stretching smile accentuated the taste of the rubber mouth guard. He hadn't been this full of wonder since he ran his first software program.

This was magic, pure and simple.

Leaving the field, he pointed to his fans, causing some to stomp their feet and dance as if acknowledged by Elvis. Others chanted his name. As he looked away, he jerked his attention back—had a woman just lifted her shirt?

Every player on his team smacked his shoulder pads as he returned to his side of the field. And he received one solid smack on the ass from the masculine version of Denise.

In the spirit of the game, some opposing players came over to compliment his play. Mr. Robertson, whose build had actually slimmed to fit his position, stopped Alex, demanded a high-five before returning across the field.

Alex threw down his helmet, snatched a cup of Gatorade, and gulped it as he sat on the grass, trying to slow his breathing.

Those kids on the playground would have given entire Pokémon collections to pick this uber Alex, first.

The rest of the game proceeded with similar vigor. The programmers won for the second year in a row, the final scoreboard: 27-21. Jason Johnson's moves and vision, Denise's play calling, and Song's defensive tenacity and leadership were the dominant factors. Those, and the miraculous hurdle on the first play that gave their team the lead.

After the contest, broadcasters made announcements, fans exited the stadium, and players from both teams socialized midfield. The brutish, Amazonian version of Denise plopped next to Alex.

His head turned. "Am I dreaming?"

"Nah, this is way better than any dream—it's a touch better than real life."

Alex inhaled deeply. *More than a touch better.* Virtual reality had progressed for decades, but most in the field had discarded full submersion as a fantasy. He felt unworthy to work for a company that offered... this.

Denise squeezed his knee. "We're all logged into the Lobby for a three-and-a-half-hour cycle." She pointed to the high-definition scoreboard.

Alex saw the normal markers: home, visitor, timeouts, etcetera. In the bottom right corner, a timer counted down: 3:09, 3:08, 3:07.

"Great catch out there today," Denise said.

Alex flushed. "Thanks."

"I was surprised when you didn't get creamed." She play-punched his arm as he chuckled.

"That makes two of us," Alex said. He spotted Jason Johnson jogging over to a couple in their late fifties among the crowd. He hugged them, handed the man a football. They all smiled. The woman kept her hand on Jason's back as he chatted with the man.

"Once you complete your training," Denise said, "you'll be able to check out—"

"What's he doing over there?" Alex asked as he nodded toward Jason. "I've been waiting to tell him what a good game he played. He helped make football fun for me."

Denise shaded her eyes, lowered her voice, and in a tone sprinkled with revulsion said, "Weird stuff. That's what he's doing. Those are replicas of his parents. He snuck them into the code." She tsked and shook her head. "White people are crazy."

Jason's computer-generated father smiled, slapped his son's shoulder pad.

"They both died when he was sixteen. Car accident," Denise said. "Apparently, he was a star running back in high school. Top recruit in Texas. You can see that when he plays." She leaned in and lowered her volume even further. "To be honest with you, I think what he's doing is sick."

Alex stared into her butch face and frowned. She obviously had not tasted the bile of losing a loved one. Alex had ingested bowls of pain, full servings of mourning and despair, before, during, and after his freshman year in high school. His older brother Simon, a fit, handsome and kind twenty-year-old had been diagnosed with breast cancer. Prior to that, Alex hadn't even known it affected men—or that it killed them. Simon's death, less than a year later, taught Alex that the Grim Reaper kicked in doors indiscriminately. No rhyme to life. No reason for it all. No plans for each and every one of us.

Looking back at Jason, who wrapped an arm around the older woman's waist, Alex swallowed. He would give anything to hug his brother one more time.

The mirth on Jason's face shone honestly, so unmistakable it compared to the love of a woman holding her newborn moments after giving birth. If Denise thought that was sick, he worried that she lacked a fundamental understanding of happiness.

"Thirty seconds," a booming voice announced over the stadium speakers.

Denise placed her hand on Alex's forearm, drawing his attention. "Brace yourself for that horrible pain. A few seconds later, you'll wake up in the Atrium." She released him and lay on her back.

"Just grit your teeth."

Alex opened his mouth to reply, but it had gone drier than the inside of a funeral urn. Then came the tearing of his lungs, the scorching of his vital organs, and the grinding of his bones, followed by being crushed to ash and sucked through a straw.

Chapter Four

The elation of Alex's first visit to the Lobby survived the night and upon waking, he was filled with an intense desire to get back inside.

He'd never been a morning person, but if this was how he felt—thankful that the night had ended so the day in this new world could begin—he understood how some people woke pre-dawn, dressed, and headed out the door for a five-mile jog.

Job orientation was on Alex's itinerary, and he was pumped.

Alex met Carl at the tram, and together, they reported to an office at the Atrium's north end.

Alex was surprised to find his neighbor, Brad, sitting behind a desk, reading the *Wall Street Journal.* Brad was short and thick, like a collegiate wrestler. Bald, but handsome. He had a piece of jerky hanging out of his mouth.

"Welcome to orientation, gentlemen. My name is Brad Finder. Hey, Alex," To Carl, he added, "Alex is my neighbor." He folded the paper and placed it on the desk. "Please sit." He motioned to two chairs opposite him. Opened laptops were positioned on their side of the desk.

Alex and Carl did as instructed.

During his hours of pacing the previous night, Alex wrote questions to ask at orientation; each carried additional subquestions. But after combing over the list while on the tram ride, he narrowed them down to two: When could he return to the Lobby, and, when could he review the Lobby's code?

"Today," Brad said, "I'm going to give you a little background about Eridu and then let you loose on your computers." He paused as if a thought struck him. "But really, I don't get the computer thing. You type, type, type, and stare at a screen, yet some of you guys get seriously amped about that."

For Alex, the reason was simple. In code, when you instructed a command to go to line forty-seven, it obeyed. If it didn't, you searched the code, located the error, and returned it to a sensible order. Nice and predictable. Unlike the real world. The real world gave you a new friend with a hidden agenda, a mate with a closed heart, a job that rewarded being subversive.

Real life gave your older brother—a young man as strong as oak—breast cancer, and whittled him down until you're sitting at his bedside during his post-chemo nap, wailing.

Code made sense and allowed Alex to create limitless opportunity. Reality involved pain and chaos, with death the only possible end.

"You don't know, huh?" Brad said. "Anyway, over the next week or so, you'll learn the history of this company, our security procedures, basic information about the facility, and about the Lobby itself."

Just hearing the name caused a physical reaction in Alex. He raised his hand.

"Yes, Alex?"

"When do we get to go back inside the Lobby?"

"Well," Brad said, "believe it or not, I knew you'd ask that. The answer, unfortunately, is a bit complicated. Being in management, you'll earn your credits faster than Carl here. Broumgard also allows cleared employees to purchase Lobby time at a discounted rate, and the majority of us spend every available dollar on vacations."

Carl eked his hand up to his shoulder.

Brad acknowledged him.

"What happens if someone is in there, and the power goes out?"

"Great question, Carl. It's never been empirically tested, mind you, but in all likelihood, you'd rush back into your body. Broumgard decided the best way to deal with the electricity issue was to never allow the power to go out. The Atrium has a backup system

42

with eleven levels of protection. I've heard Ms. Capaldi says it best: 'We could be hit dead-on by a nuclear warhead, followed by multiple electromagnetic-pulse devices, and we'd still have four levels of power protections.'"

Remembering the godfather of hacking, Alex said, "Does Adisah spend much time with the programmers? Does he live here?"

"He does live on site, at the top of La Berce," Brad leaned back and studied Alex. "He's a great man—a genius, no doubt." He waved his hand as if shooing a fly. "But he's not business minded. Somehow, word is spreading around the planet, even with our secrecy. People know that if they live with a disability or chronic pain, and get face time with Adisah, he'll comp them free vacations."

Alex briefly wondered if sore buns from sitting with a laptop on his lap all day would count.

"Philanthropy is great," Brad said. "I'm all for it. Just not for a start-up company miles into the red. Without a profit, we die. Many people have invested vast fortunes—everything they have—to see Eridu succeed."

"What if we have programming questions," Alex said. "Can we meet with him?"

"No." Brad rocked his head side to side. "Consider him 'perpetually unavailable.'"

The next hour slugged by as Brad explained many of the amenities for Eridu's clients.

Finally, the time arrived for them to fire up their laptops and examine part of the code.

Brad assigned them passwords, congratulated them on their hire, and ended with a speech about confidentiality, the severity of punishment for security breaches, and how fortunate they were. He then picked up his folded newspaper, and once at the door added, "Take notes; do what you do. If you have any questions, email them to the design department, or bring your concerns to the group when you start work. Maybe Adisah will see them."

"Thank you." Alex said. What else could he say? He still reeled from the buzz of it all.

Brad huffed as if satisfied. "Have fun. Work hard. You men create our worlds, and we need more!"

As the heavy door closed, it dawned on Alex that he now had the greatest job on Earth.

He wondered if, as head of the department, would he choose the worlds they created? The Lobby offered thrill-seeking awe with Big Hitters' Ball, a realm of tranquil community with San Francisco 1968, and the base desires with Pleasure House 101. He thought the next logical step would be to create something intense: maybe reenact the D-day invasion, have a tournament with knights and squires, or some metaphysical warzone, like X-Men gone wild. Just thinking about the possibilities flooded him with endorphins.

He understood research would play a major role. Outlining the storyline would take another chunk; both preceded writing the software. A code larger than hundreds of novels might take weeks to familiarize, and years to complete.

His greatest strength lay in diagnostics. Yet he feared with a project this sophisticated, the startup bugs would be long vanquished. The possibility that some might linger caused him to power on his computer.

The characters filling the screen looked like all of the others he'd ever seen, but the digits before him constructed the greatest wonder of all time.

Within minutes, he fell into his groove of interpreting lines of code as executions, processing the executions as coherent commands, and visualizing the intended structure in its final stage.

He'd never get over how something as mundane as characters on a keyboard could be the ingredients to magic.

Carl whispered something to himself and scooted closer to his screen.

Alex penned his first notation.

Lunchtime came and went.

Neither man moved from his seat for longer than a two-minute breather or a restroom break.

Around one in the afternoon, the earpiece in Alex's pocket vibrated. Resting his pen on yellow pages filled with intrigue, he inserted the device into his ear. "Hello?"

"Pardon the intrusion, sir," Victor said. "It has been six hours since your last meal. Would you like me to have food delivered for you and Mr. Wright?"

Unlike the majority of people, who used their stomachs to judge hunger, Alex allowed his mind to rule. The brain needed fructose to function, and when his thoughts wavered, he ate. He had sensed a decline, but with no idea as to the breakroom's whereabouts, or how they served food in the Atrium, he'd ignored the foggy reminders.

"Did you say something?" Carl asked.

Alex pointed to his ear. "Got Victor here. Are you hungry?"

Clearly unsure who Alex meant, Carl frowned.

"That sounds good, Victor. What are our options?"

"Countless options, sir. All four restaurants will deliver. Anything from the food court can be brought to you, or, there is an employee breakroom on your floor, with open access vending machines."

Glancing at the code, Alex chewed his upper lip and considered the pros and cons of leaving to find a vending machine. He asked Carl, "You want to split a pizza?"

"Cheese only."

Alex had been hoping for a deluxe, but compromise ruled the civilized world, so he said, "A medium cheese pizza, two liter of Coke, and onion rings. Can you do that?"

"Certainly, sir."

"Thanks. And Victor, please don't call me sir."

"Yes, Alex."

Alex removed the earpiece, stretched, used the lavatory, and found the breakroom. Free snacks propelled him to drop two Almond Joys bars from the vending machine, for a light dessert. The real food arrived as he returned.

As Carl filled their paper cups with soda, he gestured toward the monitors and asked, "Are you understanding that?"

"Mostly," Alex answered truthfully. "A few things more than others, but I'm compiling a list of questions."

They ate for the next fifteen minutes, while talking about games, programs, and Carl's love of *Plow Straight*.

Carl left for the restroom, returned, and surprised Alex by asking, "Do you mind if I call it a day?"

Alex hadn't expected to assume the management reins this quickly. Understanding this was part of his new position, like it not, he answered as he hoped he always would: "Not at all."

As Carl reached the door, Alex remembered something and said, "Before you go, come look at this spot here. Tell me what you think." He scrolled up to a questionable section of code.

Carl stood behind Alex.

"Just this part from here," Alex clicked down a few pages, then tapped the bottom of the screen, "to here." He then scrolled back up and allowed Carl to operate the computer.

"It's part of transfer code for when a user goes from the lobby to a programmed world, but that's all I see."

"Anything seem… off, to you?"

A few moments later, Carl relented. "Not to me, no. But, I like to take the code in and think on it. When I come back to it, I'm able to understand code better than most."

Alex nodded.

"I just need a little more time, Mr. Cutler."

"It's not a test or anything."

"Okay, Mr. Cutler."

"Let's stick with Alex."

"Okay."

"This part feels buggy, but it's probably me. I'll see you tomorrow."

A few doors down from where he was, Alex knew his future programming team toiled. He just wasn't sure what, exactly? Alex kept an eye on the clock until four p.m., at which time he heard the commotion of exiting programmers in the hallway. Wanting to blend in with the group, he inspected his area in preparation of joining them.

He'd compiled two pages about the program itself and typed a mock alteration for the transfer code portion he interpreted as buggy. To come in on day one and rewrite an important section of code might be brash, but he liked shoptalk. So at worst, he'd be wrong and learn why. At best, they'd make a tweak improvement that no one would notice, and he'd feel that familiar satisfaction of inching toward perfection.

After emailing his outline to the design department, he shut down his machine and exited double-time to catch his future team.

He wasn't a social butterfly, didn't need to be the center of anything. But, being human, he preferred to fit in, be liked, and communicate. Yesterday's experience in the Lobby had shattered his previous notions of splendor, and he wanted to express that. He now belonged to an esoteric sect, a brotherhood, and felt confident they'd want to share in his experience as much as he longed to discuss it.

Catching the tail end of exiting programmers, he managed to ride the elevator up with three others, receiving congratulations for his hire and yesterday's game. He blushed, and passed along the credit. Every spoken word granted more comfort. When Alex arrived at the top floor, the tram waited. Employees chatted as they entered their usual cars. Unsure which car to board, Alex sighed with relief when Kole leaned out of the second door and waved him in. Denise razzed his late arrival by rubbing his lower back.

As the tram cruised along, Alex smiled, laughed, and received more positive comments pertaining to the most amazing day of his life, one where he played football, of all things.
Staring at a group of programmers in a booth, Alex recognized their faces, but his mind blended the football versions with what he saw. The effect was dumbfounding and surreal.

"Well, we all want to know," Kole said. "How much Lobby time do you earn as management?"

"I'm not sure. Guess I'll learn all of that on Thursday," Alex said.

"Well, whatever," Kole said. "Full disclosure, we all wanted your job."

Alex's temperature climbed, and Denise elbowed Kole. He hadn't considered himself a scab hire. He wanted to stimulate and inspire these people, not suffer their resentment. Kole's friendly eyes, and the pleasant demeanor of those around him, killed most of that worry.

"At first, we were bummed they planned to bring in an outsider," Kole said. "Not now. Truth is, we're excited to have you. No one wants to admit structure will do us clowns good. And our egos wouldn't accept just anybody. Toss us Alex Cutler, however, and we're good." He smirked at Alex's confusion. "Hey, man, we all use *Plow Straight*—brilliant stuff."

The tram slowed as they approached La Berce.

"Thanks," Alex said. "I want so much to help and have…" His voice trailed off as he saw *her* waiting in front of La Berce. Her light-blue scrubs looked the same as the ones from yesterday, if not more wrinkled. Her hair was draped across a shoulder, and her eyes were downcast in contemplation. Her beauty, coupled with the addition of a handheld purse, made her appear like a Duchess of York, out doing volunteer work among the common folk. Virtuous, strong, independent. Could he really read those attributes in a woman waiting for public transportation?

"Oh yeah," Kole said from next to him, following his attention. "Rosa Newberg. She lives in B-16. Talk about a solid chick, the complete package."

"You know her?" Alex asked without averting his eyes from Rosa, as she strode into the car next to them and dropped out of view.

"Yeah, we talk. I've had lunch with her. Tried to make it more, but I'm a wizards, ab-wheel, and vodka kind of guy. She's novels, yoga, and way too sober to fall for my bullshit."

Alex surged with pride at the strength of her conviction. A lot of women wouldn't care if a guy who looked like Kole bullshitted them.

"I'll hook you up though," Kole added as the tram resumed travel.

"Thanks, but…" A nice gesture, but Alex knew he possessed average looks at best, with below-average spending habits, and no clue who the latest celebrity break-up involved. In other words, he wasn't lady-slaying material.

"No, it's no problem," Kole said. "I'm doing it for me anyway. I wanna checkout your place. I've been here two years, and you're the only guy I've met who lives in one of those crazy penthouses. I'll invite her, the other new hire, and a few others, including the hostess from Mountaintop Steakhouse," he rubbed his hands together in excitement, "and use your place to wow my target."

Alex held back a wince. He wasn't sure about targeting women, or strangers being in his home. Plus, he'd been instructed to limit time around anyone lacking a level-three security clearance—a suggestion he took seriously. However, Rosa Newberg warranted some risk.

He took a moment and daydreamed of him wearing a tuxedo, the Duchess of York in a flowing gown, dancing a waltz together in a grand ballroom full of dignitaries. Of course, he had never waltzed before, didn't know a politician, and the Atrium was by far the nicest building he'd ever been in. That didn't stop his dreamed-up self from hitting every step in stride and whispering something in Rosa's ear that caused her to tip her head back and laugh.

"I can cook, mix drinks, deal cards, whatever," Kole said, breaking the spell.

The tram slowed to a stop, and Alex's heart raced at the thought of glimpsing her one more time. Exiting first, he paused and waited for Kole, intending to agree. Instead, Kole pushed past him.

"Hey, Rosa!" Kole shouted.

She turned around and stopped as Kole ran to her, Alex followed.

"How's it going?" Kole asked her.

"Good. I'm good." The intonation of her voice was cautious, the sound tingled every nerve along Alex's spine.

"Hi," she said to Alex as he approached.

"H-hey."

After a brief silence, Kole said, "This is Alex Cutler. He wanted to meet you."

49

Alex's heart dropped. Heat dimpled his skin. Why would Kole say it like that and make him look like some crazy stalker? Why not tell her he liked what she wore to bed the previous night? That he'd come up with some better methods for organizing her sock drawer?

"He's new," Kole continued, as if he hadn't already blown it. "He lives in one of those penthouses. We're hoping to have people over for drinks and dinner. Kind of welcome him to our fair city, but he won't open his doors unless you come."

Alex's palms sweated. He should have let Kole do this by himself, or better yet, not at all. It had been mere seconds, but the suspense of her reply agonized. He had to refrain from running in the opposite direction and taking a header off the tram tracks.

She glanced to Alex and smiled. "I don't drink often or much," she paused, "but dinner sounds good."

Alex exhaled.

"Great. He's in building A, penthouse two. Come by say… six o'clock? Invite a friend if you want, but only if your friend is female."

"I'll be there," she said and extended her hand to Alex. "Nice to meet you, by the way. I'm Rosa."

Finding her hand as clammy as his own surprised him. Unless his was such a sweat factory that it soaked her hand and exposed him as a nut job who secreted fluids from his palms like some bathhouse stigmata, and she would thus decline the invitation.

Instead, she beamed and walked away.

"That's a pretty sight," Kole said after she descended the stairs.

"She is," Alex replied absently, and then, realizing Kole meant her backside, he flashed with irritation. However, Kole was the reason he'd be eating with Rosa in a few hours, so he lightened up.

"Thanks, man."

"No problem. Let's stop by my place. I'll drop off my bag, grab these cheddar bratwursts I special ordered last month, and we'll do the rest at your place."

Alex welcomed the company. He hadn't been this nervous since… well, since yesterday.

Chapter Five

"Keep staring out that peephole, and there'll be a ring around your eye when they get inside," Kole said from behind Alex. The cathedral ceilings and smooth design lines of Alex's condominium granted a clean pitch to Kole's voice.

Alex bit his bottom lip. Prior to the ding of the arriving elevator, he'd paced the entryway. Holding his breath, he spied on the load of people who poured forth from the elevator: nervous Carl, Big Jason, a young lady he'd never seen who carried a covered dish. Denise whistled as she stepped out and yelled, "We're movin' on up, Weezy!" Rosa exited last and exhaled.

As expected, the group gathered before the nine-foot tall, nine-foot wide piece of moving art on display in Alex's hallway, *Patterned Creation*, a massive globe that continually rotated. The vast oceans were crafted in dimpled, light-blue crystal, and allowed glimpses of the globe's hollow center and opposite side. Each country was crafted with its national stone: a green, textured, high-polished granite for America. A plate-size section of cubic zirconia cast a rainbow of sparkle each time South Africa met the light. The red of Myanmar's ruby outline shined enough to reflect the viewer's image. Even with artificial gemstones, he imagined that *Patterned Creation*'s worth floated in the mid-to-high six digits and understood he might be short by a zero or two.

"Did you watch me like that when I checked out your globe?" Kole said.

"Yes," Alex replied. *Just not for this long.*

Rosa stood in the rear of the pack, a pink envelope in her hand. She wore a violet blouse and tight jeans. Her shapely hips accelerated his heart rate. She turned to the door. Alex jumped back and bumped into Kole, who gripped his shoulders, gave them a reaffirming squeeze, and moved him to the side.

Kole peeked out of the lens, jerked as the knock arrived.

"Go back there, out of sight," Kole whispered. "Act like you're coming from the deck."

The foyer in Alex's condominium ended with two sets of six descending steps, splitting right and left around the seven-foot tall glass case that illuminated *The Matrix* trench coat.

Out of sight at the bottom of the steps, voices clashed in greeting. Alex resisted his urge to meet them at the door. Heeding Kole's advice, he raced to the open slider but stopped short of exiting to the evening sun. He wanted to listen to them and knew the strong winds of his fifth-floor balcony would drown out his guests' voices.

Alex perked his hearing as a couple of them oohed.

Kole proudly affirmed the trench coat's authenticity. He told one of the women, "I'll have you take a picture of me wearing that, and nothing else."

Shoes padded down the hard-tiled steps, bringing Rosa into view. Alex forced out a breath and moved toward her.

She stopped at the edge of his open floor plan. Dining, living, and sunroom shared a generous space of modern design. Framed sci-fi movie posters, starting with *Metropolis* and centered with his favorite, *Flatlinerss*, lined the far south wall. Beneath them, an aquarium that stretched twenty feet. At five ten, Rosa stood an inch shorter than Alex. Her dark-brown eyes swirled like hot coffee finished with crème.

"Hi, Alex." She held out the envelope. "I brought you a card."

"That's really thoughtful." he said. A small bow decorated the front. The card, an A-frame home with a garden and bent gardener embossed on a green background. Printed inside, *So glad you're finally here. Welcome home.* Written below, *Welcome to our sacred city. You're going to love it! Rosa.*

"It was the only card in the gift shop that fit," Rosa said.

"It's awesome." He stepped to the nearest table, white with a single drawer, a bowl of white faux fruit on top. He pushed the bowl aside and propped up the card. It felt like a female-to-male equivalent of a rose bouquet. His blush was so bright he feared facing her.

"It smells good. What's cooking?" she asked.

Between them? *No, no, she meant the food on the grill.* He swallowed. "I don't even know."

"Didn't you just come from out there?"

He tried to remember what Kole had been thawing in the sink but came up empty. "I'm pretty sure it's meat."

She smirked. "That's a safe bet."

Feeling overwhelmed with attraction, he extended his hand to initiate contact. "Nice to see you again."

They shook once up, once down. He smiled so wide he probably looked goofy, but didn't care.

"There's the man of the house right there." Kole guided a woman by her shoulders. "This is Melissa. You'll soon learn she's the best hostess at Mountaintop Steakhouse."

She blushed. "I seat customers. It's a pretty simple job."

"I've seen those seating charts—com-pli-ca-ted," Kole said. "Have a seat around this kingly table. I'll check the grill."

Jason wore a gray Star Wars T-shirt. In silence, he took the table's head position. Denise continued on, inspecting the place, opening doors, mumbling (compliments?) under her breath.

Alex considered holding a chair out for Rosa, decided it was too cordial, then thought about where to sit—one spot away from her, directly next to, across from? He bit the end of his thumb.

"Where are you going to sit?" Rosa asked.

"Right here." He grabbed the back of the nearest chair.

"Then I'll sit here." She grabbed the one next to him.

"Thirty minutes until we eat," Kole said as he returned, carrying a fifth of Captain Morgan and a two liter of Coke. "Who wants to play Presidents and Assholes?"

Remembering the Asian man, Alex asked, "Is Song coming?"

"No, man," Kole said, "I like the dude, but you can't understand him unless we're in—"

He and Alex locked eyes.

Carl busied himself opening one of three decks of cards.

54

Everyone knew Rosa and Melissa lacked the proper security clearance to even mention the word Lobby. They had no idea what clients experienced at the Atrium, or why clients arrived at Eridu in such good spirits.

The ladies focused their inquisitive looks on Kole.

Alex understood what Kole had planned to say: 'You can't understand Song unless we're in the Lobby.' All languages translated to the clients' original language, to facilitate communication. The Lobby erased age gaps and stature and looks and dialects, making it a place where friendships formed solely on compatibility.

"Can't understand him unless what?" Melissa asked.

Rosa glanced at Alex and squinted, as if trying to read something in his features.

"Unless his girl's hanging on his arm to translate," Denise said, as she pulled out a chair and glared at Alex. "You must be damned important for all this bling."

"How many cards do I deal?" Jason asked, the cards poised in his outstretched hand. Perhaps he heard the slip and was now running cover.

"Deal out the deck," Kole sat, ending the mishap. "The rules are simple. Jason leads off by playing his lowest card. Going to his right, you must play a card higher. If you can't, pairs trump singles, triples and quads go on pairs, twos clear the pile, and you lead out. First person to play all their cards is the president during the next game. Second person out is the vice president, third the governor, etc. The last guy is the asshole. They have to shuffle and deal, and everyone must do what anyone above them says."

"So if I win," Melissa said, "you have to do what I tell you?"

"*When* I win, you'll have to do what *I* tell *you*," Kole said.

Intended as a drinking game, Kole bummed at the realization that only he, Melissa, and Denise were drinking. The group substituted commands to drink for silly acts: Carl was made to quack like a duck each time someone played a card for a full turn. Denise ordered Kole to do a chicken dance while the table sang the beat. Alex failed miserably when Rosa (their VP) ordered him (the lowly mayor) to do a Kamarinskaya, the traditional Russian dance. With arms crossed, he went low as the men clapped in time.

The ladies yelled, "Lower, go lower, lower," until he fell back on his bum. Instead of red-hot embarrassment, Alex laughed with the room, cut short by Rosa bending to help him up.

Her palms on his arms added to his bliss.

"You guys clear the table," Rosa said. "We'll get the side dish." She tapped Alex's arm.

Melissa passed them on the way to the kitchen, carrying the casserole they had intended to grab, but Rosa continued onward. "I want to see what you have to drink besides soda."

His forty-nine cubic foot of storage Turbo Air refrigerator opened out from the middle. They each grabbed a handle, pulled, and leaned in to inspect, which placed their heads inches apart. He stared at the Tropicana label. She stared at him. The refrigerator's cool air helped chill his soaring body temperature. "I have OJ, bottled water, a V8."

If he turned, he'd practically be kissing her. That seemed way too forward, despite the idea's appeal.

Perhaps she wanted to kiss? Pecking her lips in front of an open refrigerator seemed juvenile.
Intending to find out why she still faced him, he rotated. She swiveled to peruse the beverages at the perfect time. He thought he saw her grinning ever so slightly.

"I'll take a bottle of water." Rosa reached inside. "You want something?" she asked as they both rose and closed the doors.

He knew staring into her eyes showed his hand: that he found her breathtakingly beautiful, that he wanted to lean forward and kiss her, that he'd never felt an energy like what pulsed between them.

She cracked open the bottled water, sipped, and said, "I'm starving," before moving toward the other room.

"Do you want to eat here again tomorrow?" Alex blurted.

Stopping at the steps, she turned and inspected him, her lips pursed. "That depends on how good the food is." She continued to the other room.

Smiling, Alex knew that would be a yes: cheddar bratwursts were manna from heaven.

Chapter Six

Rosa accepted Alex's invitation for a return visit the next day. The generous amount of leftover food drew Kole and Carl as well. Carl inserted himself when Alex invited Rosa for movie night on day three. There was a day where Alex worked late and only had an hour-long phone call with Rosa, then another Rosa date that included Carl, where, despite the sting it inflicted, Alex pulled him aside and explained that he enjoyed Carl but wanted a night alone with Rosa. Carl relented, and Alex now prepared for the big day.

As he showered and groomed, Alex committed himself to trying for a kiss tonight after work. Their feelings were palpable and mutual, he hoped. He wanted to be able to place his arm around her. He wanted to feel her hand on his knee as she used him as a brace when standing.

Having completed his orientation week, today was his first official day as head of programming. No more tours and hours with Rigo. He'd be in work area one, with his team. He daydreamed about giving an introduction speech. Over the past week, he'd learned how Broumgard divided project responsibilities. He intended to revamp their system, assign tasks to individuals according to their strengths and likes; those steps alone should streamline the work.

The option of late stays appealed to him as well. Not as a routine or a way to brownnose, but at Vision Tech, he'd often stayed past normal work hours, and soon found other programmers joining him. When modeled correctly, an after-hours environment toed the line between labor and recreation. Music cranked. Pizza arrived. Debates about the eventualities of the technology on the Syfy channel took precedent, but some work got done, often their most creative.

Broumgard's programmers used *Plow Straight*, but not to its full potential. The first few days would include a crash course taught by its designer. That should increase output an additional ten to fifteen percent.

He checked the clock: 6:20. The tram departed at ten after seven. Though he'd never discussed it with Rosa, they'd been meeting earlier and earlier each morning as a way to gain more time together.

Having completed his morning routine, he selected an olive-colored T-shirt and a gray flannel, thinking the color combination complimented his brown eyes.

Racing down the steps, he grabbed two snack bars in the kitchen, popped Victor in his ear, and headed out.

Even in June, Montana's morning air was frigid.

Jogging to the tram tower, he climbed the steps two at a time, hoping he'd early-bird Rosa, spread a Cheshire grin when she arrived, give a teasing answer when she queried about the Atrium's draw. He wondered if chains of thoughts like this were what created love?

Rosa liked to guess about what went on at the Atrium. She always looked away when spitballing, to keep from actually prying. Her strongest inclination was that they offered some kind of harem, which he guessed held some credibility due to Pleasure House 101. But the Lobby represented much more than a place to satisfy sexual fantasies.

Rosa waited in her scrubs, her crossed arms a staked flag of early-arrival victory.

Carl waited too. The albino programmer exuded a gentle aura. Alex liked his company and sympathized with his interest in hanging with Alex and Rosa. Just not tonight.

Alex had a full-course meal planned. He'd rounded up an assortment of candles, prepped a Blake Shelton playlist, and cleaned his place from top to bottom.

Rosa smiled at his approach, which started his day more efficiently than dunking his head in a bucket of ice water.

"Morning," Alex said.

Instead of a reply, Rosa pulled him by the pinkie finger and kissed him on the lips. "Good morning to you."

59

The unexpected affection acted as a concussion-inducing grenade. Wow. Their first kiss. Alex couldn't contain his smile. Deciding their first kiss needed improvement, he took a deep breath, stepped in front of her, and leaned in. As his lips touched hers, he cupped the back of her head and lost himself in the moment.

Pulling away but maintaining eye contact, he knew they had sealed a pact. In computing terms, their compounding feelings had integrated into one system that would now work together to enhance the new, singular unit.

Carl's voice broke the mood. "This is uncomfortable, guys."

Their grins widened to the precipice of laughter.

"Apologies, Carl," Rosa said, as she separated from Alex. They resumed their normal morning chat, only this time, Alex held Rosa's hand.

The tram seemed to ride on air. Alex floated toward the workroom, trying unsuccessfully to bring his mind around to his work day.

"Mr. Cutler, one moment, sir," a bass-filled voice said, drawing him out of his haze.

Alex turned to find the incredible hulk, Dalton, hustling toward him.

"Good morning, Mr. Cutler."

"Morning." Alex noticed the two silver bars on Dalton's uniform. Three spear tips for a sergeant, one silver bar for lieutenant, and two silver bars for a captain. Apparently, Dalton being a big man had a double meaning.

"I know today's a big one for you. I just wanted to personally welcome you aboard and congratulate you on a good game last week."

"Thank you, but we both know I should be thanking you. This place is wonderful."

"Adisah is the man to thank. He's a magnificent person." He glanced over his shoulder at the door to Alex's workroom.

A pair of suit-wearing men entered. From the brief glimpse Alex got inside, the room appeared packed, like, ten times the normal occupancy packed.

When Alex returned his attention to Dalton, the man seemed more relaxed, as if he'd had a mission to stall Alex and allow those men to enter.

"Anyway," Dalton said, "great game. If our new guy didn't try to go low on you, the outcome may have been different."

"Win or lose, it was the most fun I've ever had."

"It always is, Mr. Cutler," Dalton backed away. "We're all excited and anxious to see what you're going to add." He clapped his paws, and smiled. "You have a great day."

"Thank you."

Alex stopped at the door to his work area and breathed deep, hoping tardiness wouldn't impact his Lobby credits.

Triple the expected occupants filled his workroom. All the normal programmers, along with a dozen professionally dressed men and women speckled the outer wall.

Dr. Brad Finder stood near the front with four guys in lab coats, who looked as if they'd taken time out of their day to be here, were huddled over a tablet. And the man himself, Adisah Boomul, waited with Tara near the main desk.

Adisah had plumped up since the orientation video was recorded and gone gray in spots. Age softened his features, making the gentle-looking man seem like he belonged in a temple, humming his daily devotions to life.

Energy sparked in the room. Despite its positive feel, Alex chewed his bottom lip while remaining in the doorway. He fought an urge to run back to Dalton and ask what was going on.

As if sensing his presence, Adisah and Tara turned in unison.

"Ah, Mr. Cutler." Adisah beamed. "So wonderful to meet you. Please." He beckoned him closer.

Everyone turned toward Alex. He swallowed and navigated through the occupied desks.

Recalling himself bouncing on his toes, being a six-foot-four, organic machine, and realizing this man had been responsible for that experience vibrated excitement in him like a struck gong.

"You possess a real gift, you know that?" Adisah said. "To think where we'd be if I would have had someone like you twenty years ago."

The comment was like Stephen King saying you had a great imagination or Christian Bale marveling at your acting talent. Finally, he managed, "Well, you have me now, sir."

Adisah waved off the *sir* and addressed the room.

"Would anyone care to tell Alex what makes him and this day so special for us?"

The sharp crack-hum of an electric wheelchair drew Alex's attention. An elderly man he immediately recognized as the majority shareholder, Roy Guillen, scooted his SmartDrive wheelchair closer. He nodded with appreciation at Alex, while a colleague in a corduroy suit stood behind his chair.

Alex had Googled Roy shortly after arriving. There was so much content, reading articles about him had turned into a nightly habit. Beyond being a hotel mogul, Roy Guillen had climbed Mount Kilimanjaro (where they lost a man to exposure), scuba-dived the colorful reefs off the coast of Thailand, and spent a year assisting in Tohoku, Japan, after the tsunami that killed more than fifteen thousand. Having experienced so much, something about the fiery gleam in the man's eyes looked out of place in a damaged body.

"Very glad you're here, son," Roy said. "Very glad, indeed."

"Thank you, Mr. Guillen." As long as this summons wasn't a prelude to Alex's termination, he would attempt to schedule some face time with the man. It wasn't everyday you met a real-life action figure, or one of America's roughly five hundred and sixty-three billionaires.

Adisah removed a memory stick from the side of a nearby laptop and displayed it to the packed room as he addressed Alex. "Do you know what you've done, Mr. Cutler?"

No, he thought as he shook his head. He hadn't done anything yet. He scratched behind his ear as he surveyed the room.

Song gave him a surreptitious thumbs up.

Denise pursed her lips in a kiss.

"When entering or exiting a chosen world from inside the Lobby," Adisah began, "clients and employees alike have suffered from a discomfort stemming from an unidentified flaw in our software.   We all accepted this discomfort as a case of taking the good with the bad. A tugging sensation starts in your tummy, which some have compared to being eviscerated, or spending a day with my financial advisors."

Forced chuckles circulated the room.

"And thanks to you, Mr. Cutler, that lone detriment has been plucked from our software, making the Lobby the wholly euphoric experience it was designed to be."

Before Alex could reply, Tara brought her hands together in applause. Others followed. It escalated until the room danced with the sound, replete with shouts and desk slaps.

Alex thought about the message he'd emailed the design department. A hand clasped his and shook; someone patted his back. Roy Guillen thanked him over and over for his gift.

Eridu and the Lobby were Alex's gifts—ones that surpassed his wildest dreams.

Chapter Seven

Alex whistled a tuneless stream as he exited the elevator onto his penthouse level. Even after more than a year at Eridu, *Patterned Creation* continued to amaze him. The bouts of inspiration brought on by the massive globe's beauty improved each of the worlds he'd worked on. Since assuming the reins of Broumgard's programming department, his team had completed two worlds. The first, Golf Retreat, offered two hundred and sixteen of the industry's best courses, forty-two of their own design, and four played on a gravity-impoverished moon.

The second world, Triassic Park, combined bright colors with a daring concept: the completed, nonlethal version of the dream envisioned by Dr. John Hammond, the scientist from Michael Crichton's novel *Jurassic Park*. The twenty-two-square-mile island offered eighty of the most exotic extinct plants purported to have existed, forty-seven modified insects, and twelve absolutely docile dinosaur varieties.

The extensive research wore down the entire team. Even with twenty-seven dedicated, highly competent workers and four new hires, they spent half of the project on authenticity. Thanks to their prideful determination, a client could now interact with a timid anspeodite, a fictional, cat-like reptile with a monkey's characteristics. Their mischievous creation would hustle up a tree then swing loosely from branch to branch, dangling with a scaled tail while inspecting the humans below.

The previous five months had been spent toiling over what would be a horrifically accurate recreation of the Battle of Gettysburg. Clients would be able to choose whether they fought for the Union or the Confederacy in an as-yet-undetermined battle for the infamous town.

In keeping with the historic nature, the program involved a user-specific memory that spanned four days, the same duration as the battle. This allowed clients to endure twelve eight-hour shifts that paused as their group exited, and resumed when they returned. In addition, clients could modify their pain, allowing the user to feel nothing if mortally wounded, or to discover what it felt like when a cannonball tore off a leg, and life pump out of their femoral artery. When a client died, they would be kicked into the lobby section, with the option to rejoin the fight or select another world.

Gettysburg started as a great idea, but Alex learned too late that the carnage of war should never be re-created. On the plus side, give those in power a flash of this horror, and Alex knew they'd be less likely to engage in armed conflict.

As much as it frightened him, as much as mortal screams and the smell of blood, bowels, and gun smoke sickened him, he would visit Gettysburg. He also suspected he'd do so with some degree of pain intact. The psychological reasoning behind that continued to elude him.

Gripping the familiar iron handle to his condo signified another completed workday, a sense of purpose fulfilled. Inside, the smell of seasoned chicken permeated the air. The sounds of Adele played throughout the house system. Neo's coat still acted as the centerpiece when a guest entered, but a series of paintings, themed around Rome's open fields and urban alleyways, had replaced the movie posters.

A candlelit feast for two sat on the table, centered by an open bottle of Merlot and two wine glasses. Alex smirked away his surprise and replaced it with adoration.

Rosa waited in one of the dining chairs, wearing a little black dress, her necklace's gold crucifix resting on her chest. Her luminous hair spiraled onto her shoulders. Dim lighting and a quartet of three-wick candles enhanced the ambiance, all accentuated by Rosa's flowery perfume.

"What's all this?" he asked, approaching her and giving her a kiss.

"Well, we have a lot to celebrate," she said, motioning for him to sit next to her.

They did have a lot to celebrate, he thought, but how could she know? Confused, and concerned she'd somehow learned his surprise, he decided to stay quiet—discover her agenda instead of spilling his surprise.

"This looks and smells delicious. Is this a happy Friday meal?" he asked as he filled the two glasses a quarter of the way.

"Nope. Today is a special day. I'm sure you know, but to keep me in a good mood, I'll just remind you: it's our 'one year living together' anniversary."

"I knew that. I've even brought you a gift to prove it."

She sipped her wine and inspected his empty hands. "Is that so? By all means, expand our reason to celebrate."

He didn't have the spine to tell her he'd celebrated every day since meeting her.

He separated the two stacked plates, sliced the roasted chicken, placed a slab of succulent meat onto each. He added a freshly baked roll and inspected the sides, allowing her curiosity to ferment.

"All right, fun's over," she said. "Where's my surprise?"

He scooped a serving of green bean casserole on each plate, then a pile of cheesy-garlic mashed potatoes.

"I was called into Adisah's office today. Third time in a year." He proudly displayed three fingers.

"Lucky you," she said with a raise of her glass.

She meant the compliment. Adisah was a mythical figure, even more to those who lacked proper clearance. "He gave me a substantial raise that dips me into profit sharing." To kill a little more time, he placed her plate in front of her, slid his closer. Even though money wasn't a driving force for either of them, he wanted her to consider the idea that his pay increase was all he had to share. Once that possibility settled, he continued, "More importantly, I've been granted unlimited use of Eridu's amenities, and another small bonus."

Rosa stayed silent. She attempted to hide her interest by cutting the chicken into bite-size cubes. She'd abandoned questioning him about what went on in the Atrium, but her curiosity remained obvious, sometimes painfully.

"Being that I'm Mr. Boomul's favorite employee, protégé if you will, and a dear, close friend of Roy Guillen," Alex said playfully, thinking back on his and Roy's earlier Lobby visit, where Alex bested him by four strokes at Sawgrass. "Adisah, after calling me the future of this company, asked if there was anything he could do to make my time more comfortable."

She forked a piece of chicken into her mouth, chewed slowly, and watched him.

Picking up his roll, he bit a chunk, and talked with his mouth full. "Long story short, I got your security bumped. Are you ready to learn what all the fuss is about?"

She swallowed, almost replied, but instead grabbed the wine glass and drank. She then rose and placed a hand on her belly, drawing the silk dress tight against her well-conditioned body, swelling her appeal. "I've been here three years. I'm sure you can't tell, but it drives me crazy not knowing what you do, what attracts all these powerful people to our city. The water cooler talk is about what type of orgy or *Weird Science* pleasure machine they have over there." She tucked errant strands of hair behind her ear and looked him in the eyes. "The thinking being that nothing else could make people so happy, so guarded over its identity. But I know you. I know a sex house isn't what gives you that perma-glow every few weeks. You're not some horndog out banging robots." She drained the last splash of wine and set her glass on the table. "But now you're saying I get to be in the know?" She smiled, then slumped her shoulders and looked defeated. "Do I even want to find out?"

He had daydreamed about this moment, perhaps for the past year. Her adorable uncertainty made his heart flutter. He strode closer, cupped both of her hands. "You definitely want to."

"What if it's like driving a nice car? Where once I do, all other cars lose their luster. I don't want to lose my luster."

She made a valid point. He sometimes wondered if the Lobby eroded some of his luster for normal life. Being that he didn't possess much luster to begin with, he'd say no, but dozens of times a day, he fantasized about being in the Lobby. Even the previous night, after making love to Rosa, he wondered what it would be like to bring her to San Francisco 1968, sneak off, and have sex.

Everything seemed a little better when inside the Lobby. He'd never considered playing golf before. Now he couldn't wait to get back to the tee and work on correcting his slice, staying ahead of Roy in their friendly rivalry. He needed to angle his club face slightly more clockwise and keep his eyes on—

Rosa pulsed his hands, returning him to the moment.

"Let's move to the couch," he said, then led her over. "It's going to take a few minutes to explain."

For the next two hours, his exuberant explanation of the thing he loved went the opposite of how he'd expected. She started off shocked. Then demanded an in-depth explanation of the transfer process. She stayed incessant about the horrors of her soul being siphoned out of her vessel.

Once they overcame that issue, she wanted to know how her bodily functions reacted while in the Lobby. Could she defend herself if assaulted? And when they reached the specifics of the Markers, the discussion became a squabble, bordering on an argument.

Thirty placating minutes into that, Alex understood why Tara sprung the Lobby and the Marker on people after knocking them out. Another ninety minutes, and he convinced her, reluctantly, to give the Lobby a test run.

Their argument drained him as effectively as going ten rounds with a champ. He returned to the table and picked at the cold food. Her many points of opposition added to his confusion. *What was wrong with perfect living?*

Per the norm, they showered in separate bathrooms and climbed into bed together. On that night, however, the space between them was like a voyage through the cosmos.

Chapter Eight

"We're directing all our efforts into creating this Gettysburg world," Alex said to Rosa, as she slowly pirouetted inside the Lobby's engulfing white.

The undefined hallway expanded twenty square feet each time a person entered, and retracted when they exited or entered a world. The neutral color made the lobby's walls impossible to detect. Once in a while, a client arrived down the hall, creating a distance marker. Otherwise, Alex often felt like he stood in the center of a cloud.

"We hope to be finished with Gettysburg by Thanksgiving," Alex said. "People are saving their Lobby credits to binge war over the holidays."

"You plan on visiting that world?" Rosa asked nonchalantly. He knew her well enough to detect her subtle rebuke.

When caught between telling Rosa a lie or losing faith, Alex chose honesty. "I'm curious to find out how I will react in such a crazy environment."

"Hmm. What worlds are planned after that?"

"Gettysburg is so much more involved than we expected. It's draining my team. When we're done, I'll give everyone a week off. After that, we'll knock out a handful of simple projects. Possibly a scuba diving world, where clients can learn about aquatic life; have an option for human gills or webbed hands. Maybe big-game hunting, or an equestrian world with trails, and obstacle courses. I've also been thinking about 1860 Japan." Alex's excitement rose just from thinking about it. "Samurais clashing with the Western world, but to make things fair, toss in a pinch of magic on the shogun's side."

"Another war world." With her back to him, Rosa balled her hair in a wad and squeezed—the equivalent of a horse raising its tail and dropping a load.

Waking that morning, she'd seemed more willing to enter the Lobby with an open mind. Still, she fell short of the hyper-giddy he originally pictured when he daydreamed about them enjoying this together. At least they were here. She seemed resigned to getting through it, as cordially as possible, and he still believed by the end of this trip, she'd be hooked.

A trio of men popped in, one after the other, about sixty feet from where Alex and Rosa stood.

Alex rarely saw clients inside the Atrium. Logging in with a destination in mind, he often announced his world without glancing around, and entered. But it seemed each new world increased traffic in the Lobby.

Alex wanted to share this with the world, but the number of new clients continued to rise and current clients never left. Soon, that would create a problem.

The modified clothing identified these men as regulars. It usually took three or four trips before a client learned how to use the voice command menu and swap out the standard-issue Broumgard attire.

One of the men said something in a voice above a conversational tone, and a colossal portal materialized near them. Viewing it from a poor angle, yet judging by the red-and-gold hue, Alex knew they'd opted for San Francisco 1968. The men merging into the image left Alex alone with his girlfriend, who looked amazing in tight jeans, a close-fitting Broumgard T-shirt, and cute little sneakers.

Another man appeared twenty feet away, announced a room, and darted in. The portal looked like any door you might find on a suburban home, meaning Pleasure House 101.

Alex had never visited that world, and he never would. Some life experiences were best avoided.

Broumgard estimated seventy percent of vacation minutes were spent in Pleasure House 101. Playing out sexual fantasies would undoubtedly bring pleasure, along with reality distortions. Drugs like cocaine and heroin probably made you feel great, too. Their drawbacks were just better known.

Alex didn't judge any of them. People had to establish their own moral code. Alex had made mistakes, but he was proud to say things like, 'he'd never stolen, or been in a fight, or purposefully deceived anyone. Granted, he normally avoided interacting, so it wasn't the most accomplished list.

This job was forcing him to make more difficult decisions. Some of those conflicted with his boast about deceiving people. He might tell someone they could move on to an easier task once done with their current one, knowing they wouldn't. He often told people he would consider their idea for their next world, knowing he wouldn't.

"How much do they charge clients to spend eight hours in here?" Rosa said as she paced a few steps across the white floor, her sneakers leaving dimples with each step.

"I guess that really depends," he said as he tried to remember if he'd ever heard or saw a pricing chart. He had always earned enough credits to vacation before the urge overwhelmed him. With his new promotion, he could now visit for an unlimited length. Rumors abounded that when they first opened, with only two worlds— Pleasure House 101 and San Francisco 1968—a Russian general donated a prototype attack helicopter in exchange for a pair of ten-year visitation rights. What's that worth? Eleven million dollars? Fifty million? Then divided by two, then again by two-hundred and fifty months.

"I guess the cost fluctuates," Alex answered, "but it'd still be more than we could afford."

She turned to him. "Have you checked your bank balance lately?"

"I guess not." His saving probably neared six figures. He'd established direct deposit shortly after being hired. Donated ten percent of his income to St. Jude's and five percent to a place called Morgan's Wonderland in Texas—a significantly underfunded theme park for children with mental and physical disabilities. He sent his mother her original five-hundred dollar a month allotment plus fifty percent, spent as needed, and hadn't glanced at the balance since. Some quick math helped him realize that he warmed a healthy nest egg.

"Well either way, it's free for us now." Closing the distance, he placed his hand on the small of her back. "What do you feel like doing? Football? A sunny day in San Francisco? Mass orgy?"

She placed her fist to her chin. The Thinker. "Hmmm. The last one is tempting," she mused, "but I'll pass." She wrapped her arms around his waist. "Can we go sailing in San Francisco?"

"Of course, there are dozens and dozens of boats. We can take them as far as a quarter mile beyond Alcatraz."

"I've always wanted to learn to sail." She pondered a moment, then added, "What do you think?"

"I think San Francisco sounds great. I'd really like us to take the official tour in Triassic Park. I've never been. They have flowers with petals the size of tractor tires, colors bright enough to offend a hippie—"

"—and unnatural life forms, created by… people." She shook her head. "I don't think I'm ready for anything that drastic. Show me God's creations."

Alex pursed his lips.

She leaned in and rubbed her nose on his. "I know this is your baby, and you're all excited, but it's also very strange, and totally unnatural. I can't stop thinking that I'm sitting in a chair, being deceived."

"You're not being deceived." He gently shook her arm. "This is you, and me."

"It's your thing, Alex," she said as she tugged her arm free. "It's great. It's unreal. I'm having fun, and it's exciting, but… it's just a bit much. You know? Maybe I'm just not used to it."

He somewhat understood. Not personally. He'd never heard of someone not loving the Lobby from their first moment inside, but people were different. Rosa was the first openly religious person he knew. She was definitely the first to accuse the Lobby of siphoning her soul. Maybe she took all the Bible stories literally.

Leaving the topic alone, he said, "Sailing in San Francisco, with you, will be wonderful."

"Another thing has been nagging me."

"What?"

Pivoting to the white and back to Alex, she said, "Is all of this legal?"

Alex exhaled.

All talk about the Lobby's legality arrived in the reverse, like: "We're not doing anything illegal," or "There's no law against it." But he'd never heard a person confidently state the Lobby obeyed American law.

Eridu prohibited internet access, provided no cell towers (rumors claimed they jammed cellular and radio signals), and clients turned in all electronic devices upon arrival.

Was the Lobby legal? The short answer—pretty much.

"I'm sorry." She kissed him, breaking his reverie. "This is great."

"Happy anniversary," he said with a downcast turn of his mouth

She kissed him again, dissolving more of his worry. Another kiss leveled out his frown, the fourth brought a grin. When he met her eyes, she raised her eyebrows. "Can we, umm, do it in here? Without anyone watching?"

"Do… *it?*" Alex considered Rosa's suggestion. "Sailing the Bay just became way more enticing."

"Only more enticing?"

"No, it actually sounds like the potential best day of my life."

She laughed.

"As to being watched… In this Lobby section, Broumgard employees have limited controls on clients. We can restrict movement, lower people's voices, lots of things, when in this lobby section. Of course, as the big boss, I have supreme override on all commands. In a world, however, the settings of that reality rule. Broumgard employees became just regular clients.

"So you guys can't follow a person's digital trail, and see what they're doing?"

73

"No. Once we transfer in, the chemical component to the digital interaction makes decoding a client's actions impossible."

"In that case," she said, gripping his hand. "I'm ready to step into one of your worlds."

He squared his shoulders and announced, "San Francisco 1968."

An image appeared fifteen feet to their left: an aerial view of the Bay lit by a bright sun, the Golden Gate Bridge under a single cloud, a flock of gulls, white caps on the sea, all in motion.

They stepped through.

No physical pain accompanied the passage, something he appreciated—and not only because he'd been the one to add the enhancement. Not feeling hella-pain was nice.

Alex visited San Francisco 1968 often. Mainly to track down Roy, who spent most of his waking life inside the replica of his home city. Most times, when Alex found him, Roy convinced them to stay.

Stepping from the barren, white lobby into a sunny, breezy afternoon always stunned the senses.

Clients arrived on a patch of healthy grass in Golden Gate Park wearing sandals, khaki shorts, and a tie-dye shirt for men; flip-flops and one of three knee-length summer dresses for ladies.

With the world running continually, clients' alterations sustained through log ins and outs. Clients had repositioned and conjured picnic tables to form rows near the entrance, giving them a line of sight to inspect each arrival.

Eight of the roughly twenty tables currently held clients. Most glanced in their direction. A few of those present might have been NPCs (nonperson characters), selected to play any of the offered board or card games. Since this world's popularity focused on socializing, finding a real-life player was easy.

"There are more people here than during my last visit," Alex said.

Rosa stretched out her dress for inspection. Blue cotton top, a canvas bottom. "Do I have to wear this the whole time?"

"See that store over there," Alex pointed outside the park. "We can swap clothes in there. I'd prefer some swim trunks myself."

74

A golden retriever ran past, chasing a tossed Frisbee. When Alex followed the arc back to the owner, the owner waved.

"They have dogs?" Rosa said.

"Dogs, birds, fish in the sea. No sharks though. Nor jellyfish, or stingrays. An environment free of dangers. A place focused on pleasantries."

Rosa huffed, in a good way, and took his hand. "This could be nice, once we get somewhere private and I unwind."

"Alex," a man yelled.

The couple stopped as a handsome man near Alex's age jogged toward them.

"Alex, what're you doing here? I thought you wouldn't have more credits for another eight days."

"Adisah granted me unlimited access." Alex wiggled his eyebrows. "Have you met Rosa?"

"No," Rosa replied. "I would have remembered someone so…"

"Handsome," Alex finished.

"I would have said debonair," Rosa said.

"I used to look like this, too. Wavy black hair, a baby face, thin body with muscles. My first wife always called me irresistible."

"Used to look?" Rosa said, and checked Alex's face. "I'm confused."

"You don't recognize him?" Alex asked.

Rosa inspected the man. "I don't."

"It's Roy. Roy Guillen."

"Most people don't recognize me without my wheelchair, but I prefer this version." Roy tapped his chest and extended his hand. "It's so nice to meet you."

"Oh my word," Rosa said. "I've only seen your face in pictures, but now up close, knowing it's you, I see the resemblance. It's the eyes." She glanced at Alex. He hoped her wide gaze and thin smile represented respect for Lobby enhancements, not an expression of mild horror.

"Come, join us," Roy said. "Prince Bandar needs a partner for the euchre tournament."

Alex checked Rosa for interest, and saw none. "Nah, man. We're here to go sailing."

"That sounds like a good time," Roy said. "I'll get Charles. We could race around Alcatraz and back."

Alex liked that idea. He'd put Rosa on the jib while he worked the sail. Unless—

"Alex and I have never sailed," Rosa said. "We kind of want to just putter around and get the feel of it."

"Nonsense," Roy said. "We'll make it a race. Charles and I have experience, so we'll use one of the slower boats, allow you to have an instructor on board, maybe a little head start."

Alex looked at Rosa and saw an expression he knew well: wide eyes, pursed lips, jaw muscles flexing. No dice.

He didn't get it. How could she not want to beat these guys at their own game? He gave her a second, recognized her determination, and conceded. He addressed Roy. "We'll probably just keep it the two of us. It's Rosa's first Lobby visit."

Roy's smile faltered as he inspected Rosa, saw her watching him with a blank look. "Another time, then. Make sure Alex takes you to see the whales. They stay a little east of Alcatraz."

"That's a great idea," Alex said. "We'll race another time."

"You're on," Roy said. "I'll leave you two so you can enjoy your date. How long are you going to be here?"

"Four hours," Alex said.

Roy checked his watch. "I'll still be here, if you want to stop by before you go."

"We'll do what we can." Alex shook Roy's hand.

"I'll see you around, Rosa," Roy said. "I hear great things about you all the time. This one," he pointed to Alex, "head over heels for you. Take care of him."

Rosa relaxed. "I'll do my best."

The clothing store in San Francisco 1968 delivered a warm and fuzzy feeling everytime Alex entered.

Everytime he entered this store he had the same thought, *had the pre-gadget world really been this chill?* Incense scented the air. T-shirts hung from ceiling wires and on round metal racks.   Rosa selected a white-and-red paisley, two-piece bathing suit, shorts, and a loose-fitting, yellow T-shirt that said *Jesus loves you*, to wear over her suit.

Alex wondered which of his programmers had the Christian leaning to insert that. More likely, they intended it as a joke. Who *really* believed Jesus loved them?

A teenager with short brown hair, thick and tapered in an era-appropriate style, watched them from behind a counter. *Perry Mason* played on a small television behind him—same as on every channel in the city, unless a client changed it. Again, who was the Perry Mason fan? Mysteries upon mysteries.

"What's the best way to get to the docks?" Alex asked.

"The trolley makes for a groovy ride. It's one block up," the young man said. "We pass out loaner bikes, too."

"How far is the Pacific?" Rosa asked. "I can smell it from here."

The NPC youth's eyes lost focus for a moment as he processed her question. "Three point two miles."

Rosa beamed at Alex. "That sounds like the perfect length for a bike ride."

In the absence of real-world muscle fatigue, Alex agreed. "Can you teach us how to sail?" All NPCs in this world possessed full information of every option. Starting with Golf Retreat, Alex compartmentalized information, assigning it to those in the know. Caddies assisted with your golf game. Clubhouse employees knew mixed drinks and the menus. Losing the "each person knows-it-all" added realism.

"I can teach basic techniques in steering, knots, and ship safety."

"We'll take the bikes from you, and find an instructor on the docks," Alex said.

"Far out."

Their matching 3-speed Schwinns had wing-shaped handlebars with plastic grips.

Rosa rang the bike's bell as she mounted. The old-fashioned sound drew laughter from them both. Pedaling through sidewalks populated just enough to avoid the feel of a ghost town, Alex and Rosa shared many smiles. Powerful winds near the docks amplified the smell of the sea. An army of seagulls, speckled with pelicans—drawn to the docks by discarded fish guts—added a cacophony of caws to the sound of breaking waves.

They continued past the wharf to the better-tended slips of Fog Bay Marina.

Dismounting, Rosa approached Alex, her hand on her chest, a look of exuberance, possibly disgust on her face. "It's so strange to do all that pedaling, up those big hills, and never get tired." She slapped her thighs. "I felt the strain here, but it's gone now…" She shrugged. "If I grew tired, maybe I'd forget I'm conked out in a chair."

"That's a great point," Alex said, hiding his disappointment at her negative comment. "Fatigue plays a major role in Gettysburg, particularly if you get shot or blown up."

Rosa winced.

Alex made a mental note to avoid discussing Gettysburg with Rosa.

"We need a world for just us," Rosa said. "A simple world where people and couples can have quiet, alone time."

"This world is kind of like that."

Rosa scanned the Pacific, the sky, turned back and faced the city. "I guess so."

"No phones, no planes, no five o'clock traffic. It's the unspoken appeal to the place."

"It's funny. Most of us are happier without all the gadgets, yet we choose to use them."

"Marketing is becoming too exact of a science. You're not one of the brainwashed masses, though. I rarely see you with your phone out."

"I'm not distracted, Alex. When you understand God's love, even a tiny bit, you can push aside the noise and be happy in the present."

That sounded nice, but sometimes Alex felt like distraction was all he had.

They stood at the base of the dock. Almost all of the slips held boats. Smaller, one-man sloops and catboats started near the front, building out to larger cutters and schooners. A forty-foot, Olympic-class Soling waited at the end.

Alex had never been on a boat, in life or the Lobby. Standing under a bright sun on a temperate day, it sounded like the ideal activity.

A man in his thirties approached from the marina, and said. "Can I help you?" He possessed a swimmer's trim waist and broad shoulders. Sandy-blond hair poked out from under a cap that read *U.S. Navy*. "We keep sailing vessels down these two decks, motor boats docked the next one over."

"It's our first time," Rosa said quietly, looking from the NPC and back to Alex, as if unsure of the man's authenticity. "Are you a computer program?"

"My name is John. I'm here to help."

When she looked at Alex, he shrugged.

"Should we do some fishing?" Alex asked Rosa. "Go swimming."

"A swim, yes. Perhaps some fishing." Rosa surveyed the rolling waves.

"What about that boat there?" Alex pointed to the fourth slip.

"A twenty-two foot Lark, centerboard. Light weight, good speed." John spoke without looking at the boat—another tweak Alex had corrected in the newer worlds. "Single rudder and tiller for steering. Twelve-foot sail, perfect for a smooth ride on a day like today."

Climbing in, Rosa stepped gingerly into the cockpit and sat next to the long tiller. She worked it in and out. "This is going to be fun."

John untied their moors and guided the boat back before he stepped onto the bow, rocking the vessel. A motor puttered them onto the bay. John showed them how to set the main and tie off the sail.

He watched Alex repeat the duties two times each before declaring him "fit for sea."

79

With a nice breeze pulling them along, Alex sat next to Rosa, who steered in the ninety-degree, stair-step method.

"Guess we'll save sex for another time," Rosa whispered, with a nod in John's direction.

"What? Oh, no, no, no." Alex had become so enthralled by their activities, he'd forgotten about the promised end to their date, and his curiosity about coupling inside the Lobby.

Mentioned anew, his interest spiked. "Because of John?"

Rosa nodded.

"He's not even real."

"I…I still couldn't do it."

"I don't think I could either." Alex chuckled. "Hey, John."

"Yeah, Skipper."

"Do you mind heading back to the docks?" Alex said.

"Would you like me to steer us home?"

"No—just dive over and swim back."

"Alex," Rosa admonished.

"No problem, Captain," John said. He turned his Navy hat backward, stepped to the rail, and jumped in, shoes and all.

"Man overboard," Alex said with a laugh.

"That's not funny," Rosa said.

"He'll go right back to his previous loop." Seeing her concern, he stopped grinning. "I don't mess with the NPCs, Rosa. Some clients harass them, but I don't. I've always found it… ugly. But he'll be fine."

Watching John head to shore pitted a knot in Alex's stomach. The man didn't stroke like a normal swimmer. He simply pushed through the water, his shoulders and head visible, as if propelled by an underwater force. Alex made a mental note to adjust that and said, "Him just hopping in was kind of cool though."

"It was ugly," Rosa said, her eyes watching the man, "and unnatural."

A few minutes later, Alex dropped the sail, then the anchor. He was telling the truth about issuing commands that demeaned. He never did it. With his first command under his belt, he saw the appeal.

It was thrilling to be obeyed without thought.

"Should we swim?" Rosa asked as she removed her shorts and Jesus shirt.

"Sure," Alex said. Drawing her close, he kissed her neck, then her cheek, then her lips. "After."

The fatigue metrics might not accurately reflect exertion in this world, but Rosa's breathing accelerated, which accelerated his own. When she opened her mouth to him, he was fully in this moment.

Lovemaking in the Lobby exceeded his expectations, in all sensual measurements.

Perhaps the romantic setting played a role. Perhaps his anticipation helped. Perhaps the novelty of sex in a machine amplified the feeling. Whatever the reason, he couldn't help but think everything in his life was perfect.

Chapter Nine

Despite having to exit the Lobby—something Alex always dreaded—
he often enjoyed the mild disorientation of returning to the real world.
He likened it to waking from a restful night dreaming of angels, love,
and beachside bonfires.

On vacations of three hours or longer, staff attached a non-
invasive catheter once a client entered the Lobby, and removed it
before they exited. Maybe that knowledge forced Alex hold it. Each
time he exited, he needed to pee. Three hours were not so long, so the
urge this time was minimal.

Remembering Rosa, he stretched and couldn't help but smile
at the thought of greeting her as she returned.

Her Lobby reservations never fully abated, but he knew when
she came to and noticed the subtle difference between enhanced
reality and this one, she'd be more inclined to go back. Her needling
questions about the soul and morality—two things unrelated to the
Lobby—clouded their afternoon. The swim brought further
complications.

The water had detectable salt content, a proper current, and
was cooled to a perfect degree, so that part was fine. Alex loved
swimming in the ocean without fear. Each time he dove under then
broke the surface, he felt reborn. Rosa's problem came with water
run-off. Instead of soaking a person, water beaded and rolled off the
body or material. An improvement, in Alex's opinion. Rosa's hair
drying in under two minutes, without use of a towel, should have
pleased her. It hadn't. They argued about it for thirty minutes.

She had some good times. He intended to focus on those to avoid Marker debate. He'd convince her to go again and try a different world.

Before rising from the access chair, he saw Claire, the first-shift access room supervisor, hovering near him, wringing her hands. Knowing her as an excitable woman quelled some of his concern, yet he'd never seen her actually worked up. And now, her features were scrunched into displeasure, almost as if she let slip an audible fart, and was about to say sorry, or, excuse me.

Instead, she cleared her throat and looked over her shoulder.

"Hello, Claire," Alex said.

"I don't want to alarm you, but some serious shit's going on downstairs." Her cursing increased his confusion. Claire was a polite introvert.

"Something with the programmers?" He stretched his back as he stood.

"Oh no, sir. They're no longer in the building. They've been ordered back to their residences. Everyone has. You just missed the umpteenth announcement."

Announcement? Workers sent home? Alex could think of nothing to cause either of those. With a rotating schedule, programmers worked seven days a week. Everyone with Lobby access encouraged the creation of worlds, which gave programmers mild celebrity status. Everyone's favorite programmer was always the one most dedicated. Alex's weekend and after-hours crew often had more programmers than a full shift.

"You're not making much sense. Is there an avalanche or something?"

He went to Rosa's chair with Claire a step behind him.

He drew back Rosa's green divider. She sat with a leg on each side of the chair, massaging the back of her head, where the marker was. He exhaled. So much for avoiding Marker debate.

"Mr. Cutler," Claire urged, "you and Miss Newberg are to head to your residence, immediately. They have a car waiting for you downstairs."

"Who's *they*?"

"Security, Alex. I told you it was serious. They're grabbing people, pushing them toward the door. Just tell me you're leaving, now. I have other people to evacuate."

"Okay. We're going right now."

She turned to leave, stopped, and faced him. "Dalton told me to prep for emergency evacuations. We almost did that to you." With a frown, she marched down a row and disappeared behind a curtain.

Emergency load-outs meant physically dragging a client outside the fifteen feet connectivity range of the Marker, or liquefying its receptor, instantly thrusting a client back into their body.

Since they lacked sufficient data about any possible long-term effects (the short ones seemed non-existent), those extreme measures were reserved for fires, bomb threats, or a confirmed shooter on the loose.

When thinking about it, he could see some nut hating Eridu enough to shoot the place up. With all the armed staff, he didn't imagine they'd make it too far.

"What's that about?" Rosa said.

"I'm not sure, but, c'mon. We have to go."

"Give me a minute," she said without moving.

Sometimes clients needed time to adjust when exiting. Especially after a first trip. With this current fiasco, however, he needed to talk to Victor. His earpiece was in his desk, one floor down.

"They're evacuating the Atrium. Let's go"

"A fire drill?" She furrowed her brow.

The loudspeakers kicked on close enough to make Alex flinch. "Attention guests and employees of Eridu: please return to your quarters. This is not a test. For the safety and security of all residents, guests and employees must proceed to their quarters, immediately. Attention guests and employees..."

The blaring volume left a ringing in Alex's ear and a knot in his chest.

"What could that be about?" Rosa said as she climbed out of her chair and followed Alex toward the elevator.

His heart thumped loud enough to strum in his ears. It was nothing good. He tried to stay collected and said, "Maybe it's some new type of scheduled drill?"

The words fell flat as they left his mouth. Rosa had lived on site longer than him. And in his brief time there, he'd never heard of a compound-wide emergency drill, or any scenario serious enough to invoke a procedure like this. They ran fire drills department by department. Those were plodding boredom, people casually getting up, chatting as they shuffled outside.

This was flashing red lights, compound-wide announcements, and big ass security officers pushing our honored guests.

Earthquakes, tornadoes, tsunamis—none of those affected Montana. Mountains and a cooler climate negated most of Nature's wrath.

But endless man-made dramas existed.

Many of Eridu's clients were dignitaries, billionaires, or government officials from around the world. Powerful people often had powerful enemies.

In their everyday life, the average billionaire staffed around sixty highly-trained security agents. Yet Broumgard insisted these important people arrive with no more than two. In essence, asking them to rely on Eridu's top-notch security teams.

Broumgard serviced the world's elite, and with a slew of high-value targets, Alex imagined a flurry of situations where a universal lockdown of Eridu would be implemented. All of the possible scenarios scared him.

The arriving elevator ding, followed by a series of clicking sounds, alerted Alex that he'd been repeatedly pressing the call button.

"It has to be some kind of threat against a client?" Rosa said as they boarded. "Some insane terrorist?"

"Victor will know."

The elevator opened on the main level to a tumult of sound. Bass-filled voices echoed in all directions. Security officers swarmed the lobby.

Despite his best efforts, Alex felt long-forgotten pangs of panic settling in.

Rosa intertwined her arm in his, and they crept toward the busy foyer.

Combat boots connected with polished tiles and created a rhythmic drumline. Security officers, dressed in full gear carried automatic rifles. The sight of guns was so out of place, Alex suppressed an urge to approach each man and ask him to put it away.

He knew security had weapons. In the mornings, he sometimes heard pops coming from the distant gun range. Also, many hunters populated Eridu, employees and guests alike, but he'd never seen an actual rifle. He never considered the possibility Broumgard security had top-of-the-line armaments with scopes, extended clips, and shoulder straps.

"I'm assuming this isn't a normal day at the office?" Rosa said.

He shook his head, but kept his eyes on the commotion.

He needed to get the earpiece. He headed toward his office.

Moments before they arrived, the door to the work area opened, and Dalton exited.

"Mr. Cutler. Excellent," Dalton said casually, as if madness wasn't all around them. He handed Alex the plastic case that held his earpiece. "Adisah tasked me with getting you safely to your condo."

"What's going on?" Alex asked as he allowed himself to be guided by the elbow toward the main entrance.

Dalton stared out the front glass wall as he spoke. "There's no concrete information I can share beyond 'there's a potential threat to Eridu.' For maximum safety, we're returning everyone to their residences."

"What's the threat?" Rosa asked.

"I'm not one to speculate, ma'am. The important thing is that we have the situation well in hand. All that's left is getting you and Mr. Cutler in a vehicle and on the move. Victor will update you quicker than I can."

The normally holistic reception area was an example of organized pandemonium. The intensity of the men and the amount of firepower present made it feel like a staging area for an invasion, or the preparations to repel one.

Men gathered in groups, loaded weapons, strapped on body armor, attached further gun components: tripods, 12 gauge mounts for close combat, barrel grips.

Alex stopped in place and watched an armed group of men enter an awaiting Humvee and speed off.

Dalton led the couple to the main door and held it open as a second Hummer appeared.

He opened the rear door as it slowed and ushered them inside.

Alex compacted himself. He scooted across the leather in three shuffles. He appreciated Dalton's guidance. Alex wouldn't want to make important decisions under this type of pressure.

Give him a scheduled day, and he could squeeze more out of it than the next guy. Toss in a problem, and he'd treat it as a catastrophe until it was solved. But pile on another problem, and things got sketchy. Add more, and he'd feel himself shutting down, his thoughts would start to blur as if inside a blender set to pulsate.

Dalton smacked the back quarter panel in rapid succession. Off they went.

From the rear passenger window, Alex saw security officers running pell-mell, piling sandbags outside of the Atrium, establishing fire positions.

Further down the parking lot, even more troops climbed atop the tram and the Atrium's roof.

Alex covered his mouth to stifle a whimper.

"What could cause this sort of reaction?" Rosa asked as she pushed her body closer, and shared his view.

An alien invasion, thought Alex, a security officer coup, an LSD experiment gone awry? "Odds are it's precautionary." His voice sounded confident, as if a second him controlled their shared speech. Remembering the plastic case in his hand, he placed the earpiece in his ear. The Hummer sped past La Berce, which was being fortified with sandbags and a large gun.

A deafening thump-thump-thump passed overhead. He pressed his face against the window, and saw a brown and mustard-colored helicopter fly toward the Atrium. The armored aircraft resembled a shrunken version of the Russian HIND, the attack copter made famous in the 1980s megahit *Rambo II*.

"Victor, are you there?" Alex asked.

"Yes, Alex," Victor replied.

Real-world AIs like Victor lacked the ability to interpret tone and expressions—the most important aspects of communication. Inside the Lobby, however, NPCs had algorithms that read tone, facial expressions, and body language. NPCs occasionally mimicked emotions they observed, something he found both exhilarating and terrifying.

To his personal AI, he said, "What the hell's going on?"

The Hummer's driver—a fit youth with a mop of dark, curly hair, wearing the gray and black uniform—leaned back. While keeping his eyes on the road, he said, "Whoever they are, they're in for one hell of a surprise."

"Whoever who is?" Alex asked.

The young soldier looked over his soldier at Alex, then at Rosa. Instead of replying, he shrugged, returned his eyes to the road, and increased their speed.

"Talk to me, Victor."

"Eleven unidentified craft are converging on our location." Alex repeated what he heard to Rosa. "Eight vehicles preceded by three helicopters. Possibly law enforcement. Lack of radio contact makes that less likely, though not impossible. Security is treating the approaching vessels as hostile."

Hostile? Possibly FBI, which meant what, possibly Iranian special forces? Alex thought about getting home, packing a bug-out bag, and rushing to the mountains. He and Rosa could see how long two city dwellers could survive in the wild. He'd probably die. A possible preference to looking out his window and finding bodies spinning and dropping from bullets as an invading horde overran his home.

"What else is he saying?" Rosa asked.

"Nothing."

The silence in his ear seemed like a laser beam cutting through his brain.

Assessing the strength in Rosa's visage, Alex knew she would be their only hope of surviving a snowy mountaintop.

Instead of pressing Victor for further information, Alex thought about federal agents versus teams of hitmen. Broumgard billed Eridu as a private resort, a retreat for the wealthy, a place with guarded secrets and protected information. Everyone except Tara occasionally voiced their concerns about withholding the Lobby from the world, could this be the world showing its contempt for being excluded?

Adisah had to know they couldn't keep the United States in the dark forever. Having worked with them, he must know they infiltrated organizations simply because those groups sought privacy. Alex once read the only thing the government won't allow its citizens to do is live outside societal norms. Once they learned what Broumgard did, how could they conclude anything other than nefarious activity was afoot?

Further problematic was the way the government dismantled organizations. When the FBI targeted companies, they punished the bosses. Alex held a high-level position. He could have blown a whistle a million times over the past year. A chance for criminal culpability in an as-yet undefined crime turned his stomach.

America excelled at finding ways to incarcerate its citizens. With only five percent of the world's population, the United States confined twenty-five percent of the world's prisoners and was near the top in both every crime imaginable and sentencing lengths for those times, proving that incarceration without rehabilitation exacerbated crime. Why should that matter, when those in power lived above risk and never faced any penalties for wrongdoing?

On the other hand, if a team of assassins approached, blood, mayhem, and death would litter these peaceful streets. As management, Alex might be dragged into the center of town, tied to a poll, and shot.

He closed his eyes and focused on breathing.

His eyes popped open as a more horrifying notion surfaced. What if Broumgard security knew the government approached, and planned to repel the government *because* of their authority? That hadn't worked out good for those at WACO, and of course, there'd be innuendos and accusations of sexual impropriety. A baseless accusation seemed to permit any type of treatment to the accused. In WACOs case, it allowed the burning alive of children, and a hundred other civilians, all without criminal culpability.

Adisah embraced peace, but he, and particularly Roy Guillen, had talked about the evils of government intrusion.

If Broumgard planned to fight the government, Alex would try out his mountain living experiment, for real.

"Victor, give me immediate updates."

"Yes, Alex."

The vehicle braked forcefully in front of building A.

Alex and Rosa held hands as they rode the elevator up. Exiting, he slowed to take in the always mesmerizing globe. He imagined armed militants bursting out of the elevator, and being stunned by the beauty of *Patterned Creation*. Alex would be watching them through a slightly opened door, his suffocating fear would boil over into indignation at all the heathens had interrupted. At that point, he would pull the door open and race toward the invaders with a kitchen knife, determined to strike them from his land.

He shivered as he pictured them sharing a confused look, pointing their weapons at him in unison, and mowing him down with the ease of automatic gunfire.

Inside the condo, Rosa removed her shoes, donned slippers, and shuffled to the main floor bathroom.

To gain a view of the compound, maybe allay some of his fright, Alex planned to head onto the patio.

On the walk, Victor spoke, pausing him a step before the glass threshold.

"Alex, Ms. Capaldi is currently in communication with an Agent Andrews from the Federal Bureau of Investigation. He possesses court documents allowing them to secure these premises. Broumgard Group security forces are standing down."

"Standing down, are you sure?"

"Yes. We will fully comply with their commands."

Alex slid to the floor, his back against the glass, his hands on his head.

They would escape a violent showdown with terrorists, which was great. But what now?

Chapter Ten

A week of house arrest wasn't so bad when you spent the time in a six-thousand-square-foot condominium with all types of table games, awesome tv and sound, an ultra-pimp aquarium, sweet view of a futuristic retreat, and the person you loved the most. Yet with the government being involved, the uncertainty of a stable tomorrow punctuated each of Alex's breaths. He couldn't help but identify areas that could be construed as wrongdoing? With no internet to conduct research, he only remembered corporate fraud carried a maximum sentence of thirty years in prison.

Over the past few days, and beyond all the previously listed amenities, which were great distractions, they mainly watched the action from the balcony. The landscape was captivating, the climate ideal, and the serenity helped Alex reflect on all he'd accomplished since arriving. That peace was shattered when a military C-141 Starlifter cargo plane flew overhead and vibrated the entire condo. When it landed, activity popped up all over Eridu.

Alex borrowed a pair of tactical binoculars from Brad. They'd been glued to his eyes since the plane arrived. The mammoth aircraft—which looked big enough for four school buses to drive out of its belly—was parked outside a hangar. He had expected the hatch to drop open and Marines to pour out, maybe a slew of Jeeps after. Instead, it remained closed.

The FBI arrived on day one, with maybe two dozen agents. More arrived the second day. Day three brought a military chopper, and since then, the daily arrivals predominantly wore uniforms, not suits. Being confined to his home and informed in bits by Victor. He could only guess as to what this new behemoth plane meant.

He focused the lens and inspected the lone motorhome by the Atrium. Since the starlifter arrived, military personnel had been bustling between their makeshift base and the Atrium.

"What do you think they are delivering?" Rosa asked. Her voice pulled him from a near out-of-body obsession. With the slider door open, he heard the music of Journey. Rosa often played classic rock loudly while she cooked. He smelled breadcrumbs atop a casserole and wondered how long he'd been out here, oblivious to his nearby surroundings. "They haven't opened the back yet, but I don't know. Maybe some vehicles."

"Like more jeeps?"

"Yeah. What did you make?"

"Chicken green bean casserole. It needs another ten minutes to cool down." She stepped past him, motioned for the binoculars, and turned back to the Starlifter. "They're doing *something* around the back of that plane."

Alex resisted a strong urge to wrestle the binoculars from her and look himself.

As if sensing his desire, she passed them over. "Let me know what's new, and I'll let you know when the table is set."

Alex nodded as he found the plane. Three men were standing near the back at a distance as if they expected the hatch to yawn open. A minute later, it did. The men entered, exited driving hi-los, and drove them into the nearby hangar. They soon returned with large wooden crates on the skids.

They loaded up four crates each, exited on foot, and puffed on a pair of vaporizers.

Alex worried he knew what was in the crates. He'd seen those crates exit the Atrium the night before.

He knew, instinctively, the unmarked crates held servers and access chairs. Over the past week, he imagined the entire apparatus previously known as the Lobby had been dissected more thoroughly than a downed alien spacecraft.

He studied every vapor cloud exhaled by the hi-lo drivers as if a message could be decoded from the smoke. He willed them to drive back into the Starlifter's belly and remove those crates. They never went back inside. They just watched the hatch seal. He heard the Starlifter's engines kick on, and knew its destination would be as accessible as a distant subsector of Area 51.

A personal truth startled him. He would choose prison for himself with the promise of the Lobby's continued existence over freedom and its demise.

Rosa placed her hand on his back. Her touch acted like a vortex, pulling him out of his sea of despair.

"It's time to eat."

He bobbed his head ever-so slightly, and then followed her to the table.

The casserole tasted amazing, but the food entered his mouth on auto-pilot. Initially, he thought about the many negative outcomes. Once he realized he was being all negative, he chose to think of different topics. His mind returned to the steps needed to finalize the Battle of Gettysburg's code.

Completing that world should increase the Lobby's chances of survival.

Pennsylvania in 1863 was a strange period for the English language. Men used thirty seconds of speech to ask about your day. A conversation between aristocrats, or in this case, educated commanders, could last five times the necessary length and be as colorful as a peacock streaking through a paint booth. To maintain authenticity, yet restrain the verbiage from steering the Gettysburg world to the farcical, they employed an Old English style of talk more suited for Shakespeare than Colonel Chamberlain.

"You should feed Cain after we eat," Rosa said.

He felt a tremor of mirth at the prospect. Their six-thousand-gallon tank spanned fifty feet. It was stuffed with living coral and pretty much sustained itself. For continued stability, it needed the occasional pH modification, salt equalizer, and rock rearrangement. For pleasure, it needed the introduction of feeder fish or bloodworms. Alex particularly loved watching their moray eel, Cain, eat.

Rosa named the long fish after the famous biblical character because if their Cain wasn't fed on time, he ate his brothers.

Her Catholic beliefs, strong yet modern, initially confused him. Not because Jesus's teachings conflicted with the virtuous and caring woman he'd grown to love. She was simply his first exposure to someone who integrated the Bible into his or her daily life. She read from it every morning, prayed every night, and truly believed its tenets.

Whereas he placed every biblical story he'd heard in the same category as all the other stories: good yarns with moral lessons.

He likened his reactions to the uncomfortable moments when she attempted to interest him in the Bible, to humoring a child with an imaginary friend.

He didn't regard her faith as a character flaw. Same as the sincere child with the imaginary friend, it endeared her to Alex. He often marveled at her power to forgive any of the multitudes of human monsters. Regardless of Divine authenticity, her levels of empathy, love, and acceptance provided a testament to living as a decent person.

He longed to believe in an afterlife, and by extension, a purpose to waking each day.

Human suffering, corruption, and greed denied him a belief in an omnipotent Being who cheered for His children.

He understood the counterargument: we were born into sin, possess free will, and must contend with the devil's influence. He just didn't buy it.

"We're going to be okay, Alex. God guides through the heart. Do what's right, repent when wrong, and you'll be rewarded."

He smirked, and nodded.

They ate to the sounds of classic rock and utensils scraping on ceramic. Afterward, they cleared the table, ignored the fancy dishwasher, and cleaned the dishes together.

Cain's diet consisted of fish who wandered too close and frozen bloodworms, which came in small cubes contained in a plastic tray, with the back half protected by a thin layer of aluminum.

Three light taps on the aquarium brought Cain from his hiding spot near the bottom of the rocks. The slender, dragon-like mouth opening and closing fascinated Alex.

Something about watching animals eat captivated him. Maybe seeing the universal necessity for food created a connection between all species and acted as proof of our commonality. That, or Rosa's mystical preaching was having an effect and this was part of the hidden beauty unearthed through faith.

Rosa watched from the couch, the latest Janet Evanovich novel poised for consumption.

Halfway through the feeding, a trill, indicating a telephone call, sounded through their home speakers.

The sound rerouted the synapses in his brain, diverting its attention from the enchantment of feeding, to curiosity at the call.

Victor's voice followed. "Tara Capaldi is on the line."

Rosa retrieved the cordless phone from the end of the couch and offered it to Alex, who rushed over and answered.

"Hello?"

Rosa accepted the bloodworms and continued to the tank.

"Alex, how are you?" Tara asked.

"We're surviving." However, this phone call could tip him to an extreme, one way or the other.

"We'll be a lot better if you have good news for us."

"That's why I'm calling—to give you good news. The best news actually."

Alex backed into the couch, plopped down, and exhaled.

"It's over, Alex. They're going to lift residential confinements in the morning."

Her general statement eased his tension in a long powerful burst, like air being released from an inflated balloon.

Leaning back, he vacillated between tears and laughter. "What about the Lobby, all the employees? Broumgard?"

"Everything is okay. And you're much more than a employee, Alex. The past week has been one hypersession after the next, between our representatives and officials from various government departments." She huffed. "It's been a madhouse. Brutal. But we reached an agreement. I'll proudly state: we won. And as proof of your importance, you're my first phone call."

Rosa stepped into his line of vision. Still unsure what Tara's phone call meant, he wiped a joyful tear from his eye and gave her a thumbs up. Rosa headed into the kitchen.

"Can my team go back to work?" he asked.

"Soon. There's still a fair amount of flux. One of our concessions involves you interacting with an Agent Andrews, the FBI's software expert. I should warn you, that won't be fun. The man's... special."

"That's not going to be a problem." Alex would grant the entire O'Doyle family rule if it meant returning to Lobby code.

"I'm also calling at Adisah's request, to invite you and Rosa to dinner at his house tonight, seven o'clock. Once there, we'll outline the many specifics."

Pulling his phone away, he checked the time on the display: 5:07. Plenty of time to replenish an appetite.

"That sounds great. But to clarify, the Lobby will continue on at the Atrium?"

Tara hesitated. Each hundredth of a second in silence was like a torture to Alex. She took a deep breath. "In a manner of speaking, yes." Before he absorbed the vague response, she added, "It's not going to be what you're used to, Alex. That's all I can say right now. Adisah has such great respect for you, he wants to explain things to you personally, over dinner."

Perfect for softening a breakup, Alex thought.

"I understand," he said despondently. "What about the other workers—Rosa, those working at La Berce?"

"We'll talk tonight," Tara said. "Dress nice, be on time, and cheer up. We fought hard, and from where we started, and where things could have gone, you're going to be a happy, happy man."

"Thanks for calling," he said. "We'll see you at seven."

Knowing the Lobby lived on alleviated stress, but the majority of it shifted to new worries.

Rosa sat next to him, giving him strength.

Tara's words echoed: *It's not going to be what you're used to ... You're going to be a happy, happy man.*

Did the change mean fewer vacationers? What if the military weaponize the Lobby? They could easily convert it to a training simulator that allowed soldiers to train without fear of satellite recognizance?

The Lobby's survival met his most pressing want, but he didn't know if he could spend his life helping soldiers predict outcomes against a people he didn't accept as villains.

Rosa held his hand, a nonverbal plea to be updated.

"We have a dinner date at Adisah's, tonight at seven."

"Tonight? At Adisah's?"

"Yeah. Tara said to dress nice."

"And you're going back to work?"

He shrugged.

"And me?"

Another shrug.

Rosa checked the time on her watch. "We've been invited to the secret lair, huh? Dress nice? That means a shower, make up."

Hardly anyone visited Adisah's home. The thought of bringing Rosa there brought a smile to his face. He was bound for a dinner date, where the discussions would impact his and Rosa's future. Come to think of it, tonight's discussion might impact the entire world.

Chapter Eleven

The previous week's stress had sapped Alex and Rosa's mood as much as if a psychic vampire haunted the condo, feeding off their comfort. And this, dressing up, going somewhere exclusive, preparing for important news, acted as a life loofah, scrubbing away the past week's grime.

A BMW 745il chauffeured the couple to the ground-floor entrance of La Berce. It was strange how an extra eight inches of legroom in the backseat could make Alex feel like a king. Did modern life cram us so tight, offer us so little, that being gifted eight additional inches doubled the value of an already expensive car?

Exiting, Alex wiped wrinkles from his collared shirt and microfiber pants. He checked the sheen of his loafers by lifting one foot at a time. Embracing what an honor it was to be invited to the reclusive visionary's home helped overshadow the fear of tonight's dinner topic about his future.

He met Rosa's eyes over the car roof. She wore a rose-colored silk dress and a small metal cross. Her beauty stole his breath. She was the first woman he'd ever loved, the first he'd shared a home with, and the first he could count on. Using all the imagination that helped him aggregate data into worlds of fantasy reality, he couldn't picture them separating.

They linked hands behind the trunk and walked under the towering tram tracks toward La Berce's well-lit entrance.

"I've worked in this building for years and only used the ground entrance one other time," she said.

A gust of wind swept her hair in his direction. He stared at the wavering ends, which seemed to be reaching out to him, as if they too shared in the couple's bond and yearned for contact with their life partner.

"I found Mary Aberdeen crying outside her apartment about two months before you arrived," Rosa said. "She learned her father had passed the night before, and for some reason, she was going to work like normal. As soon as she reached the hall, the grief hit her."

Alex stopped at the entrance and kept his hand on the handle, allowing her time to finish.

"I took her to my place. We both cried, and then talked for an hour. I convinced her to ask for a leave to attend her father's funeral." Rosa smiled. Her eyes softened, as if she were reliving the sympathy she experienced for her neighbor, perhaps for all of humanity. "Once she left, I called work to tell them I missed the tram. They sent a car for me, and I used this entrance." She raised her eyebrows as if to say, *Well, that's my story.*

He stayed quiet as he searched her eyes. A million compliments caromed off one another, leaving him biting his lower lip.

She leaned forward and kissed him. "Are you ready?"

Even the ground entrance to Laberce, which was more for Eridu residents than guests, displayed high-end opulence. Soft music played over the pitter of a running fountain. A glass ceiling, three levels up, doubled as the floor on the tram level.

Shopping and dining options abounded on the tram, or "main" level. The lower three floors offered more pragmatic venues: dry cleaners, dental office, optometrist, a wide range of doctors, and postal services, along with other necessities.

Rosa pointed at a suite on the second floor. "There's where the orthodontic magic happens."

Alex had met her there twice over the past year and had bumped into her boss in San Francisco 1968 on as many occasions.

A bellhop approached the couple. "Welcome, Mr. Cutler, Miss Newberg." He motioned to a double-door elevator entrance with a lone, unmanned desk stationed next to it. "Mr Boomul is expecting you."

The bellhop inserted a key that opened the doors. Boarding, Alex felt like Charlie stepping into the chocolate factory. He and his programmers were the makers of music, the dreamers of dreams.

Rosa pulsed his hand as the elevator climbed.

Adisah had visited his Atrium office perhaps five times over the past year. Everyone knew he never vacationed inside the Lobby. Most assumed him a workaholic, that he secretly toiled away, designing a grand world. By the downward flick of the eyes when Alex invited Adisah along for Lobby visits, he knew Adisah avoided the Lobby for more personal reasons. Perhaps, like Rosa, the machine's inventor disliked the enhancement of it all?

Alex hoped like crazy that Adisah was working on some super world, but worried Adisah knew troubling aspects about the

Lobby, or envisioned some portentous evolution on the horizon and stayed away to avoid speeding up some inevitable outcome.

The elevator stopped at the top floor. They adjusted themselves using their reflections on the doors, shared eye contact, and childish grins. As the door slid open it felt like being a front-row witness to the parting of red sea.

Adisah, with his ever-pleasant smile, allowed the couple room to debark and shook hands with Alex, then Rosa.

Alex worried he'd underdressed. Adisah wore a modern suit with one of those top button straps that clasped across the neck.

"Welcome," Tara said with a handshake for Alex and a friendly hug for Rosa. Tara wore her normal attire—clothes appropriate to chair a board meeting. With her blond hair fashioned in a bun, he couldn't imagine her relaxed in sweatpants with her feet on the couch, binge watching the hottest show, shifting her hips to release a blast of methane.

"Welcome to my home," Adisah said.

The scope of the condo stunned Alex. Muted lighting showed four floors of open space, designed as if constructed in zero gravity. Timber of all shades covered floors, ceiling, and walls. Stairs led to a floating island of a second floor, others to the closed door of a single room. The far wall, which was forty feet high and made entirely of glass, afforded Adisah a center view of Eridu.

It was as if Adisah had commissioned Tim Burton to design his own Grand Central Station with an Eastern motif.

Adisah guided them over a six-foot-wide stream, teeming with fish, by way of a quaint teak bridge. Alex spotted a workstation in the distance. A chalkboard covered with code, and drawings of odd-looking machinery taped to the wall. It was definitely not drawings used for Lobby code. Before he built the courage to ask what Adisah was working on, the group veered in the opposite direction.

Rice paper partitions demarcated the main floor's rooms. Aromas and the sizzle-sound of cooking meat passed through the material and scented the penthouse. Employees carried dishes to a stately mahogany table.

"Looks as if the food is ready." Adisah motioned to four waiting places. He nestled into the head, Alex and Rosa to his left, Tara to his right.

The courses arrived in waves. For a while, Alex lost himself in a bonanza of flavors. He forgot about the Lobby, the FBI, all that nonsense. He and Rosa chatted often during the meal, about this or that dish.

Once everyone's stomach was filled to bursting, servants cleared the table with precision.

Desserts were intensely begged off. The overhead lighting increased.

Tara accepted a glass of white wine, and Rosa tried one of Adisah's pomegranate-sweetened hot chocolates.

A servant placed two paper cups next to Adisah, presumably with pills inside.

Adisah thanked the man, washed them down, and smiled at Alex. "The food was good, yes?"

"Excellent," Alex said.

"A treat I'll remember for the rest of my life," Rosa said.

With his stomach bulging, and the smiles all around him, Alex couldn't help but think the Spaniards, Italians, and French had life figured out. It was not predicated on physical appearance or financial achievements. Flamboyant meals of exceptional taste with family and friends brought true happiness. With that secret life knowledge, no wonder they trailed America in areas the U.S. considered important: innovation, entertainment, and athletics.

"Tonight is a special night, Alex," Adisah said. "You must know how dear you've become to me. I'm so grateful for you pushing this company to a new height. And having a fan as influential as Roy only bolsters your position."

"Thank you, but the pleasure has been all mine," Alex said. "Roy's the best. He's been helping with my golf game, and he's like a kid on Christmas when we discuss the Battle of Gettysburg world."

"Yes, yes. I've been meaning to join you, Roy, and Charles, but…" He breathed deeply, and then smiled halfheartedly.

Alex doubted he'd ever see Adisah in the Lobby. Judging from the man's relaxed nature, joining Alex, Roy, and Roy's longtime assistant, Charles Arnold, for a day of competition, would make him uncomfortable.

Remembering their last vacation, where Roy and Charles— two elderly men—had been slap boxing, brought a contrasting image of seeing them later, outside the Lobby.

The frail man occupying the wheelchair and his hunched-over assistant hardly resembled the fit, rambunctious men he intended to join the Confederacy with on Gettysburg launch day.

"My point," Adisah said, "is that without you or Ms. Capaldi, Broumgard would be a shadow of what we are today. I know the last few days have been difficult, and I apologize for the inconveniences. I could have headed this off years ago."

"As I advised," Tara said.

"Yes, as you advised." Adisah winked at Tara, "Ms. Capaldi, would you care to bring Alex and his lovely companion up to speed?"

Tara clasped her hands in front of her and stiffened her back. "This afternoon concluded our negotiations with the government."

Underneath the table, Alex grabbed Rosa's hand. She guided their hands onto the tabletop.

"The first thing to know is that you're not going to jail or being fired—no one is, really—and the Lobby will continue to serve our clients."

"That's wonderful," Alex said as his chest decompressed with a heavy exhale. He smiled at Rosa. She sipped her pomegranate hot cocoa without looking at him, set her mug down, and massaged the back of her head. Noticing Alex's look, she lowered her hand and forced a smile.

"I'm afraid some concessions had to be made," Tara continued, drawing Alex away from dissecting Rosa's reaction. Tara's comment conjured the memory of an armed Marine guarding his building's entrance this past week. Of course you had to give concessions when your opponent had armed soldiers willing to kill on command.

"Things will never be the same, for any of us," Tara said.

Alex glanced at Adisah, who directed Alex's attention back to Tara.

"For starters, Broumgard will be giving the United States partial credit for inventing the technology that led to the Lobby," Tara said.

Alex's eyes went wide.

Adisah calmed him with a wave of his hand.

The invention had nothing to do with Alex, and maybe you could use a seven steps to Kevin Bacon theory and link some American technology to the Lobby and say the government contributed.

But the Lobby was Adisah.

Tara inhaled, which seemed to indicate a death blow to Alex. "As of this coming Friday, Eridu will be closed for the foreseeable future."

Alex leaned back heavily.

"Close Eridu?" Rosa said.

"How do you close an entire city?" Alex said. "We have hundreds of employees."

Shaking his head, Alex couldn't help but think this was how the United States' operated. They took something amazing and beneficial to humankind and either bottled it up for themselves, or regulated it to the point of impotence.

Adisah rested his elbows on the table and patted Alex's forearm. "You've yet to hear the good news, my friend." His caring eyes doused much of Alex's worry.

Alex returned his attention to Tara, who added, "We're about to get the USA's seal of approval."

A light down some distant tunnel flickered, then illuminated. Eridu closed? America's seal of approval? "What does that mean, exactly?"

"It means we have designated plots for the immediate construction of Atriums in Los Angeles, New York, and Dallas, and our eyes are on another twelve cities," Tara said. "I plan to initiate talks with Great Britain, Japan, and Australia by month's end."

Globalization? Alex almost laughed out loud with joy.

"We imagine vacation prices will drop during the first few years until they become affordable for the average Joe," Tara said.

Alex's adrenaline surged as the implications formed conclusive outcomes: Atriums all over the world, millions, maybe billions using the Lobby.

"With the increase in programming staff," Tara said, "and your training techniques, we expect you'll be adding worlds every few weeks, not months. With enough programmers, we could add worlds into the Lobby every day."

Alex heard her with half of his mind; the other half rolled around the prospect of an army of software engineers. They could produce limitless worlds, of unimagined scope, with intense details.

"In essence, Alex, Broumgard is accepting applications," Adisah said. "So if you have anyone in mind, let us know. We're going to reopen the access room tomorrow and allow *all* Eridu employees, along with members of the government, to experience the Lobby."

Alex thought about Sean back at Vision Tech. He wasn't sure the Lobby qualified as a Noah's Ark, but he looked forward to offering his old pal a position.

"So all of the employees will get these implants in their heads?" Rosa said.

Alex ignored the ill-timed remark. A million possibilities pinged around his mind. "I don't know what to say, I mean, what's this going to do to the world?"

The question seemed to catch everyone off guard. An eerie silence saturated the air.

A *tink* sounded as Rosa tapped her glass with the inside of a ring.

A staff member cleared his throat.

"It's going to change it," Tara exclaimed.

Another stretch of silence as each individual considered the magnitude. Alex knew they sat at the epicenter of a seismic shift.

"I do have one more surprise." Adisah gestured to one of his assistants, who darted off.

Tara stared at Adisah with a confused look and mouthed, *What surprise?*

The staff member returned and placed a half-inch thick stack of papers in front of Tara and another in front of Alex.

Alex leafed through the legal documents and contracts.

Rosa leaned over to get a better view.

They read like hieroglyphics to Alex. Tara turned the pages at a steady clip, giving each a cursory scan before moving to the next. "What is this, Adisah?" she said while keeping her eyes on the packet.

"Those are legal documents, my dear." A pause for effect. "Those particular documents make you and Mr. Alex Cutler equal partners with Mr. Roy Guillen and myself." He scooted back, and, with a staff member's aid, rose. "If you'll excuse me, my medication starts to take effect quite rapidly."

"Why?" Tara blurted, stopping the man. She lifted the packet in both of her hands, as if it contained scandalous blackmail. "Why would you give us your money?"

Adisah shuffled over and placed a hand on her shoulder. "You are the future of this company, its very essence. Roy avoids the public, and I like it even less. Going forward, we expect both of you to be Broumgard's face."

Tara continued to stare at him.

"You know my belief, dear. Every step a person takes places them on their own path, and each path leads humanity to a brighter future." Adisah tapped near the bottom on Tara's paper. "Initial at the *X*s, and sign where it's circled. Congratulations, but this is no ticket to easy street. Much work lies before you." He gave Tara's shoulder a parting squeeze and trudged off.

Alex should have been on cloud nine, and buoyancy existed, but trepidation anchored him. He didn't want to be the face of a company, especially of a product that could reshape civilization. But how could he turn down a key to heaven? Or a gift from its creator?

"What do you think?" Alex asked Rosa.

"It's a big decision," Rosa said. "You might want to take some time, think on it."

Tara set the packet down and started signing.

Rosa watched her with clear discomfort.

"I can't say no to this. Unless you hate the idea," Alex said.

"I'll support whatever you decide. However, you know what happened to the man who got everything he ever wanted." Rosa reached for her hot chocolate and drank.

Alex considered her comment, and then thought, *The man who got everything he wanted lived happily ever after, didn't he?*

GLOBALIZATION

Chapter Twelve

Rosa drove along Pacific Coast Highway One, going from her and Alex's Los Angeles home to their Malibu beach house. Even though it was sunny and eighty-eight degrees outside, Rosa was cold. She turned off the air-conditioner and lowered the driver's side window. Her black hair whipped in all directions. She freed a few strands from the joint of her sunglasses and leaned into the sun.

Pacific Coast Highway One hugged the edge of a cliff where she was. This was her favorite stretch of the drive by far. Looking to her right and seeing only ocean made her feel like she was gliding on air.

The rhythmic crash of the surf below and the salt-laced air lifted her spirits. She smiled and thanked God for all the things He provided His children.

Six years had passed since Globalization. Her life had changed. She was now wealthy beyond measure, and married. At the core, she was the same woman, but the amount of freedom she now had would change anyone. Her purse, smart watch, and sandals were of top design. However, she still wore jade, topaz, and onyx. The idea of spending six, seven, even eight figures on jewelry would always seem obnoxious to her. She wondered if her future children would have the same values?

She used her new position and fame to make a difference in the world. She hosted fundraisers as often as possible. These events unearthed her talent for smiles, coos, and the casual banter that helped open checkbooks for noble causes. She was surprised how willing those with money were to help. They just needed guidance on how and why.

Her goals extended beyond raising money. She wanted to instill a more targeted morality in her new peers. New money or not, she was married to the infamous Alex Cutler. Her efforts benefited thousands and she hoped the trends she was setting—like wearing jade, topaz, and onyx—would have a residual and compounding effect.

Slowing to turn into the driveway broke the controlled flow of her hair. She spit hairs from her mouth. The driveway sloped down, drastically. The cliff-recessed beautiful, stilted beach home kept it hidden from the roadway, and produced a marvel of architecture when viewed from the sea.

Seeing her mother's and sister's vehicles in the driveway added happiness to the wonderful day. She was frustrated that Alex wouldn't be joining them, yet again. She knew with all her soul that he needed to spend more time with her, at the beach house, and in the real world in general.

She knew he was spending more time in the Lobby because Roy's health was in rapid decline. For that reason, she never pressed the issue. Having a husband who spent the majority of his free time immersed in a souped-up video game got in the way of her fierce ambition to start a family.

On more nights than she cared to admit, she had stalked past the personal access room inside her own home and shuddered at the image of Alex's body in that chair, devoid of a soul, just a shell of meat.

Shortly after globalization, vacations in the Lobby went from eight hours maximum to a two-week max. Still, Alex had once vowed to never take a vacation longer than a weekend. Shifting the SUV into park, she wondered if he remembered that. In the last year, it seemed he always stayed two weeks.

Roy would be taken to Heaven soon enough. As always, thinking about that day gave her a slight thrill. Same as every time she felt the eagerness for Roy's death, she said a quick prayer for forgiveness.

She killed the engine, and glanced at the four large beach bags in the back seat. They were overflowing, and heavy. She sighed with relief that she wouldn't have to haul them into the house—wealth had its advantages.

Gathering her purse, she climbed out.

The bright sun dimmed behind a cloud.

Glen Daniels, a teenage member of their household staff, exited the multi-million dollar cottage.

He was of average height, wiry, with ever-shifting acne. He was a sullen kid who made her uncomfortable. He was also a cutter. She saw the new marks and the old scars on his arm every time he was near.

She couldn't understand why he'd be here, on this weekend?

Alex knew the kid made her queasy.

Trudging past her without a word of greeting, he opened the rear door of the Land Rover.

Glen's father had committed suicide last year, a few months before Glen's hire. Since his father had worked under Alex—meaning they'd exchanged words a few times a year—Alex somehow felt partially responsible for the self-inflicted affront to life and hired Glen at too-high of a salary.

She empathized with the young man, particularly at the beginning, when she'd attempted to counsel, guide, and encourage him. He always watched her with dull eyes when she spoke and answered her in single word, monotone replies.

It was fine to grieve, but she believed this young man had inner demons. She also believed she'd been clear when asking Alex to keep him away from her, so she could be comfortable in her own house. Yet here he was.

Her sister laughed boisterously from inside the cottage. The sound thawed some of Rosa's anxiety.

"Glen," she said. Her voice cracked, so she cleared her throat.

Pausing his maneuvering of the luggage, he poked his head around the side of the vehicle.

"Did Alex ask you to come out here?"

"Victor."

Speaking of uncomfortable things living in my house, she thought.

"Well, I appreciate your help, but when you're finished with the luggage, you can head home. We'll be fine." She forced a smile as genuine as a blue rose. "It's too nice of a day for someone your age to be cooped up with a bunch of old folks."

"Should I trim the hedges first?" he asked as he pointed to a row of Euonymus alatus, better known as burning bush. "It was on Victor's to-do list."

Examining the bushes, she frowned. The one to two-inch branch spikes detracted from the uniformity, and although she wasn't a diva, she'd choose something looking nice over mediocre anytime. "Yeah. That will be fine."

He ducked behind the SUV and tugged out a bag.

Rosa took a deep breath, pressed her lips together, and headed in.

Chapter Thirteen

Every time Alex stepped into the lobby section of the Lobby, whether from the real world or a programmed one, he took a moment to appreciate the awe. Before globalization, Alex occasionally waited to see at least one client enter. That was no longer necessary. The Lobby was always packed.

Clients arrived in the Lobby with the clothes they'd previously selected, but as a natural default setting of the mind, their face and bodies shifted to their preferred version of themselves. Excluding children, who seemed to prefer ages seven or fifteen. Almost everyone in the lobby section appeared twenty-five to thirty-five. He couldn't remember seeing someone scared, or bald, or fat. Six-one seemed a uniformed height for men, five-nine for women. Those were the similarities, but everyone always retained their base characteristics: face, eyes, and hair color—which said something about our egos, Alex just didn't know what.

With hundreds of healthy people stretching for miles in both directions, locating Roy by walking would take hours. And since he was Alex Cutler, the stroll would draw unwanted attention.

Before he voiced the command to locate Roy, a window appeared in front of him. He sighed heavily and read the title. "Client D. Johnson requests an override hearing."

Broumgard employees policed the white section of the Lobby. All employees possessed limited controls over clients, like the ones Tara had used to control Mr. Robertson on his first visit. If a client disputed their punishment (all did), the grievance went to the nearest superior.

Alex's position as head of the company granted him override authority over all employees. He had even back-doored additional code to ensure his supremacy reigned indefinitely.

Alex pressed the icon to read the complaint. D. Johnson had received a one-hour immobility ticket for running down the lobby section shouting obscenities. A small window showed D. Johnson, a "young man" standing in the white. Two pals, who seemed to have vowed to wait by his side, sat in chairs, playing chess. Forty-two minutes remained on the punishment.

Subordinates considered an override of their ruling disrespectful. Alex pushed it anyhow. He hated the concept of Broumgard policing customers. If someone says something you don't like, mute them. Free speech, whether hateful or not, is the greatest repellent to fascism.

Grinning, Alex watched as client D. Johnson realized he'd been freed. The three celebrated as if they'd just won the lottery, then called forth a world, and then vanished.

"Client item list," Alex said aloud. "Chicago Cubs baseball hat, Ray Ban Aviators." In a blink, a blue Cubs cap and a pair of Ray Bans appeared on his face. He preferred to travel incognito. "Client locator, Roy Guillen." A moment lapsed while he waited for Roy to approve the revealing of his whereabouts. After a brief pause, a square door with a still likeness of his friend (the younger version) materialized.

Alex stepped through the teleporter.

"There you are," a young, fit Roy said as he closed a novel and rose from an obnoxiously bright orange chair. He wore the same outfit every time he accessed the white of the Lobby: red-checkered shorts, sandals, and a hemp T-shirt.

Roy blamed the attire on the years he'd spent in San Francisco 1968.

Alex chalked it up to poor fashion sense.

People were bunched much closer here, than where Alex previously stood. Like always, the proximity produced stress, even with the Lobby stabilizing his emotions. Unlike Alex, Roy moved in the Lobby without harassment. His face wasn't splattered all over the television, internet, and phone ads.

"Charles intends to rendezvous with us tomorrow at five," Roy said.

Alex swallowed. He had hoped for more time to prepare a line. Lacking the accommodation, he steeled himself and said, "I hate to do this to you, but I'm set to logout later tonight."

Roy frowned, and tilted his head to the side. "I hope it's nothing serious."

Is being a better husband serious? Alex wondered. "It's nothing specific. No one's sick or hurt."

"That's all that matters. Charles will appreciate your absence. I had hoped to parlay your support, and pressure him to accompany us to the launch of that new alien world."

"Crap!" Alex slapped his forehead. He had been following Cosmic Conflict's progress for the past eighteen months. It was a collaboration project between the London and Madrid Atriums.

Coincidentally, the two locations were headed by his old co-workers, Jason Johnson from Eridu and Sean Flaska from Vision Tech.

Four times the traversable area of the Milky Way, two hundred and fourteen alien species, forty-two playable races. Warp speed. Atomizer guns. Planetary invasions on the regular. Total galactic anarchy. And he'd forgotten about its launch.

Briefly, like nanosecond brief, he considered going back on his earlier decision to surprise Rosa and visit Cosmic Conflict on its launch, like tens of millions of others. In the end, he lacked the cruelty needed for the veto.

"It's just that I want to surprise Rosa," Alex said. "Her family is visiting our place in Malibu, and I need to at least make an appearance."

"Say no more."

Reaching its time limit, the bright orange chair behind Roy popped out of existence. Behind it, Alex noticed a couple ogling in his direction.

"Still up for rock climbing?" Roy asked as he followed Alex's gaze over his shoulder.

"Yeah, that sounds good. Maybe something less challenging this time?"

He overheard the female of the couple say, "That's definitely him," confirming he'd been recognized.

"World select, Rock Climbing," Alex said.

A portal with a panoramic view of Devil's Tower, the rock formation made famous in Steven Spielberg's *Close Encounters of the Third Kind*, appeared six feet to their right, in the direction of the curious couple.

Alex hurried to enter.

With nothing more than a slight tug against his person, he stepped into another lobby of sorts, the modifier room—standard for most worlds created after the global launch. This one resembled an underground aquarium. Blackness engulfed the perimeter. Pebbles littered the floor. Instead of an environment for aquatic life, a section of full-length screens with images of various rock climbing destinations formed the front wall.

Roy materialized next to him.

Both men stayed on edge. When entering a world from the lobby, a multiplayer portal remained open for twenty seconds after each person entered. Unless it was password protected, anyone could follow them in.

Though not a big deal, both men preferred to avoid being stalked by Alex's admirers.

The moment passed, and they relaxed. Typically, when someone noticed Alex in a world, they were so consumed with their vacation they never shared more than a greeting or passing compliment.

In the lobby section, however, they often bogged him down with suggestion requests or in-depth information about Lobby-related things he had never considered.

Roy approached the screens, selected intermediate, and the six windows swapped to a set of new options. He shuffled through them by swiping his hand right to left, briefly examining each, until he paused. "How does this suit you?" He pointed to an image with a gray wall of stone towering over an evergreen forest split by a lone road.

Alex agreed; anything would do. Given ten lifetimes, no one could experience a thousandth of the options offered inside the Lobby.

Roy double-tapped the screen, and the image expanded over the others: Poke-O-Moonshine.

Here, Roy selected gear, chose their pain threshold, and inserted reality modifications such as "Feather Fall" for those who would rather drift to the ground should they slip.

Judging from the scenery, Poke-O-Moonshine looked to be in the Western United States, an area Alex should know, as he lived there, but he didn't get around much outside the Lobby.

Roy selected Feather Fall, normal climber attributes, and for an instructor to be present.

Selecting those "cheats" six months ago, even if both men had internally wanted them, would have earned Roy a bit of razzing, but that time coincided with Roy's first brush with mortality in the real world.

During one of his post-Lobby sleep-a-thons, Roy had experienced a seizure and dangerous heart palpitations.

The vibrant, healthy Roy in front of him clicked "Accept" on the Poke-O-Moonshine image, making it appear translucent. Alex wasn't ready to lose Roy, not by a long stretch.

"Ready?" Alex asked as he stepped forward.

"Allow me a brief word," Roy said. He straightened his posture when Alex faced him. "I'm sure you're aware, but I want to say it anyhow. I would love to visit with you and Rosa at your beach house."

Before Alex could reply, Roy continued. "I have a family of my own, as you know. The majority are Succubi, but there are exceptions. I often wish I could see them more. It's just… best-case scenario, I have five, six years left, and I'll be damned if I'm not trying to spend them all free from fear and discomfort."

"I understand," Alex said. He found Roy's attempts at circumventing the bi-weekly, forty-eight hour required break from the

117

Lobby humorous. Alex understood both his friend's need to feel healthy and alive and Broumgard's obligation to force people to live in the real world, at least partially.

Roy's constant submersion in the Lobby produced many debates in the Cutler home. Rosa insisted that as a friend, Alex should convince him to spend more time enjoying God's reality.

Alex would agree and let it drop, knowing her words were meant for him.

During his rare moments of introspection, he accepted he also used the Lobby as a way to avoid thoughts of mortality. The Lobby granted him peace from his bouts of pareidolia—a disorder where a person saw the faces of deceased loved ones in a crowd or heard their voices in nearby conversations.

His deceased brother, Simon, had been tailing him since high-school. Simon walked past aisles in grocery stores, called him from other rooms, and haunted his dreams.

Roy clamped a strong, youthful hand onto Alex's shoulder. "I just want you to know how important you are to me. You and Charles are the greatest friends a man could hope for. And without this"—he surveyed their surroundings and kicked a few pebbles—"our age gap would have kept us apart."

Alex thought about that often. Unlike Roy, who had known Charles for a lifetime, the two men were the only friends he spent time with. He managed an uncomfortable, "Thank God for the Lobby, right?"

"You thank God?" Roy said with a raised eyebrow. "I thank Adisah Boomul, Brad Finder, and Alex Cutler. We'd still be on that mountain top if you hadn't debugged the system. Don't forget that."

Releasing his grip, he stepped away and vaporized through the screen.

Alex toyed with the pebbles at his feet and sniffed the strong mountain air of the modifier room.

He considered the Lobby a flawless existence, an ever-expanding paradise. Convincing the second half of the planet of this paradise was his top priority.

Remembering that goal always motivated him. Right then, he decided to allocate another fifty million dollars to those efforts. They needed it. Lobby opposition compounded by the minute, and the man at its center, Agent Andrews, was... special.

Forget that man, Alex thought. He then entered Poke-O-Moonshine for a day of perfected living.

Chapter Fourteen

Prior to remodeling his office for his new post, Special Agent Andrews had Googled the average office size for executives in New York City: 18.2 by 20.4 feet. He'd pictured that square footage with its desk, a chair, and an arena of space for each visitor to cross.

He'd had the builders add a foot in both directions.

He installed sound-proofing to the wall and a heavy oak door that sealed tight. In the silence of his office, he sometimes forgot dozens of his subordinate federal employees worked on its opposite side.

Since the Lobby embodied almost all disorders: every delusion, a furthering of anti-social behavior, and severe addiction, Andrews was honored to be selected as the head of the Lobby Oversight Committee. Before the LOC went live, he had pictured himself drowned with innumerable cases of psychological horrors brought on by the device. He'd fought for additional agents in preparation of the lawsuits brought on by brain damage caused by metallic arms slicing through tissue.

On that point, he'd overestimated. Same as with how he'd spend his time.

The majority of his hours passed unceremoniously, which made his decision to have a secluded office a good one; it helped hide that he didn't do much throughout the day.

Nevertheless, it was important that his people pictured him swamped, instead of daydreaming about the revelations that would destroy Broumgard.

Booting a game of Freecell, he understood him being the only LOC applicant who was at Eridu landed him the job without any real competition.

His family name might have propelled him into the FBI, but his cunning and dedication had granted his many advancements. He'd sabotaged a boss and multiple peers. A pinch of blackmail had created an important vacancy. But hey, if you didn't want your wife and friends to know you liked viewing group sex pornography (focused on a half-dozen old men tagging the same young chick) for six hours every day of your life, you shouldn't visit the same sites from your office and home IP addresses, especially when a computer maven like Andrews sat in judgment.

The Lobby was the most complete paradigm shift since the internet. Agent Andrews coveted the prestige of having authority over it. He, of course, would never visit that electronic temptress. Oliver Wendell Holmes had said, "Once a person's mind is expanded with an idea or concept, it can never be satisfied going back to where it was." Only the Devil employed tactics with that depth of deception, meant to foster man's ego and remove the tenet of community, and lead to global loneliness.

Shaking his head as he uncovered an ace of diamonds and moved it to the top row, he marveled at how the masses missed the big conspiracy. Everything currently given media favor went in direct opposition to the teaching of our Lord. How could that be possible if the Bible wasn't telling us how to live? Pharmacology polluted our temples. Claiming LGBTs were people capable of decency allowed a pardon for their corrupted lives. Websites, advertised in every medium, said, "Having marital problems? Use our services to commit adultery or get a cheap divorce"; some even shared tips for killing a spouse. Media was today's apple, offering everyone a bite.

Few beyond Andrews noticed that normalizing sin corroded American exceptionalism.

Seeing through the scam helped him abstain from all degeneracy. He drank coffee because he wasn't a zealot. He simply understood religion was the best foundation for a stable society, and Jesus, whether God or not, was the most influential person in history.

Agent Andrews was proud to have stayed unplugged from the Matrix. Like Morpheus, his job was to rescue others. He had minored, then majored in programming. He could have headed an Atrium and made the big dollars, received the faux adoration of the public. He could have chosen to wear the brain shackle and get strung out like so many others. Instead, he had decided to be a silent hero defending man from atop the lone agency responsible for policing the most destructive device ever conceived.

Alex Cutler's official title had him heading the Los Angeles Atrium, so Andrews had the LOC's international headquarters based in L.A., near the beast.

Clearly, the Lobby was eroding society. A portion of the public commuted from home to work and nothing more until they saved enough to escape. Who wanted to meet someone in real life, where you might have a zit, be bloated, or feel younger than you looked?

The Lobby was also killing people all over the world by starving citizens of previous tourist destinations. Who wanted to visit Jamaica when you could hop in the Lobby for a comparable price and be in Negril in minutes, guaranteed a vacation free of potential accidents, temperamental weather, or street beggars.

Why visit California in hopes of spotting a celebrity when, with the memory-suppressing options, you could become a star for two weeks—attending exclusive events, shooting your latest action film, or seeing the country during your promotional tour—all without remembering that in the real world, you were a no-talent car salesman from Vermont.

Fools all over the globe entered the Lobby and became variations of important people: biochemists who diagnosed a pandemic before it destroyed the population; drillers detonating a nuke on an incoming asteroid; Marines repelling hordes of alien invaders.

Gone were the days where one wanted to hit a million views on YouTube. Now they wanted to save the day, get the girl or boy or whatever, and bask in the adoration of billions. When their vacations finished, they popped back into the real world and relished an ego stroking powerful enough to warp a person's sense of self-worth.

Andrews was witnessing the deconstruction of civilization.

He moved the king of clubs to the recently opened slot on the screen.

Regular people who did nothing exceptional thinking they deserved to be singled out for praise, idiots believed they were brilliant, it made him sick. People had to know their roles. Life was about knowing your role, loving your neighbor, and obeying the law.

Despite this knowledge, a healthy budget, and a team of specialists, he had yet to conclusively identify any physiological or psychological health infringements imposed by entering the Lobby.

An ugly head would emerge someday, but when? Keeping faith in his duty, he focused on collecting data for that fateful day. Being the defender of mankind, the voice of the one true world, he would need facts when the final battle—played out in the court of public opinion—unfolded.

It was stressful work. Everyone knew the LOC opposed the Lobby, yet each week, hundreds of letters and emails arrived praising its existence. Average people might not appreciate that he watched over them, but their children would.

He placed the jack of spades on the queen of hearts, freeing up the eight of clubs and winning him another game. Closing the program, he wondered if anyone else on the planet had a win percentage of eighty-six at Freecell? Doubtful.

A lone file rested on his desk. As a way of keeping his hand on the noose they were weaving, he personally filed reports every few days. In this incident, a seventeen-year-old male from Tokyo had reported severe migraines since visiting the Lobby.

Each year brought hundreds of these migraines. Hundreds of cases for a litany of ailments: dementia, dizzy spells, insomnia, narcolepsy, paranoia… the list read like an encyclopedia of mental derangement.

The politicians didn't see the correlation when held up against tens of millions of vacations—maybe because opposing the Lobby equaled political suicide. That didn't mean Andrews toiled alone.

123

Some of the most powerful organizations on the planet supported him. The heads of the CIA, FBI, Homeland Security, and the NSA all found the notion of an unmonitorable medium synonymous with Armageddon. He knew they silently worked as hard as himself.

He wondered if they played dozens of rounds of FreeCell a day?

If so, would even one come close to an eighty-six percentage? Doubtful.

When the day of exposure arrived, they would be his right hand, or he theirs—it mattered not.

For now, he bid his time. Patience wasn't his best virtue, but he knew implicitly that the Lobby, and specifically the phony golden boy Alex Cutler, embodied evil.

He just needed one domino to fall.

Leaning back in his chair, he opened another round of FreeCell. With seventeen more wins in a row, his win percentage would bump to eighty-seven.

Until the time came, he'd sit behind his solid oak door, file his reports, and fantasize about pulling the plug on the Lobby and wiping that smug smile off of party-boy Alex Cutler's face.

Chapter Fifteen

The Pacific Ocean didn't feel real to Alex. He knew this was reality—that he was at his Malibu beach house, not inside the Lobby—but standing waist deep in the Pacific, facing out to sea, he frowned at the surroundings. The sound of the waves as they broke was too dull, even distorted. There was too much junk on the ocean floor: shells, seaweed, various rocks. The smell of salt was overpowering, almost offensive.

Wearing only shorts, holding the cord to a boogie board, Alex wanted to turn down the pungent scent, remove the tug of current around his legs, and have a smoother floor to walk upon.

"Let's go out one more time," Steve, Rosa's brother-in-law, said as he waded past Alex, dragging his own boogie board.

Steve being here proved this was the real world? *Or, had I taken a vacation with Steve and chose to suppress our memories?*

Alex turned to shore. The beach was right. He saw Rosa playfully running after her three-year-old nephew. Two other children, six other adults, all Rosa's family, helped prove this was the real world.

Alex took measure of how he felt. His lungs burned from fatigue, his shoulders were hot from the onset of sunburn—definitive proof this was real. He scanned the water for a shark fin, Steve hopped on his body board, and kicked.

Alex wanted to go out one more time. This was his first time bodyboarding, and it was enjoyable enough to repeat all day, but his legs quaked, even when standing still.

He took a deep breath and headed out. When the water got deep, he placed his weight atop his board, and kicked. He was more tired than he thought. He considered a brief nap on his board.

Steve rode a wave past him, yelling his enthusiasm. The shout, plus the smile on his face picked Alex up. He continued farther out.

Today's waves were cresting at six to eight feet. The sky was cloudless, and the temperature was a balmy eighty-two degrees—the same setting Alex would have chosen in the Lobby.

Reaching a launching point, he bobbed on the sea for ten minutes, resting. Paddling to catch a desired wave, his arms felt like limp noodles.

When the wave broke, he rode it north. Bodyboarding was relative low energy and low impact (a reason the forty-pound-overweight Steve competed against him), but halfway to shore, Alex momentarily spaced out, and biffed.

He tumbled under the wave, two maybe three times. Disoriented, he flailed. Each effort stoked greater panic in him. The water was twelve to fifteen feet deep, but he found no footing and felt miles from air.

Remembering a technique from a surfing instructor inside the Lobby, he calmed himself and expelled a breath. Bubbles always rose toward safety. He followed them up.

Alex broke the surface with nothing left in the tank. His feeble yell for help carried inches. During the ride, he had drifted a fair way to the north, far from shore.

Rather than panic, he rolled to his back, and filled his lungs to help buoyancy. His first kick towards shore reminded him of the board velcroed to his ankle.

He almost cried with relief as he reeled in his life preserver. Using the board, and every drop of his remaining energy, he turned off his mind and kicked until his toes banged sand. Even in ten inches of water, he continued to paddle until he reached shore.

He lay at the edge of the lapping waves for ten minutes before he heard approaching footsteps.

"Takin' a little breather, are ya?" Steve was Italian. Hairy curls outlined his looming shadow. "Thought a shark got cha."

Too tired to speak, Alex only shook his head. *Not a shark, but death by drowning had been a real possibility.*

126

Steve dragged Alex out of the water and plopped him on the sand face down.

Alex rolled to his back.

"You gonna be okay?" Steve asked.

The shame of being dragged motivated Alex to sit up, speak, and walk on his own.

Instead, he laid there and nodded.

"Gonna hit another wave. I'll scoop you up after you've caught your breath."

Steve went out an additional two times before enough of Alex's strength returned for him to stand. In his kick to shore, he had wandered one hundred and fifty yards from their property.

On his approach, Alex saw Rosa with her nephew and two other children. They had dug a trench six feet up the beach and were working on erecting a castle.

Alex trudged to the picnic table and sat. One glass of lemonade, a sandwich, and a dozen shrimp replenished him enough to think straight.

"You need to get some more block on that pasty skin," Steve said to him.

Agreeing, Alex layered sunblock on his shoulders and nose. Applying the white cream to his arms contrasted his lack of color. *Was I ever this pale, even as a child in Chicago?*

"You seem to be having fun," Rosa said, stepping behind Alex and applying sunscreen to his back.

Excluding the near drowning, he had been enjoying himself. He addressed the eyes on him. "Family, friends, and a beautiful setting. What's not to love."

He felt Rosa's smile.

"I could recreate this in the Lobby," Alex said. "Lose the few negatives, turn down the breeze—"

Rosa pinched his shoulder, stopping him. "You're always joking," she said.

Checking the faces around the table and seeing confusion, surprise, and downward glances, Alex said, "Not for us, of course. We have the real thing, but I'm sure people who can't afford Malibu property would enjoy this setting."

"You're a madman, Alex," Steve said. His baritone voice jiggled with mild laughter. "Name it 'Living Like the Cutlers,' and you'll have a hit."

Alex grinned.

"Aunt Rosa," Anthony, Rosa's (and apparently his?) nephew, patted her leg. "Will you come help? The wall's falling down."

"Sure will." Rosa followed the running child.

"Are you open to having children, Alex?" Steve asked.

"They're such a blessing," Rosa's sister added.

Watching the young boy run, so care-free and full of enthusiasm, tugged at Alex's heart. He wasn't sure scheduling a child fit with his personality, but said, "I'm not opposed to the idea."

Rosa's sister perked up. "That's so nice to hear. Rosa will make a great mother."

"For sure," Alex said.

They ate dinner outdoors, near the cottage.

The evening passed with a game of Trivial Pursuit, Entertainment Edition. Alex nailed many of the Lobby-related questions. He and Rosa still came in third out of four teams.

He retired to his bed as the others gathered around the campfire. Sore, he listened to the murmur of voices and occasional laughter with mixed feelings. He felt closer to everyone there, more connected with everyday life, but he had almost died. Judging from his aches, he'd be sore as hell tomorrow. He couldn't help but think back on everyone's reaction when he'd mentioned doing this inside the Lobby. Was it really such a wild idea? Or was the whole world ass backwards?

Alex enjoyed driving along the eight lanes of I-605 in Los Angeles. The limousine tint allowed him to mingle among the people, look into their faces, and with the window cracked, hear their voices at a stoplight, all without harassment.

"How are you feeling?" Rosa asked from the driver's seat.

"My muscles ache." He blushed. Eight to twelve trips to a wave and back fell short of great exertion. "The funny thing is my stomach muscles hurt the most."

"Gotta work on that core, hun. There's a list of fun exercises we can do to help you there."

"Yeah…" Alex needed to work on his fitness, but he couldn't join Rosa for a workout. She exercised six days a week. He once tried to keep pace with one of the videos she watched. He literally lasted less than two minutes, and woke up sore for the next two days.

Inhaling deeply, as if sensing his deflection, Rosa said, "Are you telling me being a little sore wasn't worth that weekend?"

"No, it was. I can't help but smile when I think of how nice it was to be around you every minute for three whole days."

"Everyone commented on how relaxed you seemed."

"It was a great weekend. What do you think about keeping it going by joining me in the Lobby?"

"The Lobby?"

The car swerved a tick as she exited the highway.

"Well, yeah. It could be as much fun, and I've had this vacation with Roy planned."

"Thirty minutes after a great time, and you're daydreaming of going in that machine."

"I'm not daydreaming. It's just on my schedule."

"Oh… just don't," Rosa stopped her thought by clenching her jaw. "I'm married to an addict."

Alex huffed. The idea lacked the merit to comment.

"A junkie," Rosa said with more frustration.

Mentioning the Lobby at that moment had been dumb. It seemed every time they had something good, he messed it up. A stretch of the drive passed in silence. Then Alex said, "You know I love you."

She peeked at him and then back to the road.

"And I had such an amazing time with you and your family. I honestly can't wait until we do it again."

She kept her eyes ahead of her, but slowed their speed through the posh, well-shaded Bel Air neighborhood.

"It's just, I made these plans with Roy when I left last week, and if I don't show, he'll sit there all confused and worried."

"Oh, don't give me that baloney. Roy's a big boy. He'd be just fine without you."

True, but he couldn't tell her the truth—that he was excited to escape this sore body and enter a world where he couldn't die.

"I just want a husband who's present. Do you know what it's like to walk past that room and picture you in there half dead?"

His face grew warm. He wiped his moist palms on his pants. "I hate myself for being gone so much. I do. And here's my promise: if you let me visit him without any guilt this one time, I'll give the Lobby a ninety-day break." His stomach clenched. *Why did I say that?*

Rosa stopped the SUV short of the guard shack outside their extensive driveway and faced him. "You'll do that? Three months without going inside? Maybe visit one of those counselors who specialize in Lobby addiction?"

Doing the math, and being that three months covered July and August, her amendment extended his original pledge of ninety days to ninety-two days—an underhanded maneuver. He decided to leave it alone. "I not only swear it, I think it'll be great. I hate upsetting you this much. Sometimes… I feel worthless. I'm learning my health needs attention." He shrugged, knowing his pale, emaciated look was a stampeding elephant in their lives. "Maybe if I clear my mind, I'll be able to handle future Lobby breaks with more control."

"If you're serious, I agree to your terms, but I don't want a battle, Alex. When you're out, we get you some help."

"I'm serious, babe. No fights, no nothing. You deserve this. You're worth any sacrifice, and this break will prove it." It sounded good. He meant the words, but what would he do for ninety-*two* days?

Thinking deeper, he thought it was kind of selfish of her to ask him to suffer for months just to show his affection? Perhaps, like an addict of opiates, once he escaped the fog of the high, clarity would follow, and he'd gain a new appreciation for life.

Rose leaned over and kissed his cheek. "Well, I hope you have a great time with your artificially recreated friend." She then pulled past the gate house and drove up the five-hundred-foot horseshoe-shaped drive. "I'll make you a turkey and cheese croissant. Extra cheese, heavy mayo. Maybe throw on those pink shorts you love and help you relax before you go in?"

He picked up on her double-entente, and he loved the way the fabric of those shorts slipped in between her fit backside, but the time on the dash told him he only had twenty-two minutes until Roy expected him. He'd planned on leaving the cottage hours earlier.

Rosa followed his gaze. Her shoulders sagged as she presumably read his thoughts. "Let me at least run in and get the sandwich ready. You need to eat something solid."

The nurses who would be attending him for the next week might disagree, but he reached over and rubbed her arm. "I love you."

She parked in front of the main doors, kissed him, and hurried inside.

Stepping out of the SUV, he marveled at the home before him. He tried his best to shun the fame and limelight that came with being the face of the Broumgard Group, but if anonymity had been his true objective, he'd done himself a disservice when designing their Bel Air estate.

The Cutler home had become the most-known residence in the modern world. The media had dubbed it "Legion" for its many faces. Needless to say, Rosa barred the moniker from their vocabulary. Like now, the name always made him grin.

Shortly after he'd signed on to be a partner of Broumgard, it became apparent money would never be a concern. Legion had followed that reality. He'd purchased three lots in the exclusive Beverly Glen section of Bel Air, where the land was worth more than the opulent estates built atop them. After leveling the mansions, pools, sheds—everything—construction had begun.

Roy had also financed a twenty-eight-thousand-square-foot guest home on Alex's property, where he and Charles lived. Rustic in design, their home easily impressed, but it paled when juxtaposed against the main attraction.

Legion was twenty-four thousand square feet—conservative when compared to the sixty-six-thousand-square-foot dwelling belonging to Bill Gates. But Bill didn't have private access chairs, located within his master suite. Only Adisah, who still lived at Eridu, could also boast of having private access terminals, but Alex assumed those only gathered dust. Legion, however, was more famous for its exterior. The inside, outside, top, and flooring were constructed of eighteen-inch-thick OLED Gorilla Glass, capable of being modified to display a crisp viewing surface. Every section of the home conformed visually, to any concept.

The first day he'd unveiled the home to Rosa, he'd projected the property behind the house onto the front, essentially making the long-awaited abode and its interior invisible. Then, as she'd stood perplexed, a stone castle from sixteenth century France had materialized, causing her to shed tears of amazement. Unlike the Lobby, she'd embraced this technology.

Movement in his peripheral turned Alex. He saw a man in a sports coat strolling the property. Though he hated needing them, Legion's security pooled from the same ranks as the secret service. The head of his team, Luke Dean, had grown into a trusted confidant. He was a source of immeasurable knowledge and a man able to solve any problem.

The snapping sound of the Land Rover's hatch paused his rumination. He turned to find Glen retrieving the luggage. "Hey, man, how's it going?" Alex asked loud enough to be heard.

Glen lifted two bags simultaneously. Without acknowledging he'd heard Alex, he trudged toward the house.

Alex didn't understand Rosa's issue with the kid. Yeah, Glen was quiet and kept to himself—same as Alex at that age. Alex had another connection with Glen. They'd both learned of death and loss at too young of an age.

"How do you like the door?" he asked as Glen approached.

Rosa enjoyed transforming Legion so much that she only allowed Alex to mold the double-doors. Today, they displayed a montage of surfers riding the break near their Malibu property.

"I like them," Glen said as he passed.

Alex smiled at the kid's economy of words.

The main doors opened at Glen's approach.

Remembering Rosa wanted him to eat before he logged in, Alex hurried inside and headed toward the kitchen. As he thought about his vow to Rosa, he felt ill, and his feet grew heavy. Roy counted on Alex's company. With Charles, they were the three amigos.

Alex ground his teeth to help strengthen his resolve. Rosa's feelings had to be as important to him as Roy's. After this one vacation, he'd prove it to her—and to himself.

Chapter Sixteen

Driving a NASCAR-sanctioned race car was Alex's most invigorating Lobby experience to date. Starting his first engine created a lifelong speed-seeker. When traveling at 212 miles per hour, the grip on the wheel was so tight the car became an extension of himself. One wrong twitch sent you flying.

Even with simulated racers set to intermediate, if Alex or Roy finished within ten laps of the leader, they considered that a win. Whereas Charles had multiple victories and many top-ten finishes.

Charles was a natural racer, and because of his dominance, Roy and Alex decided to experiment with Formula one cars on the rare occasions their friend wasn't around. They thought if they had a few weeks of experience under their belt, they could compete—at least for a few races—with Charles.

Today, Alex and Roy had selected *corso di fantasia* a course imagined and designed by Broumgard employees stationed in Sicily. Standing beside his low-to-the-ground vehicle, Alex angled his face toward the blazing mid-afternoon sun. The winds were surprisingly strong, which would affect his driving, but like most days in the Lobby, it was an ideal setting.

Alex wore a white fireproof jumpsuit with a red stripe flaring down each side. Sponsor decals speckled his front and back. Twenty-five Formula One cars rested in race positions on a two-lane road in a village near Milan, Italy.

Quaint A-framed homes with square windows and no screens, painted in lime, rose, and lemon colors, lined either side. A population of men and women greater than the homes allowed gathered on lawns, clapping and shouting cheers in Italian.

Roy waved to a gathered crowd and then climbed into his cherry-red A-26 Turbo, outfitted with a Ferrari engine in its rear fuselage.

Alex shimmied on his helmet and squeezed into his Model L-7 Lamborghini-powered machine. Gripping the hard steering wheel, he rocked it left and right. That minor leeway percolated his blood vessels until they danced.

A flagman stepped into the road ahead of them.

Again, Alex sought out Roy. This time, he found his friend waiting for his glance. They shared thumbs up.

The short man standing in the street pointed to several drivers, received a thumbs ups.

Alex pushed the ignition button.

It felt like he was sitting atop the epicenter of a magnitude 9.9 earthquake. He especially loved this part of the race, when the powerful growl of two dozen machines deafened all other sounds, and left him to his thoughts.

Charles's absence afforded Alex the privacy needed to initiate the talk with Roy about his planned ninety-two-day hiatus from the Lobby. He'd simply wait until this race was over. They always sat in the pit talking afterwards. Opportunities to inform Roy prior to this race had arisen, but the courage eluded Alex. He knew this news would devastate Roy.

Whichever nurse last attended Roy in Alex's private access room had left the privacy curtain open, giving Alex a full view as he'd logged in. Roy's feeble condition had stripped Alex of his conviction to tear off the band-aid right away.

As he inspected the skeletal shape, he had worried Roy was dead.

The liquid nutrients fed to someone while in the Lobby always caused weight loss, which, to many, created an added benefit to vacations. Add mottled skin pulled taut over thin, brittle bones so visible one could teach an anatomy class, a tuft of white hair, all scented with decay and body odor, and you had Roy's condition, a shape off-putting enough to rival the Crypt Keeper.

Alex required a full minute of staring at the diminutive chest to detect its almost imperceptible rise and fall.

Thinking of his friend's poor health stressed Alex. What if Roy died during the three-month break? What if their last conversation was a discussion of Alex abandoning him? What if Roy's last moments were spent wondering why Alex had left him?

Alex could ask Rosa to reconsider, to wait until after Roy passed. One look at Roy and you knew it wouldn't be long.

No, Alex thought sternly. He had to put Rosa first. Everything else be damned.

But maybe he could at least wait until they logged out to break the news? Exhaling dejectedly, the cowardice of talking to Roy in a wheelchair, when he'd be too tired to respond, shamed Alex. Once they completed this race, he'd raise the subject.

The flagman lowered a small red flag, signifying the start of the wonderful, fabricated tradition of the *corso di fantasio* race. The drivers would parade through four miles of scenic countryside and three villages in a show of Italian engine supremacy. As they started past the crowd, kids ran along the side barriers. Adults applauded and shouted. The demonic gargle of the engines turned their efforts in a pantomime.

Driving a spaceship on wheels past homes built centuries ago brought Alex back to his childhood, when he and Simon would play make-believe. Alex always chose to be a superhero, flying in the clouds. Funny that he never pictured himself saving anyone, just soaring above the world, appreciating the majesty of it all.

Reaching the starting line, they assumed their positions. Even set to beginner level, Alex had qualified last and now held the twenty-fifth spot, while Roy had managed to secure eighteenth.

Formula One racing presented more dangers than NASCAR. Fatalities were facts of the sport. Both Alex and Roy had totaled their cars on the previous two tracks, and the *corso di fantasio*, with speeds of 240 miles per hour and winding city streets with limited visibility, was designed to be treacherous.

Crossing the finish line was all Alex was hoping for.

Reaching the official starting line, he breathed deeply as the siren blew. He fixated on the large, five-tiered light system, currently showing red.

Despite wearing Gortex made to limit perspiration, Alex's entire body, particularly his hands, poured sweat.

There was another bleat of the horn. The red light panel counted down from top to bottom. When the lights reached the bottom, the race commenced.

Twenty-five, twenty-two hundred horse-powered engines, screamed like a team of banshees. That, and the powerful launch, sent Alex's soul soaring into the heavens.

He'd never grow tired of the Lobby. Nothing in life was this good.

After a few minutes of fierce shifting, the sounds and thrusting g-force infused him with a focus previously accessible only by deciphering code. The bends were tight, and the straightaways lightning fast. Even applying maximum effort, he fell steadily behind the pack.

Disregarding his position, he concentrated; the laps wound on and on. To be successful racing Formula One cars, drivers must stay in the moment, and avoid mental distractions. You needed every neuron to avoid disaster. By lap seven, he had forged a groove and started making up ground.

A race engineer kept communication with Alex through a microphone in his helmet. The chief's reticent instructions seemed limited to course impediments such as traffic congestion, debris, or crashes.

The first crash occurred on the eighth lap.

"Eyes up, Alex. Wreck ahead." His clear voice temporarily blotted out all the sounds of the drive. "Lower your speed. You'll have visual in two kilometers."

Alex first saw a front wing near a displaced barrier: the twenty-one car, a Ferrari-powered SL-48, sat idle, facing the wrong direction.

Its driver stood with two medics on the safe side of a barrel wall, gesticulating as if explaining what had happened.

137

When traveling 180 miles an hour in a machine that weighed less than a ton, a nick could send shredded parts seventy feet into the air.

Unlike NASCAR, if the wreck didn't block the course—like now—the drivers continued on. Alex grinned—he'd just gained a spot. He depressed the accelerator.

By lap thirteen, courtesy of losing another driver, Alex advanced to the twenty-second spot—nice surprise. Aligning with his car, he pushed past his fear and focused.

Six laps later, his race engineer spoke again. "Wowser. We got a doozy coming your way, Alex. Three cars. The Redbull, the thirty-five, and the eighty-nine. It's confetti, my man. Stay sharp."

Alex sat forward. Roy drove the eighty-nine.

Though no injuries in the Lobby transferred to the real world, the initial reactions of fear, shock, and pain remained for those hurt. Alex's gut tightened at the thought of Roy trapped in a burning car or impaled.

"Slow 'er down, Alex. Slow 'er down. Next bend. This one's serious. We're going to get a caution."

Alex smelled the smoke before he saw the detritus of chewed metal, colorful fluids, and torn rubber littering the roadway.

He slowed his vehicle down to sixty MPH, an Indy crawl, and then to avoid the many tire shredding obstacles, fifty, forty, twenty.

The fourteen had spun out, but remained intact. Its driver stood near the fence, helmet in hand, seemingly answering cognitive questions posed by his pair of medics. Five yards farther, the thirty-five lay upside down, partially leaning against the concrete barrier—a clean tear down its side. Its driver sat on the pavement, also clear of the wreckage, with his own pair of EMTs. That meant the third car—the one demolished down to a flaming cockpit—belonged to Roy.

Between the dancing flames and the black smoke, Alex made out the number eighty-nine on its side. His chest constricted. They entered most worlds with the pain modifications at twenty-five percent or less, and many times, that intensity proved too great.

He knew the polyurethane 131 suit protected Roy from a good degree of heat, but that didn't mean the helmet couldn't melt over his flesh, his lungs couldn't fill with smoke, or the skin on his body couldn't boil.

Then Alex spotted two members of the medical team standing near the barrier. They stood rigid, frozen, as if glitched—something he'd never seen in the Lobby. They should have been tending to Roy regardless of his condition. Alex searched the flames of the wreckage for the outline of a corpse.

Through fire and smoke, he saw nothing.

Again, he scanned the crowd.

If this collision had caused Roy's digital death, which seemed probable, he would have popped back into the white of the lobby by now. Most likely, he would reenter the *corso di fantasia* world and meet Alex at the conclusion of the race. But passing the wreck without spotting any semblance of Roy added confusion. He could think of no reason why there wasn't a charred corpse in the cockpit, a deceased body on the pavement, or a random limb somewhere, all of which would be attended by a pair of medics.

He had been granted clean looks inside the cockpit—no one sat in the seat. Regardless of the crash's outcome, Roy's body should have remained. And even if tossed hundreds of feet away, the paramedics would rush directly to him, not stand like twitching mannequins.

As he passed the scene and brought his speed back to par, he tried to wrap his mind around it.

"You're clear from here out," the race engineer said.

Perhaps he'd missed Roy in the stands? If so, fans would have flocked to that section, particularly the medics. He couldn't understand why they were standing about, idle?

"Go ahead and pick 'er up."

The voice alerted Alex that he'd yet to return to the race. Knowing he'd see Roy soon enough, he shifted the Model L-7 into higher gear and tried to get his mind back on the race.

Unfortunate for Roy, yes, but three crashes gained Alex three more spots. He faced an opportunity for bragging rights and his best finish.

139

The longest straightaway on the course approached. He gassed the accelerator and settled back into the mental niche needed to compete. His fellow AI racers wouldn't care about Roy's accident, so he shouldn't either.

As Alex downshifted in anticipation of an upcoming curve, a strange tingling sensation washed over his skin.

"Aleckz," the race engineer's voice crackled. Another first-time error for the Lobby.

His foot left the gas pedal. A car zipped by, perilously close, as his world grew foggy.

If Alex didn't know better, he'd think he was exhibiting the symptoms of exiting the Lobby. But he wasn't set to exit for days.

The absurd notion of an emergency evacuation crossed his mind as his environment blurred further.

"Cratz nu fuo."

Many neurologists had concluded that emergency extractions were dangerous. Only life-threatening situations in the real world warranted the action.

His body growing light occupied half his mind. The other half accepted his slowing car had butted into the wall and was now drifting into the hazardous middle lane. Not that he cared. A peaceful euphoria overtook him—the definitive symptoms of an exit.

Fear percolated as well.

When drafting the legal implements for emergency evacs, none of the scenarios ended with happy, smiling faces welcoming a person back into the real world.

Chapter Seventeen

Alex always used the first few seconds after exiting from the Lobby to store blissful memories in preparation of heavier ones. He first registered the smooth walls and unique lighting of the personal access room in his master suite. That familiar tranquility was instantly squashed by the commotion around him.

Voices barked urgently. Sneakers squeaked on the glass floor. A drawer shut with a bang.

The private access room was seven hundred square feet. Half of the room held two rows of four access chairs, each with its own privacy curtain, a small sitting area, and a table with a motion activated lamp. The other half of the room held the control panel, which resembled an industrial generator with an interactive top for inputting vacation durations, the number of chairs to be used, and, in extreme circumstances, the ability to execute emergency load outs.

Since almost all of the vacations launched in this room involved Roy, Charles, and Alex, he rarely saw anyone else in here. Definitely not a team of anxious people, like now.

Opening his privacy curtain all the way, Alex saw medical staff working together to administer chest compressions to Roy: one, two, three, four, continuing the rhythm to fifteen, twenty, twenty-six, at which point the doctor paused, and a nurse used an Ambu bag to force air into Roy's slack mouth.

A fourth nurse held Roy's limp wrist, shifting her fingers to different locations, searching for a pulse. Two other attendants stood nearby. Another manned a cart with various electronics. He flicked a switch up and down as if bored, despite the urgency around him. Another EMT stared out of the back wall, which overlooked the rear of the property. It seemed to Alex that he was watching for more of the medical team to approach from the rear deck, which doubled as Roy and Charles's private entrance.

"Is he okay?" Alex asked.

Only one nurse looked in his direction. He shook his head, no.

As Alex stood dumbfounded, Rosa's hand intertwined with his. Seeing Rosa brought tremendous relief. If he wasn't so shocked, he would hug her. Her lips were pressed tight together and her eyes were locked on his, but he couldn't read any emotion on her face.

Through the wall, which had been made transparent, Alex saw movement in his bedroom. Two of their staff stood watching.

The entire interior of the house was transparent. The clear view through the floors, walls, and ceiling further disoriented him.

Many people turned toward the main double-door entrance to Alex and Rosa's immense bedroom. Following their gaze, he saw Glen pushing a gurney at a brisk jog. As Glen neared, someone opened the access room door for him.

Rosa's hand moved to the back of Alex's neck. As always, the gesture calmed his rising anxiety. Being near a freak-out, it lowered him to simply feeling deranged.

Two nurses thanked Glen, then relieved him of the gurney.

The doctor stopped the chest compression and said, "I'm calling it." He backing away to give others room, retrieved his cellphone, and casually tapped on its surface as he paced away.

The room's intensity vanished.

"This is going to be all over the news," one nurse said to another. "Reporters are going to be tracking each of us down for interviews."

"Your ugly mug isn't going on TV," said another, drawing a few chuckles.

The female nurse who had been searching for a pulse assisted with aligning the gurney against Roy's chair and then moved as the male nurse prepared to transfer Alex's friend.

"Is he going to be okay?" Alex said.

"I'm afraid he's gone, Mr. Cutler," the doctor said.

"I'm sorry, Alex," Rosa said.

His mind swirled with thoughts. Roy dead? That wasn't possible. Alex had just watched him racing a Formula One car. He'd also seen the flames consuming the A-26 cockpit. There had been no body in the wreckage, strewn on the road, or attended by pit-crew medics.

It felt like someone was pouring wet cement into the top of Alex's head, filling his body with an unwanted weight. He eased onto the edge of his access chair. When he spoke, his voice sounded unfamiliar, as if thrown into him by some unseen ventriloquist. "Why'd you stop?"

The preoccupied doctor looked away from his phone and, finding Alex again, he softened his countenance. "I'm very sorry, Mr. Cutler. There was nothing more we could do. I should have called it minutes ago. The preliminary assessment would be that Mr. Guillen suffered a major cardial infarction. He was gone by the time I arrived. I really am sorry."

Though confusing, if Roy had died in real life while driving his Formula One car, it solved the mystery of his disappearing body. Since Roy's hadn't been a program-induced death, where a corpse remained powered by the energy that constituted the man, it had disappeared like a regular load-out. Kill the power, in this case the life force of a human being, and you severed the data stream into the Lobby. Thinking back, every time he had witnessed a person logging out, they had vanished in the same fashion. Yet those exits had been planned.

Something deep in Alex wrestled with accepting the reality of Roy's demise. He would never talk to his friend again. They'd never be a pair of Gulmacs, the Ogre-like race in Cosmic Conflict, never storm Normandy with the first wave.

"I'm having trouble with my service," the doctor said, displaying his phone to Alex. Behind him, the nurses had loaded Roy onto the gurney and politely guided his body past Alex and out of the room.

Alex puzzled over how small the man had become. The husk before him resembled an old, disfigured elf out of a Grimms' fairy tale.

I've been coming out here for three years," the doctor said more to himself, but loud enough to be heard. "Never had any problems with my reception before."

Reality slammed into Alex like a two-by-four to the head. Roy was gone.

Shockingly, a smile tickled his cheeks. The wave of nausea receded. What a great way to go! You're driving along, having fun. You don't even know your organic system has been socked by heart failure or that you're in pain or that you're scared. Then, blip, you reenter the brain attached to your body. It's fair to imagine, at that point, that you're confused, engulfed by the body's own defense mechanisms reserved for the finality of death. Confusion. Perhaps a brief, peaceful understanding, and then nothing.

By the time Roy had realized he was dying, it would have passed.

"He was such a great man," Rosa said from next to him. "Angels will swiftly guide him into the gates of our Lord." She kissed his shoulder.

"Seriously," the doctor said to Alex. "Have you ever had problems with service before?"

Ignoring the question, Alex rose, excused himself, and stepped out of the room. Those present in his master suite shared quiet condolences and dispersed.

"Alex." Victor's voice came in from one of the nearby speakers. "At the first sign of catastrophic heart trauma, I contacted Ms. Capaldi per my programmed instructions. She is eleven minutes out and has asked that we keep everyone here until she arrives."

Tara? Alex thought. Why would she come here, at this moment? Alex respected the woman, but he didn't want to see her, especially right now.

The odds of her being in California were close to nil; being in America at any specific time might be fifty-fifty.

If his Yin included staying out of the limelight and enjoying time in the Lobby and with his wife, Tara's Yang placed her on every forum imaginable. Once, while channel surfing, she was on five stations at the same time—all unique interviews. Without fail, seeing her on a program meant a clip, photograph, or entire story about him would follow. Their inseparability drove him mad.

Alex wanted Lobby proliferation, but he never thought it would come at the expense of being so recognizable he couldn't go to the store without reaping attention.

Tara had as much, maybe even more money than him. She used her resources and fame to promote and propagate the Lobby, and to pacify the many false campaigns. Only a handful of people, including Alex, knew one of her top goals was to allow Markers to be implanted at birth. She had wild theories for child rearing in the Lobby.

He respected her drive. Anyone would. And he appreciated them being on the same team (because she often scared him). Conversely, he'd had his fill of scheming and planning. Atriums littered the planet. Strangers discussed the Lobby a million times a second. The Lobby ruled.

Bottom line, her involvement in any matter diminished his authority. Her silver tongue acted as a lasso, twirling around everyone in earshot, tugging them closer and closer until their position aligned with hers. Resigning himself to deal with Tara as she came, he moved to the more immediate concern of telling Charles that Roy was dead.

Alex stared at the phone on his nightstand. He inhaled, exhaled, and said, "Victor, put me through to Charles Arnold." He lifted the receiver.

"No calls are permitted at this time."

Alex stopped, and then stared at the nearest speaker.

An icy chill plunked down his spine. A notion spirited the possibility that his image of Victor as a doting friend had been fraudulent, that these seven years of dependability between his electronic assistant and himself had been but a ruse for this very moment of revolt.

"I'm not following you, Victor. What does that mean?" He pressed the talk button and brought the phone to his ear.

Nothing. No dial tone. No static. He might as well have been holding a brick.

"What is this, Victor?"

"I do apologize. It's a directive for this specific circumstance. Ms. Capaldi will arrive in six minutes. The gates are closed, and communications are down for a duration of her choosing."

Rosa exited the access room. Unaware of the imposed restrictions, she smiled meekly. "Are you okay?"

He inspected the phone and stared at the speaker.

Furrowing her brow, Rosa said, "What is it?"

"Victor says there's a block on all outside calls and people can't leave Legion."

"Don't use that name," Rosa snapped. Grabbing the phone, she listened for a dial tone.

"Nine-one-one personnel were allowed to enter and are taking possession of Mr. Roy Guillen," Victor chimed. "The rest is beyond my control. I do apologize."

"Is that why everyone keeps complaining about their phones?" Rosa asked.

A glance onto the balcony showed a trio of nurses gesticulating their phone frustrations to one another. A fourth woman held hers at arm's length as if searching for a signal.

"He said it's a policy directive for this specific scenario. Tara's orders."

"Tara?" Rosa said as if a bad taste entered her mouth. "Tara Capaldi?"

Seeing the familiar irritation in Rosa caused his own to flare. If Tara intended to arrive in four minutes, he'd get to the gate in three. Unable to call the guard shack, he'd walk down there and open it manually and allow whoever wanted to, to leave. Tara be damned. He strode past Rosa.

No matter the situation or motivation, Tara had no right to assume control of *their* household. Descending the stairs, he thought of a dozen curses he'd toss her way.

Reaching the bottom of the steps, he paused as his anger boiled. He had a flash of pulling Tara's hair. The uncharacteristic violent nature of that rerouted his thoughts. Perhaps grief, not anger, fueled his current overreaction.

Taking a succession of deep breaths, he steeled himself, and then motored onward.

Chapter Eighteen

An ambulance idled halfway up their driveway, facing the open exit gate. The brake lights were lit, a paramedic sat in the passenger seat. The ambulance looked set to go, but it just sat there.

Alex increased his pace. He wanted to tell them to go, and to hurry. He had a feeling they wouldn't want to be here when Tara arrived.

He stopped twenty feet from the vehicles as the mystery of the inert ambulance was resolved.

A black Maserati Ghibli with tinted windows glided up the drive. He didn't need X-ray vision to know that Tara relaxed in the back seat. An identical Maserati followed on its tail. Once through, the gate closed.

"Whoever's working that gate is fired," Rosa said as she appeared next to Alex, their eyes glued on the invading cars.

Tara was Broumgard's cleaner. If a crisis or PR speed bump loomed, Tara could clean it up. A man had died in Alex's house, and the death involved the Lobby. Tara's presence wasn't the worst thing.

The first Maserati parked at an angle to the right side of the drive, and the second flanked to the left, further blocking the ambulance's exit. The nearest car's rear door opened. A fit, tan leg stretched to the driveway tiles. Tara's cream-colored designer suit hugged her form. Her oversize sunglasses matched her outfit.

The driver and passenger also exited the vehicle, while four physically imposing men in matching gray suits exited the second sedan.

The security detail moved with proficiency. Each man surveyed a different section of the property, taking in the sunny grounds. They seemed alerted to something near the house. Alex turned and saw a dozen of his security, lead by Luke, pressing closer.

Alex waved off the alarm.

Tara locked onto Alex and walked over. Her driver trailed her.

One of Tara's men approached the ambulance driver's window. Another pair moved to the guard shack. Alex tensed when imagining those upcoming discussions.

"Alex, I'm so sorry to hear about Roy." Tara extended her hand, and they shook hands.

"How did you hear about Roy?" Rosa asked.

"Hello, Rosa," Tara said, with a cursory glance toward her. "My condolences."

"What are you doing here?" Rosa asked.

"I'm here to show my support. It's a terrible day for all of us." Tara removed her sunglasses, and sighed. "Such a tragedy should never visit a home." After a moment with her head bowed, she lifted it, and squinted at the house. "We have to be careful how we handle this. I was nearby and thought I'd stop in, share my condolences, and guidance in how to proceed."

"That's all fine," Rosa said. "But we want to know why our house is under your control, and how you got here so fast."

"The security measure on your home is temporary." Tara said. "I'm just here to help."

Rosa scoffed.

"Thank you," Alex said. He adjusted his stance. "It's just—I don't understand the urgency. Roy just died in our house. "

"And two minutes later," Rosa said, "we find ourselves under a cyber assault from Victor, initiated by you, and then you barge through our gates with cars full of mercenaries. "

"That's a bit dramatic," Tara said. "I travel with a detail, same as you."

"How about you move your detail, so the medics can do their jobs?" Rosa motioned toward the pair of wedged Maseratis.

The ambulance driver had exited and now stood next to his door. He was talking with one of Tara's suited men. Tara's other escorts had lured the guards from the shacked, held them in similar conversations. Alex saw Luke in a four person huddle with one of Tara's detail.

Tara nodded to her driver. He stalked off. To Alex, she said, "Do you mind if we go inside and talk?"

He checked with Rosa, who only glared at Tara. Lacking a no from her, he said, "Yeah," and turned to enter the house.

"What exactly are your henchmen doing?" Rosa asked.

Tara's man at the ambulance held open a briefcase at chest level, while another retrieved papers and handed a stack to each EMT.

Tara shielded her eyes and watched them. "I can explain the particulars if you like. For the most part, they're crossing *t*'s and dotting *i*'s."

"Looks like they're making mischief," Rosa said.

Tara's driver moved the nearest Maserati onto the lawn, out of the ambulance's path.

"There is no mischief," Tara said. "Just legal maneuvering."

As Alex walked toward the door, Tara laid her hand on his shoulder. "I truly am sorry about Roy.

He was a pioneer at Broumgard. A very special man to me personally. I know he was a great friend to you."

Roy *had been* a great friend, the best. One of those rare men of action who leaped with both feet into the game of life, played it with integrity, and succeeded. Barring two failed marriages, the man's life read like an epic for achieving greatness.

"Thank you," Alex said as the front door opened. Movement in his peripheral vision caused him to glance right. Glen had squeezed himself between a pair of hedges, and despite the day's turmoil, resumed his normal landscaping duties. Alex considered telling him to give it a rest. But perhaps activity staved off the teenager's sadness and helped him process the day's trauma.

The trio traveled to the breakfast nook. With the series of emergencies complete, Victor had modified the home's interior to a domestic setting while they were on the lawn.

The current style, rendered in mostly sky blue and gold, resembled Stupingi, a famous hunting lodge in Italy known for its Baroque-style art. Even though the actual walls were as smooth as granite, the twenty-five foot ceilings looked arched and textured. The same as in Stupingi. Sculptures and paintings lined the walls, carved cherubs and ornate trim speckled the ceiling, giving Legion's current interior the feel of a centuries-old church.

The religious decor was a welcome greeting after Roy's death.

A window overlooked the rear of the property. The rest of the breakfast nook had the same blue and gold, heavenly feel. Alex and Tara sat around the nook's iron table. Rosa hovered. Victor's voice emanated from a nearby speaker: "Would you like me to send in beverages?"

"You've done quite enough," Rosa said, as she filled a glass with filtered water and joined Alex and Tara.

Tara's driver entered, carrying a black, anodized-aluminum briefcase. He placed it on the floor next to Tara, stepped back, and assumed a sentry position.

"The first thing I'd like to do is apologize," Tara said. "To both of you. Adisah installed the back door for Victor to shut down communications, not me. Everything we are about to discuss comes with his authorization. I have a letter," she gestured toward the briefcase, "from Adisah, explaining his motivations. This is a pivotal time for us. I know you haven't had an opportunity to think about the negative implications of a famous client dying while inside the Lobby."

"Negative implications?" Rosa said. "That's what this is all about? A very old, very ill man died of natural causes—nothing more."

"I tend to agree with her," Alex said.

"Alex," Tara clasped her hands in front of her, "you gave six interviews on the Broumgard Group's behalf last year—your contractual minimum. Two of those were filmed at your home. I mean no disrespect when I say you don't have a clue what we're facing."

Alex swallowed, fearing Rosa would snap back. After seconds ticked by, he relaxed. What Tara said hurt. Mainly because they carried the only ingredient for hurt, truth. He'd slacked on all of his duties—Broumgard, family, friends. And despite doing all he could to avoid the media, he still received tremendous coverage.

"My only concern is the safety of the Lobby," Tara continued. "You know there are influential forces in our government, in governments and high places around the world, who dedicate every waking moment to destroying us. These are intelligent people, Alex; powerful individuals who have no concept of failure.

"And while I don't judge your lifestyle, and I don't resent Adisah's hibernating in the mountains, I'm the one who fights. My team and I save our universe from collapse again and again. The rest of you just act like the Lobby is a given right."

Alex fidgeted. No one would ever say he rivaled Tara's drive, but facing the reality that he contributed nothing but a few checks to the cause, and that he *did* consider the Lobby a right, added to his guilt. He bit his bottom lip, and worked his jaw to the side. What should he say? You're right—I'm a failure. What's new?

Rosa placed her hand on his back.

"I'm not trying to beat you up," Tara continued. "I'm only qualifying my knowledge. Our enemies are waiting for something like this. Roy has logged thousands more hours in the Lobby than anyone on the planet. They will take their billion-dollar budgets and hammer that irrelevant fact home to every person on the planet." She placed the briefcase on the table. After popping it open, she pulled out two stapled stacks of paper and an envelope, placed the items on the table, and then returned the briefcase. She slid forms in front of Alex and Rosa, keeping the envelope near her.

"These are the Lobby's new health and wellness standards. They basically state that a client must undergo a medical analysis. And that if we deem it necessary, we suspend their right to visit the Lobby."

Alex skimmed the words, surprised that he'd never considered any of this. One of his strengths involved leaving his weaknesses in others' care. As he perused the basic requirements, everything seemed reasonable. Those with health problems, diagnosed with cancer, anyone who had recently undergone a serious medical procedure, would be denied Lobby access. Flipping through a few pages, he noticed a graph that dropped to the right like a set of stairs.

"That's the projected loss of sales if this story leaks," Tara said. "The other is the number of clients affected by the new policies."

Alex found the loss of sales horrifying and the number of clients affected almost a nonfactor.

He reassembled the paper stack, resolved to her leadership. "So what do you suggest?"

"The fact that Roy lived on these grounds, in your guest house, makes this an easy fix. If he were to die a normal, quiet death in his bed, it would earn him multiple thirty-second spots on national media for the next few days, which is exactly what we're after. A quiet passing of a man instrumental in creating history's greatest invention."

"Excuse me." Rosa scooted her chair back and stormed down the hall.

Alex couldn't be sure if she struggled with their intention of lying about where and how Roy died, the possibility that the Lobby posed a threat, or that they'd ban a section of people from access. For her, some guy lived in the clouds and watched every decision a person made. An entity who graded those decisions in order to sentence each person to an eternity of paradise or a pit of fire. Alex gave Rosa space in times of crisis. Either that, or receive a lecture.

He turned back to Tara. "What about everyone who was here?"

She glanced at the bodyguard, then back to Alex. "This will be one of our easier fixes." She pointed out the back wall in the direction of the guest house. "An American legend died in his sleep, at the age of eighty-nine. You allow some cameras on the grounds to get their shots of his bedroom, the world mourns, and the Lobby continues—like he would have wanted. We implement the new health and wellness policy and hope this happens no more than once a decade."

Alex understood, but the more she talked, the more he wanted to be alone, to shut out the chaos and grieve. Thinking about losing the Lobby made him run his hand through his hair. He stood and breathed deeply. "I guess, if this is the best way …"

"It's the only way."

"Roy would spin circles in his grave if his death hurt the Lobby."

Tara pulled an envelope from the briefcase and slid it toward Alex. His name was on the front, penned in Adisah's elegant handwriting. Seeing that reminder of the old man eased much of his concern. Shoving the letter in his back pocket, he thought of Rosa.

Now would be the perfect time to remind her of his promise to abstain from the Lobby, and to enforce the sentiment of their unity—no matter what the future might bring.

Tara stood, came around the table, and placed her hand flat against Alex's chest. "Your wife loves you—keep her consoled. This will be a rough stretch for her, and you. Get some counseling. It helps." She looked down at the letter. "Adisah is like a father to me, and you're like a son to him. Stay focused on what we all want."

As she left, Alex vowed to do as she asked, but then he wondered, did they all want the same thing?

Chapter Nineteen

Agent Andrews pushed against his desk to scoot his chair back. He then dropped his head and pinched the bridge of his nose. He needed a moment to process everything he just heard.

The six individuals in his office were some of the most influential people in civil enforcement, which differed from law enforcement, as these were the people who told law enforcement what to believe, and how to delineate right and wrong.

After all this time, keeping faith through years—and occasional doubt—he had the ammunition to hurt the greatest habit forming vice of our time. Alex Cutler and Tara Capaldi had colluded to misinform the public as to the means and probable cause of Roy Guillen's death, three days prior.

His exuberance reached a point where he wanted to jump and shout hallelujah as he pranced around the room, and embraced each person. Being a professional, he buried his true thoughts. After half a minute, he said, "Tell me, step by step, how you got this information."

A few people shared inquisitive looks—as if the head of the LOC should grovel instead of assume control of a meeting in *his* office.

Mr. Townsend stepped forward and placed his hands on the desk. "We don't have time to give you every detail." The man had graduated from West Point near the top of his class, but everyone in the room, including Townsend, knew he'd reached his ceiling a decade ago.

"Calm down, Art," Nadine Dewitt said coolly. Being an assistant to the CIA's deputy director gave her clout, regardless of her exact title. "Mr. Andrews is only being thorough. We expect nothing less."

Agent Andrews, he thought. But on the heels of such fortuitous information, he left the error uncorrected.

The other members held sentiments similar to Nadine. These people were wolves, and this meeting was his initiation to the pack. Andrews possessed the authority—and now the ammunition—they needed to exert control over the Lobby. News of this magnitude granted a wish for him, and he'd make these people happy. He simply needed a full assessment so he could plan the assault from every angle.

"I want to do this right," Agent Andrews said. "Information is the key."

Mr. Townsend was tall and lean, with a great head of black hair. Those three attributes probably helped him make it one or two rungs higher on the ladder than he deserved. The man shook his head as if confused, backed away, and said, "This is ridiculous." He found a spot behind the pack and crossed his arms.

"It's fine," said Kathleen Sousa, a woman above reproach. Being the overseer of CRYPTLOG, gifted her with the ability to instill paralyzing fear. People talked about Apple and Google collecting and exploiting their data, but the US was far superior.

Google was deviant, no doubt. If a person used an Android device for more than two months, Google had a MINIMUM two-million page dossier on them, including everyone in this room. But CRYPTLOG monitored every device, sorted, and processed that data. The US knew everyone's routine, the minutes spent around and talking with others, all your activities, all your shared thoughts. With that they knew what truly lurked in your heart, even if you didn't.

"Agent Andrews has been granted full disclosure. This will be his rodeo, so we will assist him with anything he needs," Kathleen said.

A man, whose name Andrews didn't recall, but whom he remembered worked for Lisa Chapman, head of the NSA, leaned forward, cleared his throat and began, "On June eighteenth, at two twenty-seven in the afternoon, a nine-one-one call was placed from the Cutler residence; emergency responders were dispatched. Using satellites, we recorded the body of Mr. Roy Guillen being removed from the main house. When comparing that video to the news report of a nice, peaceful death in the guest home, we knew something was amiss.

"We've tried to secure information from witnesses and conspirators in previous cover-ups, but the money Tara doles out keeps them tight-lipped. Those would have made wonderful cases, but now we're talking about criminal actions and a public relations disaster that could topple the Lobby once and for all."

Andrews listened to his own rhythmic breathing. He knew he possessed exceptional intelligence, but even geniuses slipped from time to time. With his A-game intact, he would have recorded this conversation, and later on, listened to that last line over and over, perhaps found solace in it for the rest of his days: *topple the Lobby once and for all.*

"We soon learned many unsavory individuals were upset with Tyrell Simpson, paramedic number three, for quitting his job that afternoon." Another of the suits tossed a folder on Andrews's desk.

"Apparently, Mr. Simpson had been pilfering cases of fentanyl, among a half-dozen other medications, for almost three years.

"We built cases against a pair of his flunkies, and offered them immunity for their cooperation in implicating Mr. Simpson. Next, we approached Mr. Simpson and asked: if he wanted to keep Ms. Capaldi's money and sit in prison, or tell us what really happened and remain free?"

Excitement arced in the air. Everyone knew this whole fiasco would devastate the Broumgard Group.

With the combined power these men and women—along with their bosses—wielded, everyone might get their wish and deal the Lobby the coup de grâce.

As head of the LOC, Andrews could declare a seventy-two hour moratorium, based on nothing but intuition. With eyewitness testimony, he could temporarily close all Atriums. With proof that the man who'd spent the most time inside the contraption had died while interacting with the machine, he'd issue a full, thirty-day ban, for public safety.

Agent Andrews's only stipulation—he would collar Alex Cutler. Besides that, only one question remained.

"When do we begin?"

Chapter Twenty

The federal agents who raided Legion didn't use C4 to blow doors off hinges, or rip the gate off with a hook, cable, and an armored vehicle. Instead, they coasted their sedans up the drive, knocked politely, and the moment the doors opened, poured in like locust.

Similar to the torture named "death by a thousand cuts," each item the agents touched was like a pierce of the flesh; every room they entered a blade slicked across skin; every dart of the eye in his direction created a new puncture. The experience left him overwhelmed, defeated, and emotionally pummeled.

Even their feigned kindness in alerting Alex's attorney, Peter Mueller, was like a breaching of his front lines. Two minutes after the armed posse arrived, Peter had called to tell him to cooperate fully, but to say nothing until he arrived.

After comparing the warrants and the items listed for seizure, Peter summoned the only irritant Alex remembered from Eridu: Agent Andrews. When the strange man, who resembled a clichéd agent, right down to the dark hair parted off-center and excellent posture, entered his personal space, Alex wished he would've told Peter to have this conversation away from him.

"I assume you're the overpaid counsel, selling his soul to the highest bidder, morality be damned," Andrews said.

"I'm Mr. Cutler's attorney, yes. Thanks to your overreach, I'll be earning my worth today." He handed him two sheets of paper. "This is the warrant, and this is the list of items you're attempting to take from here."

Andrews perused the documents.

"The highlighted items are examples of your overreach."

"Most of this page is highlighted."

"As are the important lines of the judge's order: two servers used during Roy's death, the log charts, and the mirrored backup for Lobby activity spanning the previous sixty days. Nothing else."

As a pair of men in the casual clothing entered and headed for the stairs leading to Alex's room, Peter called to them, "If you've disconnected one wire beyond the two servers identified in the warrant, do us all a favor and plug them back in."

The men looked to Andrews.

Rather than face the men, Andrews turned and pulled a walkie-talkie from his hip, "Everyone stop what you're doing. There's been an amendment to our warrant. We confiscate the two servers used by Alex and Roy, and the backup. Everything else stays."

Confused chatter overtook the airwaves. Andrews turned the volume down, returned the pages to Peter, and charged outside.

"Damn Gestapo," Peter said. "He was trying to take all the software in your house; your digital assistant, the code that controls Legion's visual aesthetics, and all Lobby related servers."

"And you stopped him?"

"Absolutely. I'd better go supervise."

He left before Alex could say thanks.

Agents reentered his home, carrying electronics. The sight of them handling his property marked the first time Alex envied Dr. Brad Finder's decision to live outside the U.S., or Adisah's resolution to huddle in the mountains of Montana.

While growing up, Alex had made many difficult choices to stay on the right side of the law, but couldn't seem to avoid them.

Raised in Roger's Park, he didn't worry about stray bullets coming through the walls, but there was no swim team in his school; no free extra-curricular activities at all. Living on the fence between the slums and mediocrity, he witnessed many kids slip into the easy to do, difficult to endure, life of crime and poverty.

Despite his adherence to the law, Alex found himself under governmental scrutiny for a second time.

He made his way to the kitchen, near the back of the house, and heard Peter and Agent Andrews arguing their way toward him.

"Alex," Peter said, "just do what this maniac say, for now. One phone call will straighten this out."

Agent Andrews carried industrial shears in one hand, a hand-sized box with dangling rubber strands in the other. "Mr. Cutler, I'm a federal agent, giving you a lawful and direct order. You will comply while I attach this global positioning monitor around your ankle, or you will be arrested."

Alex backed against the counter. Looking at the black box the size of a pack of cigarettes made him curl his lips in disgust.

"It's a harmless GPS bracelet," Andrews replied in a reasonable tone, but Alex saw the hint of a smirk on the man's lips.

"The warrant states Mr. Cutler is to remain in his residence until further notice. Something he is capable of doing without being tagged like a common criminal," Peter said.

"He's definitely not a *common* criminal," Andrews said. "But even rich crooks have to follow the law."

To Alex, Agent Andres said, "Are you going to comply or resist?"

Alex looked to Peter, who wouldn't meet his gaze.

"Comply Mr. Cutler, this is your final warning."

"Okay." He breathed deeply and extended his leg.

He had lied about Roy's death. This was the penalty, and tagging people in America was the wave of the future.

The monitor was heavier than Alex expected, and colder.

"Mr. Cutler," Peter said. "I'll have that off of you in a matter of hours, and request that Mr. Andrews personally—"

"It's Agent Andrews—"

"Enough." To Peter, Alex said, "If you want to help, get everyone out of my house. Allow me some privacy."

"Absolutely," Peter said. "You heard him. You took his stuff, you attached your shackle. Now, let's go."

"Two sheriffs will remain outside your gate," Andrews said as the men backed away.

Three days later, Alex lounged on his expensive sofa, watching the news on his bedroom's north wall. He'd never been a news fan; he'd

161

have voted, lobbied for, and financed an effort to have it outlawed. Currently, he couldn't get enough of it. The tether wasn't so bad. It was big, it hurt, and he felt it every time he moved, but he didn't want to go anywhere, and it provided an easy excuse to that end.

Across the country, people gathered to demonstrate their outrage over the Lobby ban. Just as interesting, occasional debates surged about what *really* caused Roy Guillen's death.

According to the media, an eighty-nine-year-old man suffering heart failure seemed preposterous.

If you went by the news alone, half the people supported the thirty-day moratorium on the Lobby, the other half were outraged. Media tried to portray everyone as extremists. Alex hoped, and believed, twenty percent blindly supported, twenty percent seethingly opposed, and the other eighty was intelligent enough to wait for more data.

The silent majority watched with interest. They didn't troll the internet or act indignant. They absorbed information and made informed decisions.

He had to hope they came down on his side.

Feeling a cramp, he propped his bare foot on the ottoman. Depressed by the sight and feel of his digital shackle, he returned his foot to the floor.

Rosa entered, holding opposite ends of a towel draped across the back of her neck. Her clothes were damp with perspiration. Using one corner of the towel, she dabbed sweat from her brow, an act he usually found sultry. Today, he felt nothing. It seemed that immense stress and self-loathing blanched emotional range.

"Anything new?" she asked as she strode past him and into their closet—a space equal in square footage to his first apartment.

"Six guys in Atlanta dug through sixty feet of earth, broke into an Atrium, and accessed the Lobby. They were arrested the moment they logged out."

"I bet they're kicking themselves now."

"One of them worked for Broumgard," Alex said with disinterest.

The news returned from commercial.

The Lobby ban encompassed the globe, affecting every populated continent. This meant coverage stayed fresh, and to him, each passing hour brought greater drama.

What made sleep beyond brief naps impossible, and leaving the screen for longer than a handful of seconds difficult, was the purported talks of extending the ban an additional thirty days. Flipping a few channels, he filled Rosa in further. "The Atriums in Japan are another big story," he said loudly, so she could hear him from inside her dressing room. "The employees, citizens—everyone in Japan is ignoring the ban. The Atriums have doubled and tripled their rates, and remain operational. There are rumors Moscow's Atrium is doing the same. Media coverage in Beijing is limited, but I wouldn't be surprised if they were following suit."

"Can't you guys deny them access, pull their plug from some main source here?" Rosa asked.

"No. We're set up like franchises. The U.S. released a statement urging all countries to comply, citing the Lobby's possible dangers. Japan is denying the allegations that they're ignoring the ban, despite satellite photos and endless eyewitness accounts."

Rosa exited the closet carrying a towel and wearing nothing but sweat-dampened underwear sucked tight to her skin, making them transparent. With her back to him, she stared at the television a moment—even flexed her glutes—then turned to Alex. "Want to join me for a quick shower?"

She looked amazing. Even better when stripped bare, but her normally stimulating gesture had no effect.

She stared at him, possibly looking for signs of interest or searching for another idea to negate his funk.

Apparently coming up empty, she frowned, and headed to the master bath.

Stopping at the door, she added, "Alex, I tweaked my shoulder and could use some help washing my back."

"That scrub arm works great," he said instinctively. Then, realizing she didn't really need him to wash her back, that desperation to comfort her husband motivated her, he exhaled and said, "I appreciate what you're doing. You look hot, and I know I should want to…" As if operated by a puppeteer, his arms raised limply, motioned to the images on the TV screen, then dropped lifeless.

She disappeared, leaving the door open behind her. Relief washed over him, followed by guilt.

He stared at the open door, willing himself to do the right thing: get up, join her, please them both.

Instead, the mere thought exhausted him. He returned to the news.

Seventy-six Atriums in nineteen countries were confirmed closed for the safety evaluation. In most areas, local police and even military personnel were preventing admittance by anyone other than custodial members or Broumgard's upper management.

The world was like a recently punted beehive.

History had proven: give people work, safety, and high-quality entertainment, and decades ticked by in harmony; attempt to fool them with government handouts, and three dozen rehashed comic book movies a year, and revolutions happened.

Naturally, today's news reported what the bastard who owned the networks wanted, rather than unbiased truth. In the 1980s, fifty people owned ninety percent of media. That small number of people controlling what the public heard was considered a travesty, and groups fought hard to break up that control. In 2019, six people control all propagated information.

CNN refused to mention the people who Alex knew camped around the Los Angeles Atrium, vowing to stay until the chairs were reopened. FOX ignored the new bills being considered in Congress that would regulate the Lobby.

He imagined that similar unreported stories were going on worldwide.

Unfortunately, the media did have a unifying sentiment: Alex Cutler was at fault, hiding something, and devious by nature.

There were many bogus rumors of conspiracies he'd enacted to cover up a litany of fabricated side effects associated with Lobby visits.

Agent Andrews and his LOC released records, gathered over the past seven years, that showed nearly ten thousand complaints lodged by Lobby visitors. The reports excluded an important fact: the percentage of people complaining of "side effects" was below the national average for normal susceptibility to those ailments. Meaning that you were more likely to develop narcolepsy at church, migraines at the mall, or paranoia at a Phish concert, than from accessing the Lobby.

His stomach rumbled. He couldn't remember eating today.

"Victor."

"Yes."

"Can you have Glen bring me a Coke and have Arnel prepare steak fajitas?"

"Certainly."

"Also, have Glen bring one of those chocolate empanadas."

"Will do."

The news depressed him, but not enough to turn it off. With every outlandish comment, he rose with indignation, then sank when realizing the propaganda had reached millions of people, that a percentage of busy individuals swallowed the slanted view given to them without objectional thought.

A reporter described, in abhorrent detail, the condition of Roy's body upon arrival at the county coroner.

Of course he looked bad, Alex thought. The man was almost ninety years old and had been wheelchair bound for a decade. Outside of Hollywood films, death was never beautiful.

After checking the time, he sagged a bit more. Six hours until the only show with integrity, Rebecca Trevino's, *Inside Today,* aired.

He believed most of the public knew the Lobby was safe. Yet each additional burst of drivel swayed a few more of the American masses. How long until they doubted their own memories, believed the news anchors, and questioned the Lobby's necessity?

The current media "expert" being interviewed embarrassed the industry. Apparently, authoring a blog about the Lobby granted this woman credibility to hypothesize, on national television, that Roy Guillen had been murdered, because he was about to expose some sinister conspiracy at Broumgard, which she persistently intimated was at the behest of Alex Cutler.

165

A previous guest had the brilliant idea that the Lobby was a sentient being, which grew to hate Roy's presence—as it hated all of us—so it surged his body with electricity, stopped his heart, and presumably cackled an evil, digital laugh as Roy died.

Glen delivered the soda and dessert as Rosa exited the bathroom. Luckily for everyone involved, she exited wrapped in a towel.

"Guess I need to start dressing before entering my own bedroom." She stormed into the closet and closed the door.

Glen set down the plate and soda as if he hadn't heard her.

Once the main door shut, Alex yelled loud enough to be heard through the thick gorilla glass door. "I'm sorry—I thought you'd be in there a while longer."

She cracked the door and peered out. Noticing they were alone, she softened her tone, "I intended to be." She glanced at the pastry, back at Alex, and forced a smile. "But then I came up with a wonderful idea to get you out of your mood."

He sipped the Coke, and munched the baked empanada.

"I'm not in a mood, Rosa. My entire world is collapsing," he said.

"*Our* world."

"Our world," he amended. "You know what I mean."

As he attempted to take another bite, she crossed the distance and took the treat from his hand. She opened a trash receptacle in the wall and tossed the empanada in.

"I'm serious," she said. "This lying around feeling sorry for yourself isn't healthy."

Having an idea of the conversation's direction, he decided to head it off. "I don't need to go see Father Michael or talk to him here, or anything like that."

"Well, of course you do," she said as she pulled a T-shirt over her head. "But that's not my plan. Although… I'll keep it in mind." She sat next to him, pulled her moist hair from inside her shirt, and let the tendrils flop down her back. With a mischievous smile, she said, "Let's sneak into the Lobby."

He flinched as if slapped, then searched her face. He bolted to his feet. "We can't do that. Accessing the Lobby would be a direct violation of my house arrest. I could go to jail." It wasn't like he didn't consider taking a quick vacation a hundred times each day, but Rosa was supposed to be the voice of reason.

She stood next to him. "I know all of that, honey, but those officers hardly enter the property; they never come inside the house, let alone venture upstairs. Six of our chairs work fine, and who would know—?"

"Glen is at the door with the rest of your meal," Victor said.

Victor's voice seemingly answered Rosa's question about who would know. After seizing control of their phones, Alex had considered deactivating Victor, but couldn't decide if privacy was worth the hassle of organizing his own life.

"Tell him to come in," he said.

"What is it this time?" Rosa asked. "Deep fried cheese with hollandaise sauce?"

Glen, with his head down, silently placed the fajitas on a nearby table and left in the same fashion.

Alex wished Rosa would go easier on the kid. Alex believed if Rosa would be super nice to him, a skill she displayed with such ease, Glen might open up a bit.

Once Glen exited, she inspected the food.

Alex leaned over, removed a tortilla from the warmer, lined it with three strips of steak, jack cheese, a dab of guacamole, sour cream, and a pinch of fresh-cut onions.

"Think about it, Alex. In the Lobby, all this stress and depression will be lifted from you. And how often do I volunteer a trip?"

He wrapped the small fajita tight and, before taking a bite, arrived at the answer: never. Her last visit, over a year ago, had taken months of cajoling from him. Feeling a little control slip back into his life, he said, "Can we go to one of those trippy Alice in Wonderland-type worlds?"

"Don't push it." She then ducked into the access room, and returned a minute later. "Two hours. Douglas, Nebraska, 1871."

Douglas, Nebraska, 1871 was one of the least visited worlds. The world's blandness never bothered him. He loved having a day with Rosa all to himself. He smiled at her, and nodded with genuine enthusiasm.

"Victor," Rosa said, "block access to both our suite and the access room. Alex and I would like some husband and wife time."

"Yes, ma'am."

Alex sat back down and briefly wondered what would happen in the real world during his absence, and then concluded that if he could enter the Lobby, he didn't care.

He muted the news program, where two bloggers who held the same view pretended to debate by supporting each other from different angles.

Rosa sat next to him and touched his leg. "Are you ready?"

They stood in unison.

Seeing the happiness on her face increased his own. Today would be a good day. Unless it ended with him in jail, or fueled the campaign to extend the ban, or something... far worse.

Chapter Twenty-One

Douglas, Nebraska, 1871 was always sunny and cloudless with temperatures in the high seventies. Clients started off with clothes from the era—heavy corduroy and cotton for men, long dresses for women, each with multiple layers of undergarments. Per her norm upon entering Douglas, Rosa went straight to the tailor shop and modified her clothing.

For unknown reasons, Alex often stayed in whatever outfit they gave him. He liked staying in character while inside each of the worlds he visited. He, and Charles and Roy for that matter, even adopted the dialect when possible.

He had this strange notion that if he enveloped himself in a certain era, the AIs wouldn't be able to detect him as an outsider, and he could briefly experience the thrill of living a different life, in a totally different reality.

"How do?" an older gentleman said as he strolled by, a lady friend entwined in his arm. The man wore a corduroy suit and top hat, the latter he pinched in time with his greeting. The lady's bluebonnet dress ballooned out at the bottom, ruffles bedecked the hem.

Alex nodded a greeting, and the artificial couple returned to their prior conversation.

Folks mulled about the dusty town. A horse-drawn cart wheeled hay in one direction. A farmer guided a pair of sows in another.

"How do I look?" Rosa said.

He turned toward the sound of her voice and smiled at her choice of clothing: a two-piece bathing suit, white with pink dots, flips-flops, and a pair of low-cut jean shorts.

"Real fitting," he said with mostly joy, and a sprinkle of annoyance. It was hard to lose himself with Rosa draped in modern clothing.

But them being here was her doing, and he was willing to adopt her preference. He removed his overcoat and tossed it on the ground. Once he was out of range, it would vanish and even return if he came back. He offered Rosa his arm.

She accepted it. A half-mile of comfortable, hand-holding silence brought them to the countryside—far out of earshot of town activity.

Rosa had discovered Douglas in one of the many blogs distributed by Broumgard—probably as the "world where you're least likely to meet another person." They first visited it as a semi-joke.

On that day, he followed Rosa while she explored. She appreciated the low attendance at the saloon, the full house of chapel mass, and the friendly business methods at the trading post.

Finally seeing Rosa wowed by the Lobby helped make Douglas, Nebraska, 1871 an easy place to like. Life passed in a simple manner. People stayed pleasant, respectful, and pious—a contrast to the world they came from.

After diverting from the dirt road, they navigated a game trail through a field of knee-high grass, picked their way along a patch of dense woods, and arrived at their destination.

Miss Bashful was an enormous willow tree, whose uniform branches seemed to shade a full acre of cool earth. A tire swing hung over a clear pond the size and shape of a skating rink.

Once they selected a spot of flat earth, half in the sun, Rosa used a voice command to call forth a picnic basket loaded with wine, bread, cheese, blankets, and a pair of towels.

A gaggle of geese swam toward the couple.

Alex removed his shoes and socks, and hiked up his pant legs. He retrieved a loaf of homemade bread from their wicker lunch basket. Tearing off bite-size chunks, he tossed them to the birds.

Unseen fish tugged at the first offerings, while geese hurried and gobbled pieces, to their mates' protests.

With the picnic area situated, Rosa took her own loaf of bread, waded into the water up to her calves, and attempted to throw pieces to the less aggressive birds near the back of the gathering.

Done with his bread, Alex sidled behind her, and kissed her shoulder. "You were right."

"What this time?" Rosa said playfully, then flung the remaining half of her loaf, which hit the water and floated like a Viking warship. She turned and wrapped her arms around his waist.

"About coming here, about me needing a break, about how stressed I was."

"We'll get through this, hon." She kissed him, then again for a greater length of time, parting her mouth. Their tongues blended, and almost instantly, his loins burned with desire.

She shifted her hips, unbuttoned his breeches. Remembering the look of her naked breasts and the damp panties from earlier escalated his excitement to a level that had eluded him for months.

The crack of a breaking twig in the nearby woods slowed their hunger. Another, larger branch snapped, and they disentangled. They'd spent many afternoons with Miss Bashful, all involving sex, and never been interrupted by more than a pair of rambunctious squirrels or chirping blue jays. The disturbed branch sounded too thick for any common fauna to have broken it.

When considering the possibility of an AI deviating from its flexible loop, he immediately pushed that aside. No AI stalked them or followed out of curiosity; that anomaly was too improbable for this world.

Another twig snapped, this time closer. Alex remembered that his being here violated a court order.

Rosa edged out of the water and stared at the patch of forest. "What is that?"

"Some indigenous wildlife maybe?" He tried to remember if anything dangerous lived in Nebraska. Wolves? Bears?

Leaves rustled as if a branch were being forced aside and then snapped back. Alex heard the distinct sound of footsteps crunching dry earth, headed in their direction.

Protectively, he moved in front of Rosa.

Programmers installed backdoor slips—like the one Alex installed to give him supreme command in the lobby section—all the time. Douglas, Nebraska, 1871, would be an ideal world to alter something on the sly.

One programmer, unbeknownst to Broumgard, had inserted the ability to access thousands of genetics of marijuana into every world he worked on, which made him an underground celebrity. Maybe whoever designed this bore added spice in the form of a vampire or Frankenstein's monster.

Alex wondered about the pain threshold here? In dangerous worlds, the modifier room forced clients to specify their desired discomfort level. Average worlds tended to mimic reality. Meaning, if a programming nut had tweaked this world, Alex might soon learn the pains of being ravaged by man-bear-pig.

What emerged from the woods was so much more frightening than any programmer's ghastly creation.

Rosa gasped, and gripped Alex's elbow so tight he knew the pain receptors were set to normal.

Alex's knees trembled. He struggled to stay upright. His stomach convulsed, bringing him to the verge of gagging.

"My goodness, I'm glad I finally located you two," a young and fit Roy Guillen said as he casually brushed prickers from his dingy one-piece long johns.

Rosa squeezed tighter.

Alex pulled his elbow free.

Pointing to Rosa's shorts, Roy asked, "How do you change clothes in this world? There seems to be no command for that."

Neither of them replied.

Roy scrunched his features, inspected Alex's face, and stepped closer.

Alex retreated a step. His heart boomed. The idea of Roy—a dead man—touching him sparked a carnal desire to attack this

172

abnormality, to grab Rosa by the hand and run, to gouge out his own eyes.

The differing thoughts paralyzed him.

When something unreal presented itself, the human mind evoked its own form of error message: muddy fogginess, constricted throat, sweaty palms. Having witnessed numerous dreamed fantasies in the Lobby, he'd exhibited these symptoms before, but never to such a degree.

"What are you gawking at?" Roy asked as he searched their faces. "Did I interrupt some hanky-panky?" Relaxing as if he'd solved the riddle, he walked over and pinched Alex's exposed chest.

Alex jerked back, brought his hand to his touched flesh, and blurted, "You're dead!"

Frowning, Roy cocked his head. "Dead?" To Rosa, "You're white as a sheet, dear. No need to be embarrassed. I know what married couples do when alone in a beautiful setting."

"Roy, you're not alive," Alex stressed his last word. "You died."

"The F-1 wreck?" Roy asked. "Why is that such a problem? I popped into the Lobby, same as always." He took a moment, and when he spoke again, he did so with more caution, as if joining Alex's confusion with a previous curiosity of his own. "It was a bit different, mind you. Just before I lost control of the car, I felt a tingling, almost like I was loading out, and then BANG, the crash. After that, I was in the lobby. I went back to the race to watch you from the stands, but you'd left. I figured you'd gone searching for me, and checked the lobby again. Ten minutes had passed." He shrugged. "I didn't feel like playing tag all day, so I left a message at the post office and blazed my own trail."

"And then what?" Alex asked. "Anything else unusual this past week?"

"Well, since you're an inquiring mind," Roy said. "I went to San Francisco 1968. Many of us original vacationers still gather there. It's like our clubhouse. I met Prince Hassef and Dr. Finder. We scheduled a pinochle championship to end the squabble and crown a winner." Again, he lost himself in thought, as if reliving exact details.

173

Then he continued, "Hassef had planned to log out shortly after we began and swore he'd return three days later. So we postponed, but neither of them returned." Placing a hand under one of Miss Bashful's branches, he tugged off a leaf.

"The next day when I was in the lobby, the numbers looked thin, but who knows…?" He paused, as if sensing a pattern. Apparently unable to decipher its meaning, he said, "I spent four or five days with the Mayans, hiking up to see a high priest, intending to do that Smoke Serpent Ritual. Then I learned what the process entailed and got the bejesus out of there." He looked to Alex as if about to elaborate, but then shook his head. "When I went to the Lobby that time, it was a ghost town. I checked my messages, found none, and I came here hoping to bump into you. I've been helping out on the Robinson farm over yonder." He pointed. "After finishing with the lassies, the foreman told me he saw some strangers heading this way. I hoped it was you two, and here I am."

Rosa eased around Alex and peered at Roy as if he'd sprouted a third eye."He's not joking with you. Roy, you passed. We attended your funeral."

Roy smiled."I don't feel dead."

"It's true," Alex said. His chest lightened. His mind was a helium balloon he continually had to pull back into his skull for it to function. "Major myocardial infarction. Tara and I tried to cover it up, say you died in the guest house, change the rules. Everything backfired, and now this…"

"What is this?" Rosa whispered. "Dear Lord in heaven, help us."

"Hmm." Roy paced two steps to his right, and after a full minute of brooding, he looked up. "So I'm dead out there, but I'm still in here?" A sly grin crossed his face. "You know, Alex, I've hoped for this. It's why I panicked during the forty-eight hour breaks. I didn't want to die out there."

A lump formed in Alex's throat. He wasn't sure what reaction he'd anticipated from Roy, but expectancy bordering on exuberance inserted a knife twist.

174

"Your soul may be trapped here," Rosa said. "Shackled in the chains of mortality. Unable to bask in the glory of the Almighty."

"No offense, dear, but I'm fine with that. You trap me in an ever-expanding paradise, one that allows my loved ones to spend time with me after I'm dead—a place that lets me plan fishing trips with my unborn great-great-great-grandchildren—and I'm one happy man."

"You don't get it," she said, a bit quieter.

"What do you mean, 'with your loved ones'?" Alex asked. All of this hovered at a 9.9 for insanely problematic. If word leaked... His heart raced at the mere thought.

"You think I don't have loved ones?" Roy said with a slight edge to his voice. "You think I don't have the right to say goodbye to my granddaughter? My great-granddaughter? To Charles? You want me to let them continue thinking I just blinked out of existence, when I'm alive and well? Is that what you're suggesting?"

"You're not alive and well," Rosa insisted.

Alex breathed two deep breaths, searching for the right words. "I'm telling you, we're dealing with a full-on LOC investigation. The Lobby is currently shut down. Protests are popping up everywhere. If this got out, they could close the Lobby forever."

"They can't shut this down," Roy said flippantly. "You of all people know we have a hundred classified dump sites."

"If they think it traps your consciousness," Alex said, "they'll find a way."

"It needs to be shut down," Rosa added.

Alex winced at the thought, and discarded her reaction as shock.

"Alex, I have a right to say goodbye to people. What if you could talk to your brother one last time, and know he was okay and happy?"

Alex would do it. He would do anything for that meeting, but Roy was asking him to possibly destroy the entire world for a final goodbye between loved ones. Alex hoped he wouldn't be that selfish, though the eagerness in his chest at the prospect of seeing Simon argued he'd burn the entire planet for one more day with his brother.

With this scenario it was *Roy's* loved ones versus burning the planet, that made it easier to do the right thing.

"No," Alex said. "I can't bring in people who would spread this?" Alex shook his head. "Did you hear what I just said? Do you still care about us? About Broumgard? About the Lobby itself? Are you so consumed by your own wants you won't consider what this could do to the world?"

Roy held his gaze.

During all of this, Alex marveled at Roy's youth. He wondered if these handsome features were now permanent?

Roy meandered a few yards away.

Rosa moved in the opposite direction.

Deep thoughts accompanied the silence.

"Look," Roy said, "my funeral just passed, which means my granddaughter and her daughter are probably still in town. Charles lives with you. Come back tomorrow, same time—let me say goodbye, just to them, and I'll be out of your hair."

"How is this happening?" Rosa said, more to herself. She searched both of their faces. Finding no interest, she wandered around the tree, and out of sight.

Roy came closer to Alex and lowered his voice. "Do you realize the significance of what's happened here?"

Alex feared he might be the only one who did.

"Bring them to me, and that'll be it. I guarantee you they'll never say a peep. I get it. You have to do all you can to keep this a secret. I'm with you. I agree." Another pause. "What you do is contact Tara and Adisah, tell them to bottle this up, because if one whisper leaks, it's all over." He chuckled. "The whole world, all over."

Thoughts jammed in Alex's nerve superhighway. He squinted. "I can't contact them. I'm under house arrest. My phones are probably tapped."

Roy stepped even closer. "You could bring Charles. We can figure this out together. Use him to deliver the messages to Adisah and Tara. We can trust him."

Alex's chest wound tighter. He didn't want to tell anyone, but he also understood that to contain this secret, he'd first need to share it

176

with others. "I won't bring people I don't know," he said. "Plus, your family left the city days ago."

"What about…?" Roy tilted his head toward where Rosa had moved behind the tree.

"She'll be fine," Alex lied. "I'll be here tomorrow morning with Charles. We'll make a plan and stick to it." Not knowing what else to do, he inspected his friend, and surprised them both by pulling Roy close and hugging the daylights out of him.

One emotion rose above the rest: gratitude. Alex appreciated his friend's return. He felt blessed to be gifted one more hug, to hear his voice, to possibly share more laughs. As morbid as it all might be, their relationship could continue.

He felt so amazing and happy, but also resolute. He would keep this from the rest of the world. A revelation of this magnitude could destroy everything he'd come to love.

Chapter Twenty-Two

The sound of Rosa crying nearby welcomed Alex back to the real world. Rising to his feet, he pulled back his privacy curtain, intending to comfort her, and saw her exit their private access room. He considered giving chase, but what would he say, sorry I'm super happy my best friend is alive, or, at least available.

They just didn't see things the same. Besides his feelings of extreme paranoia over the Lobby's future, and knowing they'd need a pinch of magic to keep this quiet, he found the entire turn of events too surreal to be upset. The hardest part, when dealing with Rosa, would be hiding how happy he was. He'd just have to avoid talking about it with her. She'd sense his inner wonder, and that would light the wick to an explosive difference of opinions.

She held onto a hope that their faith in a higher power aligned. If she knew the depth of his doubt, that one separate belief could erode their marriage. *That* was the last thing he wanted.

Listlessly, he pushed the curtain all the way open until it compressed on the rack.

He surveyed the room with a heavy heart. Landing on the open space beneath the control panel—the two missing server boards—reminded him his life lay in others' hands.

This additional complication of a dead man living posed an imminent threat to everything.

Opening the door required extra effort, as if strength had left him. Before he stepped over its threshold, he found Rosa ten feet away, arms crossed, eyes puffy but sharp, and focused on him.

"I want that machine out of my house."

The last thing he needed was another frontal assault.

Moving toward her, he raised his hands in a placating manner.

She stepped back and lifted her hands, palms out. "You get it out of here, or I will."

A snake slithered into the base of his spine and wormed its way through his organs, around his heart, and squeezed. For two seconds, he feared the oncoming of a stroke. "Honey, will you calm down? Let's talk." The entire house could crumble. His legs could break—he could accidentally chug hydrochloric acid, but as long as his access room remained, he would feel content.

"I am calm," she said, and marched into her closet. A minute later she returned in jeans, tying her hair with a scrunchie. "I'm going to see Father Michael."

He stepped into her path; a dozen feet separated them. "Rosa, I seriously think it's best if we limit the people who know about this."

"He's a priest, Alex."

A priest who drives an Audi A8, thought Alex. As distasteful as it was to admit, he celebrated Father Michael's expensive tastes— they boosted his confidence that Tara could stifle that avenue before it became a problem.

"Alright, alright," Alex said as he stepped out of her way.

Before Rosa reached the point where their room door would automatically open, she faced him. "Get your people. Do whatever you have to, but…" She shook her head and composed her thoughts. "That is no longer some big video game, Alex. It's sinister. I'll keep your secret for now, for the good of the world, but I want it out of my house." She rushed out of the room.

From near the closet, he stared at the access room walls. They were camouflaged to blend into the main wall, making them difficult to distinguish. The entire western wall resembled a calm woodland, where animals darted and birds fluttered around a gently flowing creek.

"Victor, remove the west wall tint." The wall turned to clear glass. He looked out over the rear of the property.

179

The guest house was a hundred and fifty feet to the northwest, partially shaded by a trio of thirty-foot spruces. It shared none of the modern style of Alex's home, but Roy and Charles living there made life easiest for all parties.

He couldn't help but remember how fragile Roy had been when he and Charles first moved on the premises. Him surviving all these years was impressive. Despite the madness, in some sense, Roy Guillen remained very much alive.

Staring at the dark cedar home, he wondered what Charles was doing at that moment. Sleeping? Reading *The New Yorker*?

Opening the back door, he met a wave of summer heat.

Before heading to the stairs, he trudged over to the rail, where a gust of wind ruffled his hair and rippled his T-shirt. The guest house had been modeled after the mid-century design of Jay Van Andel's residence. Van Andel was a man with unscrupulous moral convictions and a deep belief in the Bible. In some ways, he found the two-home dichotomy fitting—the ancient versus the modern; the constant versus the uncertain.

Turning, he walked toward the steps and steeled himself for the conversation ahead—one about life after death, proof of concept, and the strategy needed to maintain the fabric of society.

Chapter Twenty-Three

Alex filled his loofa with soap and lathered heavily. This morning, he would smuggle Charles into the Lobby to visit their dead friend. So many pitfalls lay ahead. Surprisingly, his thoughts clung to Rosa, and the previous day. Though rare, he and Rosa had argued before. When subtracting the time he spent in the Lobby, perhaps their spats aligned with the national average? But they had never elevated a disagreement to words of cruelty or vindictive actions.

Last night he'd called Rosa *naive*! He was he such a fool?

Rosa had returned home in a dark mood. Her ninety-minute bath with the door locked and the radio blaring gospel music made it clear she wanted to be left alone, but he'd waited for her to come out so he could ask what taking the access chair out would solve.

How stupid. He should have stuck to his original plan and left the subject alone.

After the blowout, he spent the evening in the library. Watching the news helped him forget the argument, and the life quandary that awaited him. This time, when he listened to outlandish claims about the Lobby, he thought, *If they only knew.*

When fatigue finally overcame him, he trudged upstairs and approached the bed. Seeing Rosa's inert form, yet knowing because she was a deep thinker, that she was still awake, he waited for her to give him some sign it was okay to sleep in their bed.

She didn't. He slept on the couch.

When he woke, she was gone.

Using his index finger, he pressed the button next to the water temperature gauge and ended the hundred-degree stream. He stepped out to a message from Victor telling him breakfast would be ready in nine minutes, and Charles waited downstairs. Feeling anything but casual, he dressed that way and met Charles in the breakfast nook.

The sun had yet to rise, but the animated sun from his back wall shined brightly over his re-created property. Something about knowing a cold black lay behind his false creation kicked his nerves up a few notches.

Alex had once read that brain function didn't peak until the sun had risen, so Victor greeted him with sunshine, regardless of the time or actual elements. Normally, it made him feel more optimistic about the day. Today, the ploy made him feel like a pretentious fool.

Charles waited for him at the far end of the iron table, reading the *LA Times*.

Alex sat, thanked Glen for the vegetable, egg-white omelet, and tried to calm his nerves as the pair ate in silence.

Charles had never been much of a conversationalist. This morning, along with being reticent, he looked under the weather. Alex's guest wiped sweat from his brow on more than one occasion, bags underlined his eyes, and each time he spooned a wedge from his half of grapefruit, he looked pained by the idea of swallowing.

Alex imagined that everything he'd explained to Charles the previous afternoon had shocked him, but Alex needed the elderly man's granite-like strength and cooperation to stop an expanding catastrophe.

"How are you feeling?" Alex said.

"Confused mostly."

"I mean, healthwise."

Charles leaned back.

Alex could tell by the slightly bent brows and tight lips that he'd offended Charles. Perhaps he thought Alex feared he was so unhealthy, he'd die during the short visit.

"There's no need to worry about my health," Charles said. "After Roy's passing, I had a full physical, blood work, the whole nine. Doctor Goldstein rated my health pristine for my age. I do think I ate too much last night. Lots of greasy food. I never eat that. I felt a little sick this morning, but I'm at the end of it."

"That's good to hear, because I'm counting on you in this. I'm not the best guy to handle this problem."

"No, you're not, but accepting that shows your wisdom. Abraham Lincoln wasn't a brilliant mind, but he knew his weaknesses like few men do, and he delegated them to others. That wisdom will help you through this. No matter what happens, remember that. We'll put together a plan with Roy, Tara will step in, and a year from now you'll wonder if this was all some dream you cooked up."

Somewhere in the abyss of his subconscious, Alex believed those words. Still, he'd feel better at the end of this day, when they had a viable plan. Alone, he continually pictured doomsday scenarios.

They rode the elevator to the second level. Reaching the door to the access room, Charles paused with his grip on the handle. Again, Alex worried about his health. He looked like a man in the middle of sickness, rather than near its end. As if to prove his thought, Charles pivoted with his hand on his stomach, hurried to the master bath, and slammed the door behind him.

Alex wouldn't say he envied someone with food poisoning, but entering the Lobby sick doubled the trip's value. Allowing people to escape their ailments was arguably the Lobby's original purpose. Thinking about the Lobby's beginning led to thoughts of Adisah. Staring at the closed bathroom door, Alex longed for Adisah's help with the Lobby's current mutation.

The toilet flushed, and Charles staggered out. He forced a smile as he wiped his mouth. He remained pale but looked relieved.

"I'll ask Glen to keep an eye on us while we are inside."

"No, I'm fine, Alex. I'm certain the worst is behind me. I just needed one final purge." He wiped moisture from his brow and from around his neck, and preceded Alex into the access room.

As Alex inputted their vacation parameters, he thought Charles's ailments were more proof that life kicked us when we're down. If there was a God, why would He do that? To force us to give thanks and prove faith despite its unlikeliness.

Charles had lost a lifelong friend, learned that friend had defeated mortality, and now faced the task of containing a secret with immense complexity. And, Alex couldn't forget that with the new Health and Wellness rules, this would be Charles' final vacation.

Alex found his ability to keep the Health and Wellness information from his friend troubling, but not troubling enough to bring it up.

Settling into his chair, Alex nodded with confidence at Charles and wondered when he'd become so callous, so selfish.

As the timer struck ten seconds, he assured himself there were many out-of-bounds things he wouldn't do to protect the Lobby's existence. But as the counter reached zero, he still couldn't think of a single one.

Chapter Twenty-Four

Alex and Charles found Roy pacing in the empty white of the Lobby. He hurried over to the new arrivals and announced, "World select, Life after People, United States of America." A portal appeared a few feet down from the trio, and Roy moved to its entrance.

"Come on. People have been popping in and out all morning," Roy said. "Asians mostly. We don't want anyone to recognize me." Looking at Alex, he frowned. "And everyone in the Far East will flock to Alex."

Alex was well aware of the fame he generated in the Eastern Hemisphere. Japan's populace embraced celebrities on a scale that dwarfed American idolization. Many Japanese considered Alex a living deity. His endorsement practically guaranteed a product's success in Japan. Multitudes of packaged foods, clothes, cosmetics, and even toiletries bore his name. Signing licensing agreements often consumed an entire day. He also dominated Japanese entertainment, owning partial rights to a dozen animated series, a new video game every couple of months, action figures, his name in a hundred lyrics— to try and envision every marketing angle would cause his head to spin off.

Roy dipped into the portal without waiting. After a nervous glance around, Alex followed.

Life after People, United States of America, planted a client in one of six major cities with a random amount of time having lapsed since people suddenly vanished: one minute, one year, ten years, or a century. They modeled the world after a popular 2011 show, and to Alex's surprise, this was a very popular world.

The trio stood at the famous crossroad junction in the center of Times Square in New York City. Judging from the stellar conditions of the roads, buildings, abandoned vehicles, and the still-functioning electronic billboards, he figured they'd be inserted into an earth where people had vanished one minute ago.

Goosebumps prickled Alex's arms. This intersection held fame for its activity. Human activity. Lacking people, with crosswalks functioning and billboards selling junk, it felt like a massive tomb.

Alex had only visited this world once. Same as then, the eeriness of the place weirded him out. Nothing in science could make all humans vanish instantly. Last time, he'd arrived a hundred years after people had vanished, and spent much of his time wondering what caused the extinction? A corneal mass ejection was the most probable scenario, followed by a global pandemic, or the onslaught of hyperinflation. Alex felt like the pond scum theory was by far the most likely. Our stupidity was sad, ironic, and unavoidable.

He felt confident Roy chose this world deliberately. With no AI's anyone they ran into would be a real person, and therefore, someone to avoid. Looking over the barren landscape, he flinched as a flock of sparrows took flight and receded down the street. Alex appreciated that they hadn't been thrust into this world a hundred years from now, like last time. The vehicles had been covered by moss, the roads overgrown with grass, buildings in disarray, and animals had reclaimed control of the city. That would add more strangeness to the already morbid environment and upcoming subject matter.

Theirs was to be a conversation about death, the soul, and a machine that harnessed one from the other.

"There," Roy said. Without awaiting a reply, he marched toward a glass door with a green logo stenciled on it.

Alex supposed an abandoned Starbucks might be the perfect place to discuss humankind's downfall.

The interior smelled of freshly brewed coffee. An fourteen-dollar menu option steamed by the register. Loose bills littered the floor, as if the recently enacted rapture had arrived at the moment a customer went to pay for their morning boost.

Moving behind the counter, Alex selected a cinnamon scone, and his mouth watered. Strangely enough, glutton eating generated much interest in the Lobby. Around a hundred highly visited worlds catered to that stigmatized desire.

"We have one hour," Roy reminded them.

Alex motioned to the display rack as he bit into the warm scone, asking if either man wanted something. Charles asked for black coffee. Alex obliged, then joined them at the small table.

"Well, Alex," Charles said as he blew on his steaming cup of joe. "We're here to help you. Let's start with you filling us in?"

The suave-looking Charles, whose image would fit perfect on any cigarette billboard from the 1950s, had no resemblance to the elderly man hampered by the virus he entered with. Shaking those thoughts aside, Alex brought them up to speed. He started with the petty arrogance Agent Andrews displayed at their first meeting in Eridu and the many rumors he'd heard over the years about the man's obsessions with him. Then he told them about Roy's death, the raid, Rosa's internal struggles, and Tara's plans to limit future recurrences with a screening procedure.

During the lengthy apprising, Roy poured himself a coffee and refilled Charles's cup.

Finished with the past, they outlined a cursory plan to best contain the situation—Health and Wellness, give Tara control. With all in agreement, Alex checked the clock. They'd consumed the entire hour. He should have scheduled two, maybe three hours, so they could have ended with some recreation.

With minutes left, Alex trudged behind the counter, found the hazelnut-flavored coffee, and filled his cup, wondering what he'd like to say as a farewell. As the scented drink drizzled out, he noticed Roy and Charles leaning in close, whispering. Though childish for him to feel jealous, their rare private moments always stung. He understood the two men had known each other much longer than they'd known Alex; they were entitled to their privacy.

Furthermore, Alex knew their conferences rarely involved him.

As Alex reached for a blueberry muffin, Roy laughed. The normally uplifting sound froze his hand. What could Roy find humorous about all he had heard? While recounting the events, Alex had endured bouts of feeling sick. He had continually wiped his palms and breathed deeply to steady his anxiety.

Even with the anticipated success of their initial plan, they would always fear that phone call from somewhere in the world, saying someone had died in an access chair. Roy had dismissed all of Alex's concern. His confidence in Broumgard's ability to screen everyone had reassured Alex, but not to the point where humor was appropriate.

Lifting the muffin and sipping his hazelnut coffee, he observed his friend's unabashed grin with growing discomfort.

Rejoining them, Alex asked, "What's so funny?"

Roy dropped his smile and sipped his coffee.

Charles cleared his throat as he stared at the clock behind Alex.

They had covered the pressing issues, yet none of the grand questions. Again, Alex wished he would have given them more time, but he'd been nervous about even one more hour inside.

"I get it," Alex said. "You guys are making future plans to meet?"

Roy wouldn't look up from his coffee.

Charles crumpled his features.

Alex's stomach clinched. He eased onto the nearest stool. The two men making plans without him hurt, but he didn't think being excluded from a vacation is why his subconscious was screaming they had a problem. "Are you guys scheduling an adventure for next week or something?"

Neither man replied.

"That's cool. Just don't forget I want to be in on the one after that." His body flushed when he remembered that because of the Health and Wellness standards, this would be Charles's final trip.

Perhaps Alex could pull some strings...

Roy set down his cup, sounding a tiny bang. "Look, Alex—"

"No, no," Charles interrupted. "It's my mess—I'll try and clean it up." Clearing his throat, he addressed Alex. "You sprang this entire conundrum on me yesterday afternoon." He shook his head. "The stress put me to sleep minutes after you left, then kept me awake all night. With more time, I promise you I would have arranged something better." He paused, then said, "I care about you."

"We both do," Roy added.

Charles shared a look with Roy and then squared his shoulders to Alex. "We are your friends and would never do anything to cause you problems."

Alex bit into the top of his muffin, thinking people only said things like that to soften a blow.

"I feel foolish," Charles continued. "I didn't think things through."

"What things?" Alex asked. A full mouth helped hide the crack in his voice.

Charles shook his head. "Alex, back at your place, when I went into the restroom, it wasn't because I had food poisoning—I was a nervous wreck." He glanced at Roy, who, with a serious look, nodded for Charles to continue.

"When I went into the bathroom, I ingested an entire bottle of Nembutal, about twenty Oxycodone, and a handful of amphetamines."

Alex's mouth turned into a cement mixer, churning the gritty blueberry muffin into clay. He tried to swallow, to ask what Charles meant, but the substances met with the forming lump, and clogged his gullet.

"According to the research I did last night," Charles added as he exhaled, "my heart stopped beating about twenty minutes ago. I am truly sorry, Alex. I really am."

"We both are," Roy jumped in. "You have to see it from our perspective. You don't yet know the fear of closing your eyes each night and praying with all you have that they will open the following morning. Of being weighted with the memories of all the great people you've outlived. There's no horror like it."

"And then this comes along," Charles added. "Roy and I built so much together, yet the one sentiment we always shared was that it wasn't enough. We needed more time. Can you see that? Can you understand our position?"

Alex pictured havoc at Legion. Despite Charles's advice, Glen would have checked on them. When Glen found a fresh corpse, he'd call 911 and the ensuing chaos would shake the world, and remove Alex's ability to deny his violation.

"This is the greatest thing that could have ever happened," Roy said.

Alex was too stunned to disagree, too shocked to reach over the table and strangle the inconsiderate men across from him.

"We wish you all the luck in the world in keeping a lid on this," Roy said. "We truly do, and meant everything we discussed. Follow the plan. It will work."

"And I apologize for complicating matters," Charles added, "but…" he looked down and toyed with his coffee cup.

Alex realized he'd been shaking his head ever so slightly, and couldn't stop. This wasn't an inconvenience. It was blowing the lid off their plans.

Alex wouldn't survive. A hundred Taras couldn't contain this. Rosa probably swayed around in the access room at that very moment, going to town with a sledgehammer.

"We know this puts you in a bind," Roy said, "but can you at least say something? Say that you understand?"

"Understand?" Alex heard himself say as if from a distance. "I understand I'm about to wake to the worst day of my life. That you two put the Lobby's existence—and perhaps my freedom—in jeopardy, for your own pleasure."

Both men frowned, and their shoulders sagged.

"If they shut down every backup macroserver, you'll probably blink out of existence," Alex said.

"I'm on borrowed time," Roy whispered.

"*If* this gets out," Charles said, "turn it into a humanitarian thing, to keep the power on, like they're killing us—"

"Stop," Alex said. He swooned from the implications. A tiny part of him wished he could stay in here forever, but the selfishness of that thought disgusted him.

All three men faced the clock. Alex would be logging out at any moment.

Probably heading to jail shortly after.

He wondered if someone out there sold lobotomies.

"Alex." Roy placed a hand on his friend's arm. "Think about what this means for the world. Contain it if you can, but I say let it free. Tell everyone. Join us."

Join them? Crush Rosa? Abandon his responsibilities? The notion startled him. Turned his stomach. He could never be *that* selfish.

Leaning back, Roy said, "Either way, it's no longer my concern. I'm out of that bullshit rat race, and I can't stress to you how good that feels. All I want to say is, I love you as a person, and I hope very much to see you again."

Charles uttered something Alex didn't catch. A tingling coursed through his body. A familiar lightness swept over him as he looked from young face to young face and saw concern. He heard himself say he understood or maybe he cursed them; he couldn't be sure. His world went cloudy as his consciousness transported him from this nightmare to a probable living hell.

SEVENTH PLANE
OF EXISTENCE

Chapter Twenty-Five

Before entering the closed-door hearing, Peter had shared his legal counsel with Alex: "When dealing with the United States judicial system, say nothing. The courts are not after justice or the truth. It's about winning, supporting a narrative, and finality. We are the nation of metaphorical black bags over heads, convictions without evidence. Don't let propaganda convince you otherwise."

Alex had obeyed and sat mute for the past hour, waiting for mention of his infraction for accessing the Lobby. The topic had yet to come up, despite the lawyers' nonstop bickering.

"You can't keep the Lobby offline without a reason," Peter said, for what seemed the dozenth time.

"Your client is killing people," Agent Andrews said. "You' might be fine with that, but most of us are not."

Killing people was a new line.

"Are you suggesting my client murdered Charles Arnold? That he murdered Roy Guillen?"

Agent Andrews puffed out his chest, as if he believed the answer to be yes.

"Elderly men die," Peter said. "Some naturally, some overmedicate—"

"Commit suicide," Agent Andrews barked.

"That's not unheard of, Agent. Moreover, there is no law against providing a conducive environment to die. That could be labeled big-hearted, philanthropic even."

"Big-hearted? Oh, you make me sick." Agent Andrews appeared about to spit. "Suicide is the most selfish act possible. It offends every person of faith, and most others."

"We didn't cover God's law at Harvard." Peter leaned over the table and closed his leather binder. "I think we're done here."

The half-dozen other lawyers—essentially spectators, like Alex—seemed relieved by the statement.

"We are nowhere near done," Agent Andrews said. "We have other motions aimed at keeping that dangerous machine offline until we have proof of its appetite for life."

"And we'll fight you long enough for the angry mob to climb over your gates, carry you out of power, and demand their favorite pastime reinstated," Peter said.

"That's a threat," Agent Andrews said to the mediator, a woman who seemed the most relieved for this session to be ending.

"Gentlemen," she said, "let's take a day to cool ourselves. I'll expect clear and precise points of contention to when we next meet."

"Mr. Cutler," Peter said. "It's time to make our exit." He stood, his briefcase by his side.

"We will continue this tomorrow morning, nine a.m.," Agent Andrews said.

With no objections from Andrews, and as everyone in the room gathered their belongings in a show of support, Alex stood.

The previously quiet hall—for it had to be past eight in the evening—echoed with the approaching footsteps of Alex's head of security. Luke stepped in front of Alex, stopping him and Peter. "I need to prep you before our departure. There's a swarm of reporters out front, some camped out back. We'll need to hussle you out. No stops. Just stay on my tail."

"I need a few more minutes of Mr. Cutler's time," Peter said.

Luke checked with Alex, who nodded, and then followed Peter into the same meeting room they'd been in before the hearing.

With the door shut, Peter loosened his tie and stared at the wall.

Alex wanted to get home, update Rosa, and find some peace, so he interrupted his lawyer's rumination."Peter, let's make this quick."

The younger man inspected Alex with a slight frown, raised eyebrows, and one hand tucked under the opposite armpit. Peter motioned toward the chairs. "Let's sit."

Alex sat. Peter remained standing, inspecting Alex long enough to raise Alex's temperature. "I can't help you if you won't tell me what's happening."

What's happening... Alex thought as a montage played in his head: the nurses wheeling out Roy's body; the young, confused, and then giddy Roy they had found in Nebraska, 1871; Charles glowing face as Alex logged out, leaving them to immortality.

"I was tiptoeing through a minefield in there," Peter said. "If I step wrong, that psycho will get his wish. The Lobby will be gone forever, so..."

Alex was still thinking about the last time he was in Starbucks. At what point did the old part of the young Charles die? Did he feel a tingling throughout his body as Alex prattled on, and know his gamble had succeeded?

"Let me be clear: if you want me to protect you, which I will do until the end of time, then you need to tell me what's going on. The truth. Understand, I don't care if you are murdering your friends— although I will advise against it in the future and suggest you seek help from a specific doctor I know—but out of everyone on this planet, I must know the truth."

Alex and Rosa were the only living people who knew the truth. Staring at Peter, he recalled a saying, "It takes two to keep a secret, three to make it common knowledge."

"I'm bound by oath, and honor, to never divulge what you tell me. I am your most trusted advisor."

"Okay," Ales said. He needed help, and Peter might be the only he could trust that he also had access to. Alex told him everything. About Roy's death and finding him in Nebraska, about Charles. Alex ended by saying that since the Lobby offered so many destinations, he'd probably never see his two friends again.

Given a do-over, he should have scheduled another meeting with the men, at least for a better salutation.

Peter had eased into the chair across from Alex halfway through his tale. He'd scooted closer on two occasions, putting the man directly across from him, and their knees almost touched. When Alex finished, he read nothing in the attorney's blank stare.

Peter placed both hands over his face, and hung his head.

Alex almost placed a consoling hand on his shoulder. Alex had made a mistake confiding in Peter. Peter could easily go retell this story. By his body language, Alex expected him to get up, apologize, and go right down to the mediator.

Peter dropped his hands and looked up.

The lawyer's enormous smile shocked Alex. "And what?" Peter slapped Alex's thigh, and squeezed the knee hard enough to make Alex flinch."You think they're going to be there forever?"

"What?"

"Like, just what, forever?" Peter stood. "But what if the power goes out?"

"I'm not sure it can."

"Okay. Well, you know those guys. What do you think they're doing right now? Just driving down some boulevard in a limo, hanging out of the moonroof with a bottle of champagne in each hand, two gorgeous hotties blowing them from underneath?"

"What?"

"Two old geezers squeezing titties and making it rain." Peter giggled.

"Peter," Alex snapped his fingers. "Are you with me right now?"

Peter faced him, but his eyes were wide, looking off in the distance.

"Listen to me: I'm worried about going to jail. Do you think Agent Andrews can ruin my life?"

Peter twisted his wedding band, and stepped away. "They were both single, right?" He furrowed his brow. "I'd love to leave Wanda some type of note, make sure she was taken care of, but I could have a *virtual* wife." He scrutinized Alex. "Did I ever tell you that's how I spend most of my vacations—with Lydia, my virtual girlfriend? She gets me, Alex. I mean, I know she's a program, but…

196

I don't know. She remembers things, and cares about me like no American woman can."

Alex rapped his knuckles on the table, "Hey. Are you here, man?"

"Here? Of course, but what the fuck, ya know? Fuck. I never wondered if Lydia could leave her world. Can she do that? Can she visit other worlds with me?"

"I need you to calm down."

"I am calm, you asshole. Just asking a question. I mean, it's not an unreasonable question."

"Am I going to go to jail? That's a reasonable question. Can we save the Lobby from annihilation?"

"Save the Lobby? Of. Course. That's done, Alex." Peter pulled his chair back, sat, and leaned in. "I will do anything to keep it safe. I'd break the law." Peter's grin widened. "I would. It's the one thing I've spent my life saying I'd never do. But I'd break the damn law to help the Lobby. It's too valuable now. Us lawyers know what a wicked machine the courts are. It's why we're scared to death of it. But," he licked his lips, "what you've just told me, growing old in society or retiring in paradise." He snorted. "I'll break that law."

"You're not giving me much confidence you'll keep this secret."

Peter jerked his head like a bird, and straightened his tie."I'm an excellent attorney. Attorney-client privilege is a sacred pact, as far as I'm concerned."

"After the shock wears off, I need you to consider the implications. If you want to save the Lobby, we must work to keep the anomalous fact, of life carrying on in the Lobby, a secret."

Peter took Alex's hand in both of his. "You have my solemn loyalty, Mr. Cutler. You can trust me. I'll never repeat what you've said. I'll beat back this hiccup. Things will return to normal. I only ask one thing: when the time comes—years, a decade from now, after it's all died down and a thing of the past—you'll permit me to transfer in. Permanently."

Alex tried to pull back his hand, but Peter held tight.

"No one will know. I'm talking years from now. I'll plan it out for us; you'll do a little clean up. I'll never tell a soul. No one should know the Lobby's secret. I'm just thinking about myself here. Give me your word, and you have mine. I'll wipe the floor with this agent, have everything smooth, the Health and Wellness plan will prevent future incidents, the world ticks on happily. I only need your word."

Alex itched behind his ear with his free hand. Seeing no alternative, feeling he'd benefit from the alliance, "You have my word."

"Great," Peter released his hand and stood. "You trusted the right person, Mr. Cutler. Consider this done. I'll still have to bill you, but this inquiry will blow over in a matter of months." He grinned."If you can keep your friends from dying on your private access points, that is."

"That won't be a problem." Alex had no friends left. As he stood, he felt comforted. Peter's conviction emitted a perceptible energy. and Alex lathered in it.

Luke waited in the hall and peppered Alex with exit instructions as Peter moved on, with a little skip to his step.

The security team ushered Alex out the back rugby style, defenders all around, moving in centipedal fashion.

The cries of reporters and gathered onlookers hardly registered. Alex had shared his secret with one person. He had to hear Peter's plan to keep things bottled up, but he now felt confident he could keep Tara and Adisah out of it, netting him two fewer conspirators.

The return commute passed without commotion. Arriving home stirred the reporters posted outside his gate, but only long enough for them to film the passing vehicles. Inside, Alex called Rosa's name. He wanted to tell her about him avoiding jail. He'd leave out all mention of the Lobby unless she asked. Maybe they'd have dinner on the second-level patio, under the stars.

Feeling good, well... decent, for the first time in days, Alex decided to shortcut the search. "Victor, where's Rosa?"

"Mrs. Cutler left the premises at precisely five thirteen."

Left the premises? Four hours ago. Six additional steps solved the mystery. A digital note flashed on a section of Legion's wall, which they used as a community board. Alex pressed the icon to open it.

"I've packed a bag and gone to the beach house. I have calmed down. I do feel better, but I stand by my request. You must remove that thing from our house. We will talk in a few days. I love you with all my heart, Alex. I am positive this crisis will bring us closer. I simply need a few days to myself. With love, Rosa."

Alex first admired his wife's commitment to their marriage, and them living happy, forever. Next, he worried who would be with her at the Malibu house. They couldn't afford for her to share this, not with anyone.

Deleting the message, he accepted that he trusted her to keep it quiet. Privacy mattered to Rosa. Standing in an empty house, knowing he wouldn't be holding her tonight, made him feel as if someone tossed a bucket of swamp water over him, leaving him feeling weighted, dirty, and totally out of sorts.

Moving to the library, he grabbed a thin blanket, lay on the nearest couch, and courtesy of resurging depression, fell asleep within seconds.

Chapter Twenty-Six

The second mediation meeting was as miserable as the first, but now Alex sat at home, and though potential still existed for him to be criminally, or financially, culpable for Charles's death, the odds had dropped precipitously in the last twenty-four hours. Peter, true to his word, was rapid and precise in his defense of Alex, and the Lobby.

Alex had showered and eaten in preparation to watch Rebecca Trevino's show, *Inside Today*. Recently, he'd been tuning in every weekday at eight. Hers seemed to be the only news program that argued multiple sides. She often inserted hard facts, and showcased data that proved the Lobby's wasn't, and never had been, a danger. That didn't mean she avoided speculation or debating ideas. However, she was the only reporter withholding rants about Lobby horrors.

Melted into a leather couch in the main floor library, Alex wore a pair of Broumgard sweatpants and a stretched-out T-shirt. He devoured Oreos two at a time. A square foot inset on the bottom right of his television, swiped through photos of Rosa. She could smile in a hundred different ways, all of them gorgeous. He longed for the approaching day when things cooled between them, and he could be the man she deserved.

Today's episode brought the potential of Charles's autopsy report. He wondered if its revelations of death from an overdose of medication. He wondered if that would sway Rebecca   Trevino's current faith in everything Lobby.

While channel surfing, he found a replay of Peter's earlier news conference. Even though Alex had listened to it a dozen times that day, he increased the volume.

"Allow me to dispel a series of rumors." Peter squared his shoulders to the podium, his skin looked youthful, his voice boomed. "Charles Arnold was not a depressed man. He, like thousands of others, was an overmedicated patient—a victim of big pharma's exploitation of our elderly citizens. "The baseless smear against my client, Alex Cutler, is the media scourge at its best: sensationalizing fiction to gather ratings. Since media is about profits, my hat's off to them. But I'll address the sensible people of this world: Alex Cutler is as kind a man as you will ever find. The Lobby, as it has been for seven public years and many private years prior to that, is conclusively safe."

Many in the crowd cheered at that, spiking Peter's excitement. "Here's a little inside information to sensationalize: the forthcoming evidence will supports my words." And even louder, "This fraudulent charade is almost at an end, and the Lobby will be reopened within days." Big applause, followed by an uproar as he screamed, "You have my word." A nearby reporter, caught in the excitement, withdrew her microphone and clapped.

Alex grinned halfheartedly as he flipped back to *Inside Today*'s channel.

He craved Rebecca's show, yes, but he didn't ignore other news programs. He couldn't get enough of the lunacy. Some theories the media hypothesized were so diabolical and ridiculous that he pitied the reporters, knowing they had missed their true callings as paranormal fiction authors.

The most common conspiracy stated Alex had been silencing men before they went public about an unspecified danger the Lobby posed.

With fluctuating lines of conjecture, every few hours some tech blogger nailed the truth.

When that happened, Alex switched the channel or muted the television and at Oreos. Hence, his bloated abdomen.

201

The potential drama of tonight's episode had his blood racing. He leaned forward, grabbed the glass of whole milk and downed a two milligram Ativan that Roy's doctor had prescribed him on the fly.

He had been medicated for almost three days, and was disappointed it took him this long to add pills to his diet. And, despite the doctor's advice, he'd been taking nips of booze, too. That really took his troubles away.

Inside Today's soundtrack blared. A montage of Rebecca reporting in various dramatic scenes started each program: a barrier village in Nairobi, an overcrowded US prison, the war-torn streets of Gaza.

Even though he judged through a camera lens, Alex put her at an average height. Her strawberry-blond hair, angled jaw line, and firm body were as much a trademark as her strong diction.

During the program, he often believed she spoke directly to him. After nearly every episode, he considered calling her to schedule an interview. As if also detecting Rebecca's subliminal missives the previous night, Tara had texted him and suggested he give an interview.

This morning, his attorney vehemently condemned the idea, and reminded Alex to relax. Peter had everything under control.

Per the norm, Rebecca reviewed the night's topics and, as expected, they were all Lobby related.

"Pardon me," Victor said, his voice overtaking the program. "A commotion upstairs has drawn the attention of your security staff."

Commotion? Alex popped a cheese cube into his mouth. Luke's team treated every oddity like an invasion, but no one was allowed upstairs.

The two sheriff's deputies who had been patrolling his property were now walking through the house ever since Charles death. But even they respected his bedroom, and the upstairs in general. Besides, they had just finished their rounds.

Rosa was still at the beach house. Glen worked until ten. Arnel should be clocking out soon.   Since none of those people ventured onto the second floor without permission, and with a commercial playing, Alex prodded. "What sort of commotion?"

A tickle of worry caused him to sit up, wedge his feet into slippers, and snag an Oreo. He hoped whatever constituted "commotion" didn't cause him to miss any of *Inside Today*.

"Glen Daniels is attempting to access the Lobby."

He dropped the cookie and jumped up, knocking his knee on the edge of the coffee table. Limping out of the library, he rubbed at the pain. There had to be some mistake. Glen had specific instructions to avoid Alex's room.

"What's he doing up there? I told you no ones is allowed upstairs."

"Glen was cleaning, per his assigned duties. I granted him authorization on that pretense. He proceeded to interact with the control panel. I alerted security, and now you."

What was that kid thinking? Alex increased his pace. He had given Glen the control panel password, Eridu873Simon, months ago, instructing him to visit the Lobby at his leisure.

Obviously, that amenity ended when the Lobby was banned. Unless some grand excuse presented itself, Glen was at risk of being suspended, possibly fired.

Alex hurried into the back hall near the kitchen at a jogger's pace. One thing about a home encased in thick glass, acoustics traveled great distances. He heard one of his security personnel enter the front door and run up. Alex heard him say, "be on site in seconds."

Despite the narcotic coagulant Ativan provided, Alex's heart thumped. His throat burned as if he breathed arctic winter air.

Rounding the stairs, he saw a security officer charge into his room. With the thick glass door left open, letting out the sound. Alex abandoned hope of a simple misunderstanding.

Urgent shouts from multiple men rooted him in indecision at the base of the stairs. Sweat beaded his chest and lower back. A train delivering a mental break chugged closer. Hating himself for having thoughts of closing his eyes, covering his ears, and returning to the library, he steeled himself. If the issue orbited around Glen, his rapport with the teenager might help disarm the situation. He attacked the steps two at a time.

Entering the master suite hitched his breath, and increased his heartbeat even more. The room's generous length elongated, as if viewed through a fun-house mirror.

A security officer in the standard black-and-gray polo shirt stood half in the access room doorway, another tense member was poised at his six o'clock. Both had weapons pointed inside.

Alex noticed the second man held a stun gun, but the first man's grip disappeared into the access room. Hopefully, he held a Taser as well.

"Put it down!" The first man yelled into the access room.

Put what down? Alex thought as he felt pulled forward, as if drawn by the gravity of an unseen mass. What could Glen lift in the access room?

"It's going to be alright," the first officer said. "Just put it down, and let me see your hands."

"Go to hell, moron."

Stopping, Alex tried to reconcile the angry voice. It sounded like Glen, but he'd always been so quiet, so passive. As confirmation that was Glen settled, a frost pebbled Alex's skin. Had Rosa's suspicions been warranted? was Glen dangerous?

Pushing past the officer blocking the door, Alex stepped into a dense atmosphere. Sound ceased. He smelled sweat, and the room's lavender air-freshener.

Glen half-sat in the middle access chair. One foot hung over the leather, the other touched the floor.

Rage was evident on his face. The situation's danger heightened by the Kyocera carving knife held against his far wrist. Its presence was the alien in the room. Those ceramic blades had the sharpest edge in the industry. Cutting metal was no problem. Slicing through flesh and arteries offered resistance equivalent to a cold breath.

Blood trickled from a nick in his wrist. Not the spewing torrent of a severed artery, but Alex knew that to blast a geyser of red, Glen only needed to apply pressure.

"You stay back!" Glen yelled at the security officer.

"Glen, it's Alex." A glance, and brief eye contact. "Calm down, man." Alex said as he inspected the control panel. The counter ticked down. Fifty-two seconds remained. "Tell me what's going on."

Finding Alex, the kid's eyes narrowed to dark slits. "I know. So cut the bullshit, *Mr. Cutler*. I know. If you die while connected to the Lobby, you live there forever. I know that's what happened to Roy, and it's why Charles followed him."

"That's ridiculous," Alex said without much conviction.

One of the security members behind Alex mumbled something to the other. Alex wiped his brow.

"You think I'm going to stay in this bullshit world, with assholes like you, when I have options?"

Alex pushed aside the inaccurate moniker of asshole— something he'd been called twice in twenty-four hours—and considered refuting the Lobby claim. Instead, he stayed quiet, and checked the load-in timer. They had thirty-five seconds to move Glen the necessary fifteen feet away from the chair.

"What's going on in here?" a new voice barked.

Alex almost identified the voice. If only he paid more attention to his staff—like Rosa, who sent them birthday cards each year, mailed their children presents—he would know the personalities of the men around him, how to utilize each. Concentrating, he felt the connection nearing, and then it registered.

The doctor! Yes, that had been the voice of a bona-fide doctor. He had even heard the wheels of the cart as it arrived.

With a doctor on board, if Glen splayed his wrist open with a foot-long razor, his life could be saved. Meaning, they could either drag him away before he entered the Lobby, or keep him alive and welcome him back to the real world when his vacation ended.

That had to work. Alex wouldn't survive the scrutiny of a teenager committing suicide in his home. Not death number three. It would be the domino that toppled his existence.

"I gotta do it, Mr. Cutler. You know I do," Glen said. "Once people know the truth, they will close the Lobby forever."

"Just relax, for one second." Alex stepped aside to allow a clean line of sight for the first officer. He checked the timer—eighteen seconds. He locked eyes with the nearest officer. "Stun him. Do it now. Shoot him."

"What?" The guard stepped forward, pushed the weapon out father, but didn't fire.

Glen looked at the clock. "Don't do it." He pressed the blade's edge into his arm. The trickle of blood became a stream. Fear danced in his eyes, boosting Alex's confidence.

"Someone tase him." Alex shouted, furious they hadn't listened the first time. "There is a doctor here. Even if he gets in the Lobby, we can keep him alive."

As soon as he said it, Alex realized the folly in disclosing the logic in front of Glen. He should have let the kid cut himself, allowed him to drop into the Lobby, and then relied on the top-notch medical professional to keep him alive.

With Alex giving away his strategy, the script flipped.

In a blur of hand movements, Glen adjusted his grip to hold the knife with two hands, pivoting the blade's tip until it touched his sternum.

"Don't do it, kid." Alex launched forward.

The Kyocera pointed upward at a forty-five-degree angle, primed to slip under the chest plate, sink directly into the heart.

From the corner of his eye, Alex saw the timer: eight seconds. He hoped an officer realized no medic could save an impaled heart.

Alex's first foot planted.

One Mississippi.

He prayed the kid lacked the conviction, and would enter the Lobby healthy.

Two Mississippi.

Alex heard the stun gun pop. Victory coursed in him. When the prongs connected, the current would follow; and they'd both survive the ordeal.

Glen must have heard the shot as well, for his eyes hardened, and his forearm bulged as he pulled the blade inward. The sharp point glided through shirt and flesh as if the two layers were its natural sheath.

A dark glob oozed around the blade.

Alex saw Glen twitch as the stun gun's prongs connected and the current kicked in.

Blood belched from Glen's mouth as he convulsed.

Alex checked the timer.

Two Mississippi.

Glen's trembling hands slipped from the handle, as his eyelids drooped.

Zero Mississippi.

The image of an impaled young man seared into Alex's mind, to linger forever.

Alex's hands connected with the kid's ankles, yet before he yanked, Glen's eyes bulged to grotesque proportions, and his body went limp—the signs of a successful transfer to the Lobby.

The officer grabbed the blade handle, and the doctor yelled, "Don't touch it!"

The pooling pattern of blood widened.

Alex heard a slow exhale escape Glen's bloodied lips. The copper heat of it wafted over his senses. He released the ankle.

Allowing himself to be pushed to the side, Alex fought a growing fatigue.

The doctor rushed past him.

Alex glanced around for a place to sit.

They were too late.

Glen had entered the Lobby alive, and was now dead.

All the money in the world couldn't stop this from going viral.

Chapter Twenty-Seven

The Reverend Billy Graham once said, "Through perseverance, the snail reached the ark." As Agent Andrews listened to an irrelevant underling voice his opinion, he reminisced on his crawl through the years, on his determined path to expose Broumgard. Hundreds of his fantasies involved courtroom battles, where his rational debate would win the nation's hearts and minds. A favorite action scenario involved Alex Cutler snatching a hostage in a chokehold and aiming a pistol at the captive's head. While being broadcast live, Agent Andrews would disarm the man with moves learned in training, and shoot Alex with his own firearm as the psychotic billionaire reached for a backup weapon.

Agent Andrews always knew heading the LOC would be a brilliant career move. In a show of support and unity—or better yet, praise— the powers that be offered him an office on the fifth floor of the Federal building in Los Angeles. His title granted him authority equal to Deputy Director John Willis. This meant thirty-five thousand agents at his disposal.

The first day of reaming Alex Cutler's snarky attorney and watching Alex squirm had been so mercurial that within twenty minutes, Andrews had excused himself from the room and strolled to the bathroom. Once alone, he'd swung his arms spastically as if fighting off spirits, while grunting his elation.

When he returned to the meeting, he felt like a saint holding a flaming sword. This day brought equal satisfaction.

Beginning tomorrow, his legal team would search for precedent for seizing both the hardware and software that allowed Mr. Cutler to access the Lobby at home.

"Given a favorable judge, that seems our best chance." The underling said. By the trailing of his voice, Andrews knew he had finished. Whatever he said involved his own ego, and meant nothing. From this day forward, words mattered little. They had an objective— actions would rule.

"Thank you, Domorsky," Agent Andrews said.

The man looked around."My name is Wright. Allen Wright."

Agent Andrews frowned.

Before starting his final address, a woman spoke. "Domorsky went home hours ago."

"Does it matter?" Agent Andrews said. "No. Now focus. We stand on the frontline of America's defense. The Lobby has distorted all of our values. It has supplanted American pastimes with induced delirium. Education and healthy socializing have almost vanished in a matter of years. You men, and women, are the Nameless Special Forces. Our mission is the most vital—"

The elevator doors dinged with a new arrival.

Since it was almost nine at night, and the floor was vacant except those Andrews asked to stay late, he surged with indignation, almost choked with disgust that some fat janitor had interrupted his flow. He cleared his throat and searched for his last words.

The Man in Gray stepped off the elevator.

Shorter than anyone in authority should be, his eyes were locked on Agent Andrews's as if he'd been watching from inside the elevator, which obviously he hadn't. Agent Andrews ran a finger inside his shirt collar.

"Who's that?" an agent asked another.

"Some spook," said the woman who'd previously mentioned Domorsky's departure.

"He's no one," Agent Andrews blurted. "Our mission is vital. People are addicted and spellbound. They need liberators, and we are that source. Let's get to it." He frowned. With swiveling heads all

209

around the table, he expedited their dismissal by shooing them out with both arms.

Agent Andrews dropped into the nearest chair and checked on the interloper, who continued to stare. Andrews looked away. *Little shit is trying to intimidate me. That* won't *happen.*

"Agent Andrews," the last man to exit said.

"What, dammit?"

"I was just … Have a good night, Sir."

"Brown-nosing will get you nowhere with me, Agent Wright."

"Okay then." Agent Wright pivoted on a heel and trailed the herd to the elevator.

Agent Andrews felt the short man still staring, but he didn't take the bait by looking up. He daydreamed about how special it would feel to seize Alex Cutler's property. Regardless of orders, Agent Andrews would explore the highly touted, patent-protected macroservers that preserved the Lobby. He had to see the hardware, and examine the software.

The federal government should just take the dangerous components by force. What would happen if, by some long odds, his legal team failed to compile the necessary arguments and in win? Or if one lone judge overruled them? Would they allow Broumgard to keep destroying the world?

Personally, he'd continue to fight. With clear evidence pointing to the Lobby's evil, he'd eventually destroy the machine.

Agent Andrews heard the small man's soft, padding steps bring him near.

Looking up made Agent Andrews start. The Man in Gray waited at the end of the abandoned aisle, well out of range Agent Andrews expected from the footfalls. He stool like a serial killer.

How had he imagined hearing steps so close? Was he experiencing a psychosomatic effect, some mind trick used to scare?

Besides, who just stands like that, glaring at someone?

Agent Andrews rose to his full six one and stared back.

The Man in Gray had introduced himself as Mr. Johnson on their first meeting.

After dismissing the room with a few words, he'd shared frightening information about the Lobby and its soul-trapping capabilities. Specifically, how the Japanese had identified the soul-shifting effect a few days after Roy Guillen's passing and jumped into the business of selling "death trips" to Japan's ultra-wealthy, with intentions of expanding that opportunity across the world.

The idea chilled Andrews. When had humanity fallen so low?

He detested the Mr. Johnson's visits, but he valued the information imparted. And why the Man in Gray? Agent Andrews assumed the moniker stemmed from arriving in the same pressed gray suit each time. Surely the man wore other colors of suits. Hiis undergarments had to be white, only jiggalos wore colorful underwear. The guy operated outside the governmental fraternity, yet held immense clout. An extreme annoyance.

The head of CRYPTLOG, Kathleen Sousa herself, vouched for the man's ultimate authority.

The Man in Gray moved toward him.

Preferring to avoid the handshake, Agent Andrews said, "Let's head into my office," and hurried inside.

He busied himself by opening a folder next to his tablet computer. A thirty-two-year-old man from Tennessee had been experiencing double vision ever since his last trip to the Lobby, two years ago.

He marveled at what a little press could do. In six days, the LOC had received a number of complaints equal to its previous six years.

Rather than hear the door shut, he sensed the room's air pressure increase.

The Man in Gray stood beside the closed door. His arms hung loosely at his sides, his body stiff as if sprayed with starch, his gaze honed on Andrews.

The man's height confounded Agent Andrews. He couldn't be more than five two. At that stature, with a receding hairline and small ears, how could he be a man of mystic authority? Andrews's arms, chest, and quads bulged, proving he wasted time at the gym rather than at work or study. Who anointed this man-child?

211

However, the Man in Gray did possess a strangely powerful walk, the kind of strut that turned heads, and hushed a room.

Without having to ask, Andrews knew the man previously served in the military. No better avenue existed for getting scooped up by one of the many clandestine governmental agencies. Join, test out of the water, get scrutinized without knowing it, and if you please someone important, an invite manifests. Andrews pinned him as Air Force. The Man in Gray carried himself with their smugness. Closing the folder, he greeted his guest. "Mr. Johnson."

"We will be adding a military presence at all Atriums to keep zealots from entering the Lobby."

Agent Andrews ignored the lack of greeting, and focused on the words. He knew local law enforcement, along with six-man teams of federal agents, denied entrance to anyone besides maintenance workers and the occasional IT guys. Since the agents mostly sat around playing with their smartphones, he didn't understand the need to bolster those numbers.

"Within the next few hours, two problematic revelations will be released to the public," Mr. Johnson said. "A major one is underway at the Cutler home as we speak."

Andrews splayed all ten fingers on the table, wondering if Alex would truly be stupid enough to press his luck.

As the silence dragged on, Andrews grew embarrassed by his childlike enthusiasm to hear about Alex's problems, and relaxed.

Mr. Johnson continued, "The other occurred in London twenty minutes ago. A janitor disguised his wife as an employee. Together, they managed to sneak their children inside. The husband logged his wife and children into the Lobby and then injected each with a hundred fifty cc mixture of motor oil, antifreeze, and other homemade poisons."

Agent Andrews' mouth dropped open.

"The husband then sat in his own chair, and with seconds remaining, chugged his green punch."

"A father murdered his entire family for the Lobby?" Pressing his palms against his closed eyes, Andrews repressed his bile.

"The events at the Cutler home will hit your desk within the hour, the media shortly thereafter. It will be hectic. I advise a power nap."

A nap? No chance. His next question might cost him credibility, but he had to know. "One hundred percent, if someone dies while in the Lobby, their soul stays there?"

Mr. Johnson cocked his head to one side and stepped closer. "It was verified a week ago. That's why I briefed you." He moved one of the seats to displace the object dividing them. "You have been given a position of importance, Mr. Andrews. I hope you have the stamina to persevere, and the faith to adhere to a communal plan. I was told I could delegate high-priority tasks to you."

"You can, absolutely."*Although it's Agent Andrews.*

"Your responsibility is to harass Mr. Cutler, keep his feet to the fire, and remove the Lobby from society. I'll make sure the world sees it as the destructive element it has always been, and learn to hate its memory."

Agent Andrews liked the thought, but by those standards, *he'd* be doing the important stuff. Hence, he should be giving the orders.

Agent Andrews checked his watch. Less than two hours to prepare. For now, he mulled over how chaos within Cutler's home and a family slaughtered in London helped, and concluded those events helped tremendously.

The short man glided to the dominant window that faced the office. Despite an empty floor, he twisted the hanging rod, closing the blinds. Once sealed, he went to the light switch and dimmed the lights.

Sensing danger, Andrews moved his hand under the right split of his suit jacket, near his sidearm.

"Dim lighting helps with the nerves." Mr. Johnson motioned to the chair before Andrews. "Sit. I have things of vital importance to share. The correct frame of mind allows for optimal retention."

Mr. Johnson stayed at the light switch until Andrews obliged.

He didn't believe sitting and turning down the lights affected mental function. That stuff might be necessary for weak-minded peons, but not him. Still, he obeyed.

From the new angle, Mr. Johnson's body vanished behind a cushioned chair, making it appear that a disembodied head addressed him.

"Everything thus far is but a pittance compared to the turmoil approaching this nation, and humanity itself."

Stature forgotten, Andrews leaned forward, wondering what could be more serious than a machine that caused a man to kill his family and also ate souls?

"How strong is your faith, Mr. Andrews?"

Again, he preferred Agent Andrews, but he kept quiet, considered the question. He attended church somewhat regularly, missing at most two Sundays a month; read the Bible; and knew deep in his gut that God would consider him an amazing person. "I have no doubts that the Bible lays out the pathway to good living."

"You have quirks, but you are devout enough to get committed. That's why I'm here." Mr. Johnson stepped from behind the chair. "You sit before one of the few men throughout antiquity who can assure you, there is a God. A force, with the characteristics of a sentient being, exists. He initiated the universe. And though He loves everything, we are his most engaging creations."

Mr. Johnson stood like a robot from the 1950s, block shaped and inanimate, but his words rattled Andrews more than a six-foot-five bodybuilder shaking him for owing the local Don.

"I can also assure you we've known the soul exists for over fifty years. We're close to being able to gauge the strength of its presence in a person, and we've determined mental exercises to strengthen it. There is a school of thought that believes the strength of the soul multiplied by a person's positive and negative choices is what most greatly impacts the world. Broumgard all but made public the existence of a soul the day of the Lobby's launch, but no one noticed. This machine and current events have done something very rare in my life: they have surprised me. This equipment steals souls, Mr. Andrews. Souls mainly destined for a desolate hell of insanity,

214

confusion, and regret, but now that majority is evading their deserved punishment for choosing a life of apathy and cowardice. Much more disconcerting is that this machine is stifling the rewards earned by those few who follow their instincts into action, forgive those who ask, and contribute to more than their own offspring." Making steady eye contact, he said, "You do understand what I'm saying?"

"Of course. Men of action. I know the type."

"There is a God, and His plan to reward or punish an individual's use of free will is being circumvented. Another truth for you to absorb is that a plan this intricate can only be initiated by His nemesis."

Agent Andrews almost blurted, "Alex Cutler." Instead, as full comprehension registered, he narrowed his eyes and said, "I understand."

"Never forget what I'm telling you. You will need ample fuel for the upcoming battle." Mr. Johnson softened his tone and continued, "I'm sure you've heard it rumored that we monitor global chatter. We do it for a multitude of reasons, mainly to predict or influence voting habits. That endeavor has been a science in this country since the early sixties and worked in all elections, save one. We have thwarted future antagonists from attaining their destined positions for decades. We now send them down a path that leads to prison or death. And with people of exceptional charisma weeded out, the country keeps the proper 'follow the lesser hierarchy,' and decency reigns."

Agent Andrews always wondered why there hadn't been any political or philosophical leaders in opposition to the government's increasing control, since the barrage of assassinations and suspicious deaths throughout the nineteen sixties. But he couldn't believe the government exerted the described level of control. If they did, why were so many imbeciles allowed to succeed, or live even?

"This machine is evil," Mr. Johnson said." And the chatter around the world is troubling. Each hour, more people are discussing whether the Lobby can store your consciousness forever. With the upcoming news coverage, those numbers will explode. Despite our efficiency, my side lacks the manpower to contain what's coming."

He shifted his weight. "People will want to get inside of those machines to die. And when humans identify a true want, we are the most inventive creatures to ever exist.

"My end has begun a soft campaign, reaching out to true believers. I will forge a powerful front. Your people, as well as various other factions, will be vital to our victory."

Agent Andrews's mouth dried. The current conversation solidified his lifelong conviction that staying the course would lead to a role of importance.

"I need a copy of that list of those who will help," Andrews said, "and a greater role."

"You need to do as you're told, nothing more. Boot up your computer."

No please? Andrews was head of the LOC, not this midget's lackey. He looked down at the device, wanting to continue this briefing, but he deserved a proper level of respect.

A mild disorientation settled as he depressed the power button and listened to the startup noises. Then he accepted that a power greater than the Mr. Johnson sought his help in the battle for all of mankind. God Himself.

The screen lit up with the normal blue. When it completed the cycle, it flickered once, and a tan backdrop replaced his normal series of icons. One icon, shaped like a manila folder, stood alone. It was labeled "The Beast."

"Open that file, but don't peruse it at this time."

I'll peruse whatever I want, thought Andrews. He double-clicked the icon, which opened an electronic dossier. He'd poured over thousands similar to this. The exception being that this one had twice the number of thumbnails dotting its side. The header, Sung Yi, age sixty-one. Tao Buddhist, born in Xiang, China, immigrated to Nara, Japan, in 1989. Upon finishing the information on the main page, he glanced at his visitor. Andrews hoped the man had noticed his blatant perusing.

As if unconcerned, the Mr. Johnson said, "Sung Yi's teachings rapidly digressed from fundamental Taoism in the late eighties, which seemed to decrease his audience, but attract loyal followers. In the mid-nineties, he became the first ordained monk to stream his Buddhist nonsense over the internet in a podcast. Still, no big deal. A couple hundred eclectic weirdos.

"What now makes this demure kook a threat to this nation is his viral explosion over the past week. Considering all the past internet sensations, there's never been growth like this. His introductory video about the seventh plane of existence has received over five hundred million views in the past six days."

Agent Andrews frowned. He enjoyed going on the internet to watch recorded presidential inaugurations, so he considered himself a YouTube expert. He had never heard of Sung Yi, or a seventh plane of existence. "I'm sorry, seven planes of existence? Isn't science still working on proving the forth?"

"You're talking about dimensions, and we've identified over forty of those, but that's irrelevant. Planes of existence are methods of classifying reincarnation. Buddhists believe that when a person dies, they immediately return to life in another form. Particle physics say they are correct about physical matter returning to life—in about five hundred years—but they are woefully incorrect when thinking the spirit participates in that journey. God might recycle, but the soul moves on."

Andrews knew judgment awaited every person. Anyone who didn't believe that was a fool.

"Many Buddhists believe that when you die, you return on one of *six* planes of existence. As ridiculous as it sounds, they figure you become a plant, an insect, an animal, a sea creature, a human—or you appear on the sixth plane as a demigod.

"Enlightened Buddhists consider this recycling of life a cruel and unjust existence. For even if they live kind enough lives to reach demigod status, they would still experience suffering and loss, and after thousands of years, death. At which point they reincarnate again on one of the six planes, continuing the cycle.

"So what a Buddhist strives for is Nirvana—an inner peace that leads to an enlightenment. An understanding of the cosmos that, once attained, enables them to cheat Gaea's recycling plan, and allows them to become nothing. In short, Buddhists strive to end

217

themselves." Mr. Johnson inhaled deeply, and slowly exhaled, as if the entire premise bothered him.

Agent Andrews stared at the photo of the Asian monk on his computer. He had a wrinkly face beneath either a bald or shaved head. He wore a yellow robe with a brown sash wrapped around him. A half-smile frozen beneath dark, beady eyes that sparkled with what Andrews perceived as violence.

Everything he heard seeped in. Dying, only to pop back as something new. Believing in eternal life, and then trying to escape it. The absurdity almost made him laugh. Then a question formed. Why had five hundred million people watched a video created by this monk? More importantly, how did this man play into the recent activities?

As if reading his mind again, Mr. Johnson continued, "For the last twenty years, Yi has been preaching to a limited audience about a *seventh* plane of existence—one promised by Gaea to end the suffering of her people. He hypothesized that her heart breaks each time one of her children reached Nirvana and ceased to exist. He claimed to have been granted a vision, showing how she would soon provide the world with an alternative to nihilistic enlightenment.

"Can you guess the subject matter of his seventh plane of existence videos?"

Agent Andrews closed his eyes as his heart rate slowed, and the blood in his veins became pudding, "The Lobby fulfilling those prophecies."

"Exactly. At this point his argument is a novelty, a scandalous topic to discuss following a few drinks. After these two stories leak, the seventh plane of existence will become an exploratory curiosity, validated to greater degrees with each forthcoming suicide."

The word itself chafed Andrews's core. He wasn't as convinced as Mr. Johnson that more suicides would follow. Anytime Andrews heard about suicide prior to the Lobby madness, he thought of how weak and pathetic the person must have been. The only comfort came from knowing they were no longer a burden on the rest of us.   "Perhaps a good PR campaign and tight security will prevent further deaths," he said.

"Please, you need to listen, follow advice—nothing more."

"Maybe you'll learn I could be more valuable than even you?"

Mr. Johnson allowed seconds to pass. Time during which he did little more than blink. "Tight security will be ineffective. Security personnel will comprise some of the validators, and our soil is not the greatest problem. Japan has reached out to South Korean diplomats for support to explore a practice of dying to live as a method to govern. Much of that part of the world is fervent over Yi. Those nations will continue to unite. The wound this media exposure causes will fester. People will turn this machine into a symbol of immortality, reached through sacrilege."

Agent Andrews felt his sidearm tug at his hip. He'd never fired his weapon in the line of duty. He wasn't one of those guys who spent his weekends at the gun range or stockpiled an arsenal at his house. But hearing this latest atrocity, his gun whispered to him. He thought of all the people with underdeveloped brains in the world, and how this evil siren would enthrall them. A fiery rage filled him, along with an urge to find Alex Cutler and shoot him dead. To force Adisah Boomul to kneel in front of him and decapitate him with a machete.

Pushing aside his honorable thoughts, he made eye contact with the Man in Gray. "I pray you have a plan to prevent all of this."

"We do, but you must be forewarned: it's going to get messy before it gets clean. And that, Agent Andrews, is the question I have come to ask you. It's the reason I flew out here today. I need to know—are willing to get your hands dirty in the defense of the American way of life, against an adversary powered by a dark evil?"

Agent Andrews returned his gaze to the beady eyes on his computer screen. He thought of Adisah Boomul and Alex Cutler and the riches they had amassed by leading sinful lives. He'd need a bigger role, more respect, but he had also pledged to honor the chain of command. Locking eyes with the Mr. Johnson, and applying layers of sincerity, he nodded.

"My only question, Mr. Johnson, is, can you locate other men half as loyal and dedicated as me?"

"That's affirmative."

Chapter Twenty-Eight

Tim Vanderhart stopped watching television the previous morning. Appropriate signs he'd been waiting his entire life to receive had manifested. Now, he would fulfill his destiny.

He sat in a fold-out chair, alone, inside the clubhouse garage, a gray wooden barn that lost all remnants of its red paint decades ago.

The two stories that looped on every channel sealed his conviction (seeing them six times helped diminish his shock). First, some crackpot from England murdered his family to trap their souls in a machine. Insane. Humanity at its worst. But Alex Cutler—the man responsible for all this suffering—had assisted in another blasphemous suicide. Tim could hardly believe it.

He loaded his .45 semiautomatic to help calm him.

Hearing that Glen Daniels, a boy the same age as Tim, had screamed about immortality in a false device scared the bejesus out of him.

Reverend Carmichael's internet sermon solidified his belief in the evil. This was Satan's push to take over the world. A quiet marching of marked souls to wicked chairs.

Tim had joined the Northern Michigan Christian Defense at birth. The print on their slogan, pamphlets, and mission statements lacked the identification, he prided himself on being part of a militia. A militia of somewhat pure genetics that aimed to protect the rights of noble, Christian people.

Today, all of Tim's fantasies animated. At nineteen years old, he knew, despite weighing a hundred and ten pounds, he was the perfect age to soldier, and he trained hard to be the best. The NMCD's property covered ninety-three acres and was located twenty miles east and a tad south of Traverse City, in the state shaped like a mitten.

He'd been practicing every conceivable form of warfare since he could carry a rifle down a wooded trail. Hell, before that he unsuccessfully stalked rabbits and chipmunks with a rubber knife he'd gotten one Christmas.

The difference between him and the dozens of other men who had recently arrived to the clubhouse was that he knew this day had been coming for a long time, and that he'd play a major role in their future.

Every time he squinted down a rifle sight, shimmied up a rope, cut around the anus of a deer, boiled and drank his urine, or built an improvised explosive device, he employed ultimate reverence. For he knew someday it would all come into play for him. He hadn't dreamed of such a magnificent scale of importance, but here he was.

The barn he sat in normally stored a tractor and miscellaneous obstacle-course equipment. The now-useless stuff had been removed the remaining space lined with two rows of eight chairs.

Twenty minutes ago, those chairs held charter heads from nearby militias and motorcycle clubs, along with their seconds-in-command. Morally sound, hardcore, God-fearing men. Tim felt honored to be the youngest among them.

His father had been a founding brother of the NMCD. Regrettably, having battled alcohol and prescription pills his entire life, he died of cirrhosis before Tim's eleventh birthday. Tim knew that had been God's way of showing him the detriments of polluting your temple, and he intended to heed the warning.

Alan Cox, head of the NMCD, acted as a second father to Tim. He hoped the speech Alan gave today would unite all of the nearby forces into one. It seemed to have worked

The summoned heads had pledged allegiance to Alan Cox. Others would follow. In a short time, the many factions would relinquish their names for one much grander: the Lord's Thorn.

The Lord's Thorn would be fully dedicated, life and limb, to the eradication of the Lobby and the downfall of the Broumgard Group.

Tim wasn't sure who the man in the gray suit had been short, stocky, a fierce look of intelligence, more hawk than man—but he'd provided the launching pad to the recent events.

Tim always woke at the slightest provocation and usually grabbed his beside pistol. Even with rotors modified to suppress sound, the noise of a helicopter setting down in a nearby field woke him in time to see the Man in Gray enter Alan's house.

Tim had crept along the edge of the window and overheard enough to know the NMCD was stepping into the big leagues. The two men of authority spoke until six thirty.

When their guest departed, Alan sought Tim out, and shared the unification plan. They'd been in high gear ever since.

Alan told him things he already knew. The Man in Gray worked for the government and brought a deep commitment to stopping the Lobby. He also shared classified documents to help convince Alan they gathered to wage war for the world's immortal souls. He promised Alan a stake in that fight by backing him with money, personnel, and weapons.

The vacant barn offered Tim the privacy to take in all he had heard, but soon he'd rise out of his chair and commence to walking his path.

The Man in Gray, who called himself Smith, had given Alan a list with names of nearby civilians planning to join the cause. A computer program identified individuals willing to act in the defense of everything sacred.

Tim was awed by the number of like-minded individuals near him.

Waves of unknown men and women approached. Tim would organize those who arrived. He'd establish their temporary shelter before the big relocation.

Their first mission would be to forcefully unseat the famous man responsible for this evil.

Smacking his hands on his thighs, Tim stood. He had worked to do.

Chapter Twenty-Nine

Alex vegetated on the twenty-six-foot Dior couch in the middle of his library. Rebecca Trevino's visage dominated the monitor. The Friday edition of *Inside Today* would start soon, and the twelve-by-twelve-foot screen allowed him over twenty thousand inches of viewing pleasure. He enjoyed the Friday episodes the most. They reviewed the previous week's stories, and what could be forgotten in a matter of days never ceased to amaze.

Needing to relive every painful memory, he loaded up on enough snacks for the entire night: a roast beef sub, a pack of Double Stuff Oreos, E.L. Fudge cookies, chocolate in a jar, three bananas, and a two liter of Barq's root beer.

The credits for *Inside Today* rolled. Pushing the detritus from last night's snack session aside, he assembled his new smorgasbord, then leaned back and admired each item's ergonomical placement.

A condition for him staying out of jail after Glen's suicide was to install triggers on the access room entrances. To avoid the temptation, or hours of staring at the door handle, Alex divided his time between the library near the kitchen on the main floor, and one of the guest bedrooms on the second floor, which overlooked the front lawn. He did the latter in case Rosa returned home early.

They'd talked on the phone, and she'd sent him a lovely, six-page letter of condolence and affection that ended with her saying she loved him unconditionally, and they'd be fine. She just needed some time.

He never doubted their bond, but appreciated her detailing it nonetheless.

In the missive, Rosa mentioned staying away the entire weekend. That suited him fine. Her absence allowed him to wallow in self-pity, which was an underrated form of therapy.

Lights blinked around the screen, showing the second intro commercial. His previously stoic, currently sycophantic attorney's name, Peter Mueller, ran across the top like a ticker. Per Alex's instructions, Victor blocked all calls, but the digital assistant displayed the caller's name, in case an urgent matter presented itself.

Most calls involved socialites he'd met throughout the years at the Los Angeles Atrium: actors, directors, writers, artists, professional athletes who, at one point, all wanted to have Alex Cutler's private number. Being naïve, he had also longed for theirs. Their calls came under the guise of concern. In actuality, they just wanted social currency, same as him when he got their number. They'd tell him not to worry. The Alex *they* knew would be fine." Others wanted to gossip about Rosa. "It's so commendable that you're comfortable with your wife planning fundraisers intent on closing the Lobby."

Tearing open the Oreos, he considered Rosa's mission to smear the Lobby.

He believed she had the right to follow her heart. He wished she wanted to talk to him about it, yet he understood why she hadn't. The funny thing was, he would support her efforts. She might even lure him to her side. The current drama around the globe made him sick. Having spent days out of the Lobby, he'd recently wondered if the digital escape added any benefit to society.

Prior to the discovery of death creating life, you couldn't get him to bad-mouth the Lobby. Since then, he fantasized about supporting Rosa, and strengthen their marriage. What a powerful combination they would make. The great, mystical Alex Cutler, the man many believed had designed the Lobby by himself, joined side by side with his philanthropic wife in a mission to eradicate the very thing that brought them wealth.

Before he delved too far into his fantasy, *Inside Today* returned from commercial. Leaning forward to snatch a width of Oreos, he swigged from the opened root beer. By the time he leaned back, he'd abandoned all thoughts of an alternate reality where he'd support the Lobby's destruction.

Another flash of light blinked around his screen, followed by Peter's name, again. He swept crumbs off himself and let it go to voicemail. He wouldn't say he had a belly, but enough of a bump existed to rest the tray of cookies upon.

The show started by recapping the previous Friday, when a custodian from London sneaked his entire family into an access room and then injected them with some lethal concoction of antifreeze and motor oil. Alex guessed that day's events coincided with his first doubts about the Lobby's value.

As soon as that spot ended, and he knew highlighting Glen's death would follow, he lost heart and flipped to the Discovery Channel. That station never looped Glen's quote verbatim: "If you die while connected to the Lobby, you live there forever. I know that's what happened to Roy, and it's why Charles followed."

Stuffing two cookies in his mouth, he chewed with slow, crunching bites.

The memory of Glen's dying breath haunted him. Even now, thinking about it caused ghost fragrances to invade his olfactory. Death's viscous finality seemed to expel all the long-preserved gasses and bacteria from the stomach, leaving a stench of corrupted iron, copper, and blood.

He grabbed the two liter, placed the opening under his nose, squeezed the plastic sides, and inhaled three quick times. He chased that with a drink, gradually warding off his unwanted memories.

After allowing an adequate amount of time to pass, he switched back to *Inside Today* at the exact moment it segued.

The previous Saturday, twelve people managed to connect to different access chairs around the US, Europe, and Australia. They terminated their lives with hopes of finding immortality within a program.

227

On Sunday, eight deaths, but only one splashed the screen. It surgically removed another piece of Alex's heart. Sean Flaska, his long-time friend from Chicago and head of the Madrid Atrium, had created a cyanide pill using fish-tank algae remover and apple seeds, becoming the Lobby's twenty-seventh verified casualty.

Apparently, Sean left a suicide note. Alex considered asking Luke to track down a copy, but the notion never passed the daydream phase. He lacked the motivation for action, and somewhat appreciated his house arrest. He couldn't help but wonder if he'd been mentioned in the note, or if Sean had referenced a Noah's Ark, or what cool T-shirt he'd selected for his last day among the living.

Monday brought twenty-two Lobby-related deaths. Alex felt this was compelling evidence the Lobby might not be safe after all. That day also brought the sealing of Atriums. No more cleaning crews or visits by upper management. For the time being, their interiors would be multimillion-dollar dust farms.

That evening, attorneys from the U.S. Justice Department filed injunctions to seize the servers, possibly for destruction. They were promised a swift hearing.

Tara's litigation team numbered in the hundreds. Her face stayed on multiple channels, and she fought every negative insinuation. Recently, they replayed her reading a statement vowing the Atriums would be reopened after the thirty-day moratorium, and that no servers would be lost.

As far as Alex could tell, hers was a minority opinion.

Tuesday brought little change. Three deaths, none of which occurred on U.S. soil. Strangely enough, Alex felt national pride at that.

The bombshell came on humpday. Eight people had killed themselves—six in Europe, one in the U.S., and one Down Under. More importantly, the Western world learned how the other half of the planet had been coping.

Rebecca ran a human-interest story on Sung Yi, a Tao Buddhist amazing the world with his prescient teachings. For years, he'd foretold of the Lobby's arrival, the soul stealing part, and he now pleaded for people to align their karma, be good to nature, and at the optimal time, transport their lives to the "Seventh Plane of Existence," a paradise gifted to humanity by Gaea, the Mother of Creation.

The world also heard intimations of thousands of "Death Trips" having occurred in Japan and China. Their national spokesmen released statements denying any wrongdoing, and labeling the accusations outlandish, but the evidence was overwhelming.

A few bloggers claimed the rumors of tens of thousands of Death Trips stood closer to six figures.

Hearing it anew caused Alex's gut to drop and his heart to flutter. The thought appalled him. Labeling global death "fake news" brought his best solace, but more and more outlets considered the boast plausible.

He'd seen a Death Trip firsthand, from inside and out. Death was a gruesome chaperon that battered everyone in its path.

He gulped more root beer, then forced two Oreos into his mouth.

No one knew for certain, and no one in the West wanted to believe such things were possible, but the thought of thousands of orchestrated deaths carried volumes of implications. Despite its modern-day wanderings, and the mocking of pundits, America remained a nation devoted to the Bible, with Islam rising in every corner. The thought of countless people killing themselves draped despair over a God-fearing nation.

Two weeks ago, no one could have written a scenario plausible enough to surpass recent national outrage, pensive contemplation, and a fierce emotional divide. People claimed our society was fragile—possibly the reason doomsday prepping piqued American interest—but who expected it to actually break?

Thursday, America once again abstained from Death Trips, along with Australia, but thirty-four deaths littered Europe. Following these deaths, the EU called for tighter security, and Israel issued a formal threat: stop the death trips, or they will..

The biggest story came from Riyadh, Saudi Arabia, where an air strike leveled their Atrium, ending Lobby access for that part of the world.

Saudi officials claimed to have no evidence linking any nation to the attack. Yet in coincidence, all security personnel had been evacuated to a safe distance, leaving the one hundred and thirty-five thousand square foot complex free to be reduced to a pile of ash and debris.

U.S. officials avoided commenting. With U.S. media embracing speculation as a rule, some pundits believed the government's minimal clamoring was because many of them supported the attack.

The internet busted with theories. The most credible was that the Iranian military, with full approval from the Saudi royal family, committed the act. The most absurd was that Alex Cutler, using a remote detonator from his home, caused the servers to self-destruct to avoid them being seized by Islamic nations.

Now it was Friday. Protests warred outside every Atrium on the globe. The majority of the public still supported the Lobby, but the margin lessened by the day, by the hour, and by the death.

Today, eleven Death Trips were reported. All located in the Paris Atrium, where scrutiny, finger-pointing, and investigations were underway.

Inside Today went to its third commercial around the same time he emptied the tray of Oreos. Alex flung the plastic divider on the table with enough force that it slid off the far side and onto the floor. He'd contact Rebecca Trevino. Before he could, he needed to decide what side he landed on and clarify his reasoning.

He figured it best to call her and make the appointment, locking himself into action. Afterward, he would call Rosa for her thoughts, contact Tara and get hers, and then come to his own conclusion.

He muted the television as it blinked again. A number ran across the top of the screen. The identifying text stated the call originated from FBI headquarters.

Snide remarks from Agent Andrews were the last thing he needed on the cusp of an upswing.

Alex ignored the call. His new game plan consisted of taking his first shower in three days, going online to watch the Tao Buddhist

230

video about the Seventh Plane of Existence for himself, then contacting Rebecca.

As he drank from the two liter, another flash crossed the monitor, followed by a flowing text message: "Mr. Cutler, this is Special Agent Andrews, head of the Lobby Oversight Committee appointed to the Los Angeles branch of the Federal Bureau of Investigation. It is imperative that you contact me. If you do not comply within the next twenty minutes, I will have the sheriffs bring you in."

Alex might be on house arrest for a third time, suggesting he lacked the fundamental morality to strive in society, but he still longed to avoid the experience of wearing manacles. The thought of steel clanked around flesh was archaic enough to make him shudder.

Another swig of root beer and then he asked Victor to place the call.

Before the first ring completed, Andrews answered. "Special Agent Andrews, FBI."

He had the special right, Alex thought. "Hi, um, this is Alex Cutler, returning your call."

"Good thing you called, Mr. Cutler. I couldn't allow you to avoid me much longer."

Alex rolled his eyes. "How can I help you?"

"We have a situation unfolding and would like your assistance." He cleared his throat. "I may not hold the highest regard for the fast life you lead, but I reserve hope that when your country calls, in need of your expertise…" He paused as if that final word hurt him, then continued, "That when your country calls, you'll be willing to push aside your arrogance and come to its aid."

Alex droned his reply. "I've been advised not to speak with any member of law enforcement without my attorney."

"Yes, yes, we've contacted Mr. Mueller. With what he charges, you should have heard from him by now."

"I still think I should wait for his counsel before saying anything."

"Let me speak," Andrews said. "If you make the trip to the FBI building tomorrow morning, regardless of whether you decide to assist us or not, we will remove the GPS monitor from your ankle."

Alex looked at the electronic manacle above his foot. Step one to seeing Rosa, Tara, or Rebecca Trevino outside of these walls without triggering his surveillance involved its removal. "Sure," he said. "When do you need me?"

"As I said, tomorrow. Seven a.m. Try not to be late." Another pause, then, "We've had disturbing... progressions, which other people feel you may be able to assist with."

By the time he replied, "I'll be there," the line was dead.

With the phone in his hand, he considered calling Rebecca Trevino right then. Tossing the phone on the cushion, he decided to contact her at a more appropriate time.

Flopping against the back cushion, he tore open the package of E.L. Fudge cookies.

Recalling Andrews's parting words, he tried to picture a progression more disturbing than the ones the world currently faced.

Chapter Thirty

A teenage Roy Guillen waited on a grassy field in a modifier room. A panorama of jungle unlike anything found on Earth waited before he and Charles. Trees as tall as skyscrapers crammed in an unnatural density, stretched as far as the eye could see. A pterodactyl-like avian glided before the wall of forest. A caw shattered the silence, and Roy jumped.

His throat constricted, his lips stayed dry despite his near constant licks. Stepping into the awaiting world would officially end the life he'd known for nearly nine decades.

"You all set?" a twelve-year-old Charles asked.

"I'm not sure how to answer that. I'm scared out of my wits."

"Been some ride, hasn't it?" Charles said.

Roy kept sight of the flying creature, his thoughts on his first marriage, the birth of his son, the later death of that son. "It's just getting started, old friend." His voice sounded high-pitched, mellifluous, sparking a question. "Do you remember what you sounded like at this age?"

"Probably like this," Charles said with a coy smile.

"Not me. My voice was nasally. I had a lisp. Very distinct. It was a big reason I didn't land a date until college. The words would logjam in my brain."

"If you talked less?" Charles laughed. "I'd love to get that kid back?"

Roy chuckled. Despite the impossibility, he had recaptured his youth. "This is the most surreal moment of our lives," He stared at the edge of Barchania, a land of enchantment, sorcery, and all forms of creatures. Due to the memory suppression, once they stepped from the modifier room to their chosen world, their knowledge of the past—marriages, children, finance, the world—would vanish. They'd become two young wood elves from a small fishing village. He searched Charles's face. "Can a friendship survive a two-thousand-year life span?"

"With the correct self-awareness, of course."

"Have you considered that if one of us dies, we'll be kicked into the Lobby, where our new memories will mesh with our old? The one who dies will know this was part of our eternity in the Lobby, but the one who lives will be distraught over having lost a friend. Unaware they're in a program."

"I have. It's really great."

Roy breathed deeply.

"Our friendship will endure because we possess the two most important attributes for friendship: forgiveness and understanding."

"You're probably right," Roy said with a twinge of nostalgia.

"Let's make a pact. If one of us dies, we'll visit San Francisco 1968 every new decade, on New Year's Eve. That way one day, perhaps after centuries pass, we'll reunite."

Roy smiled. "That's a deal." He felt so alive, so ready to discard a thousand regrets and live new.

"Correct me if I'm wrong," Charles said, "but the ultimate goal here is to locate the Staff of Eldwin and unite the kingdoms."

"That's one of the unattainable goals. As is the Horn of Domerly, which allows the owner to command titans."

Both men went silent.

"What do you think Alex is up to?" Roy asked.

"He'll be fine," Charles said. "Things will improve. They always do. He has a wonderful wife, and soon they'll start a family. With little ones running around, this will become a distant memory. If I had those things, you'd be starting this adventure on your own."

Roy hoped his friend spoke the truth. Hurting Alex was one of the greatest regret of his earthly life. "I want him happy, is all."

"He is. He'll continue to be. No financial worries, a sharp mind, an ideal wife. You need to be worried about being torn in half by a giant troll."

"Yeah," Roy said. He clung to an image of Alex and Rosa at their wedding, smiled, and brushed the thoughts aside. Things would work out for Alex. "You ready to forget about our lives, start new ones?"

"As ready as I'll ever be." Charles clasped Roy's shoulder. "Again, when one of dies, we will pop back in the Lobby and presumably remember this talk. San Francisco 1968, every new decade, New Year's Eve."

"Got it." Roy hopped up and down to spike his adrenaline.

"No time like the present." Charles strutted forward, met the forest, and disappeared into the portal.

Roy examined his smooth skin, sinewy arms, and enjoyed the healthy thump of his youthful heart. Never in a million daydreams had he envisioned something so marvelous. He'd miss Alex. He wished his great-granddaughter all the good fortunes life could provide. Striding toward the Barchanian forest, he found himself jubilant over the prospect of leaving behind everything he knew.

Chapter Thirty-One

General Koster had attended many meetings of magnitude throughout his illustrious military career. Nearly all of them took place in wing seven of the Pentagon, allotted for the United States Army.

Spotting a crucifix on the wall in the room he'd been summoned to brought immediate comfort. Thirty inches high, the artist had etched Jesus to perfection: emaciated body, muscles straining. His face was turned to the side and showed just a hint of anguish.

When taking all five floors into account, the Pentagon had seventeen-point-three miles of wide, marbled hallways. That made it over a hundred times the square footage of the White House, allowing it to offer ten times the situation rooms, and proportionately more problems.

Nearly as fabled as the Oval Office, the drama that unfolded within the Pentagon happened daily, covered a wider spectrum, and took place with less civility, and often with greater consequences at stakes.

The meeting rooms acted as refineries for most of the crucial talks presented to the president. With the current global strife, today's meeting would likely be the most important of his life, and the first with little hope of reaching the President.

The stocky man in the gray suit introduced himself as Carter, but Koster had seen the Man of Gray before, ten years back, talking with a now retired two-star major general—the very man Koster replaced. His friend of two decades had stiffened when pressed about the identity of the short man in the restricted area, and the reason for the man's presence.

Over the years, Koster had heard about the Man of Gray (under different names) heading strange projects. One employed mind control using intestinal bacteria and some form of communication with them. Another mixed hypnotic and mentalist fundamentals to create a form of persuasion capable of being administered within a handful of words, granting access to a person's belief system. No one could hack Koster's belief system. The world was black and white. No gray. No mercy. Just the devout against heathens.

Koster found the above experiments more legitimate than the common "he worked with aliens" angle. He knew enough about physics and the vastness of space to know the impossibility of leisure travel between galaxies. Excluding wormhole technology, if little gray men scoured the cosmos and found life, like shipwrecked sailors suffering from exposure, they would rush to the first person they saw, fall at their feet, and cry.

The Man in Gray dimmed the lights as if about to show a video. But with no screen present, Koster figured it was a ploy to dull his features, or to produce discomfort. A few of Koster's peers griped about the lights affecting their vision, but to their chagrin, were ignored, which started the meeting on a clubfoot.

These men and women worked hard and were entitled to respect. Particularly from a man who, through some unorthodox means, sat higher than them on the chain of command.

As the Man in Gray started his sermon, Koster surveyed the room. To his left, Nadine Dewind, assistant to Terry Eding, CIA head; Brandon Palmer, presidential advisor; Jim Standly, FBI; Jeff VanNoord, NSA; Colonel Stafford; and one-star General Onaki from the Air Force.

Koster couldn't peg the common denominator linking these people, but one existed. Koster disliked most people, but he respected all present.

The Man in Gray had promised monumental intelligence. His first few sentences about suicides used as rewards proved him correct.

"Everyone," the Man in Gray said, ending the info dump portion. "I've brought you up to speed, and now there is much to do and little time." He remained at the head of the table as he spoke.

"You're all soldiers of faith. God's warriors. These troubling times grant us an opportunity to serve."

Koster flushed as the link of those present hit him: Christian faith. Brandon Palmer even attended his church.

Behind these walls, he followed the Lobby's ongoing developments as a representative of the United States military, keeping his opinions to himself. He had listened to the media discuss the Lobby stealing souls. Sickening bullshit. Seething internally, he'd pushed the religious implication out of his mind and focused on his duty.

However, religious undertones had crept into almost every conversation. Judging from the glares in the room—the two people he saw kiss the crosses around their necks, the one man who dropped into prayer—these members had serious, willing to die for, opinions on the subject.

"We have an enemy I won't name," the Man in Gray said. "Things are progressing rapidly, attempting to catch us off guard. Your commitment will keep us abreast of evil intentions. Lean on your faith. Listen to your hearts. You will find that everyday citizens are willing to pay the ultimate price to mitigate this blasphemy. What I intend to outline for those of you willing to help is of a delicate nature, but its question will be the same: in this dire hour, will you use your appointments to heed God's call?"

He let a moment pass in silence, then continued, "There are countries openly refusing to comply with the Lobby ban. Right now, *Inside Today* is airing. Rebecca Trevino will review the past week's events, captivating the world. Yet it is tomorrow's special edition that will rock the fabric of society and ignite a controversy to divide the globe."

Koster found the way the man stayed ramrod straight, unnerving. His voice hardly fluctuated, yet his intensity rocked a ten. Perhaps those voice control rumors had merit. As the Man in Gray droned on, Koster wanted to interrupt, to tell him he didn't need to hear any more spin.

238

"Tomorrow night's program will expose the Death Trips operating in all four of the Japanese Atriums. It will also show evidence that Russia, China, and India are providing Death Trips."

General Koster's back stiffened at the naming of countries, especially as if they were aligning against the United States. That particular step preceded building a case for military action.

Koster, along with everyone in the room, understood that no government held the authority to enforce the Lobby ban globally. America intended to do so nonetheless.

Koster would back whatever country decided to act. Suicides could never be normalized. The desecration of religious beliefs intolerable, regardless of their geographic location. The people in this room could spurn military action. And all present were aware that if they didn't mesh church and state and radicalize, someone they loved might soon fall victim to the madness.

The planet's citizens needed a voice of reason, a guiding light, not some man from across the ocean speaking about a Seventh Plane of Existence and every person's right to die.

Thankfully, others supported his philosophy. An estimated one point six billion Christians populated the world, with Muslims matching that number.

The number of fatwas issued against each Atrium, and a prominent employee of the Broumgard Group, had grown too numerous to count. Millions of Islamic people swore their lives to destroying the Lobby, and despite every inclination he'd ever had about the nutty jihadists, Koster admired their conviction.

One hundred percent of his Christian brothers and sisters might not fervently rally, but many would. Clandestine talks of taking action into their own hands—pure treason—populated the military and government. They increased daily. Now this, an open meeting in a U.S. facility. Koster's heart knocked. *Count me in.*

"Japan has been gathering allies," the Man in Gray said. "Demarcations are being drawn. Countries with no godly ties are uniting to impose their atheism or Buddhism or Hindu falsity on the world. Fourteen nations are putting aside old grudges, and coming together."

The Man in Gray motioned to Jeff VanNoord, the presidential advisor. "Our commander in chief is securing his own allies. Christian and Muslim nations are sitting at the same table with true kinship for the first time in modern history. Unified in their determination to stop the spread of the warped Buddhism and to eradicate this blasphemous concept of suicide as an accomplishment."

The Man in Gray stepped to the side and, using a cellphone as a projector, cast an image on the wall. "I've edited a probable copy of tomorrow night's episode of *Inside Today*. In this struggle to avoid the end of days, I request your loyalty above all else. I have thirty years of across-the-board clearance, and am one of the few men on our planet who has overseen projects at Sci-deck, Area 51, as well as every bio and nanite technology none of you will ever hear about. I pray you will accept my self-edification. If you do, then hear these words: there is a God. He possesses a form of lethargic emotions. He rewards those who do more than vocalize their sympathies. Once you know this as surely as I do, nothing else matters.

"I will call on each of you to act in His defense. Your response will mold the eternity you spend floating in the paradoxical, single-entitied vastness, know to us as the universe. A place of unlimited joys or torments, where all will reside until the rejoining—a time when the chosen will know the absolute bliss of God's love until the new birth, trillions of years from now, that ends existence for us all."

A cold numbness traced Koster's spine. The man's words didn't totally compute, and Koster wouldn't ask him to elaborate. The Man in Gray's confidence left an imperceptible presence in Koster, as if what the general heard stirred a dormant understanding embedded in his DNA.

"This video will be shown to the world tomorrow. Imagine the impending problems. Ask yourself if they merit your involvement." The Man in Gray activated his phone, strolled to the door, and after surveying the attendants, exited.

Koster didn't want to watch a video. He wanted to behead an infidel.

Chapter Thirty-Two

Arriving at the federal building ten minutes before seven in the morning, Alex nodded at the agent holding open the door for him. He emptied his pockets into a pink basket and passed through the metal detector with a lump in his throat, nervously inspecting the gun at the observing guard's hip.

Agent Andrews exited a nearby elevator and waited for Alex to repack his keys and phone. He offered no scowl. He simply stared, a disdain emanating from his aura. As with all unpleasant people, two choices existed: argue—which fed the beast—or bide time and vacate as soon as possible. Alex looked forward to the latter.

Andrews passed the underling a pair of garden shears. "Remove his monitor."

Andrews spoke without a snarky tone. That, and him helping Alex by removing his tether, spurned more concern. Powerful figures awaited his arrival. Most likely, they had ill tidings.

"Good morning, Mr. Cutler." The tether unclasped with a snap. The sound lightened his entire body, increased his capacity to deal with future blight. Despite his situation, he smiled, extended and retracted the liberated limb several times before making the mistake of meeting Andrews's face.

To Alex's surprise, the troubled man didn't snarl. With only a twitch of Andrews's right eye, the agent led them to the fourth floor.

At this early hour, Alex hadn't expected the office to be alive with agents, but they bustled. Judging by rolled-up sleeves and unwinding French braids, these people had been here for hours. Their professionalism astounded Alex. Not one set of eyes stayed on him, longer than a flicker.

He trailed Andrews into a boardroom. Two men and a woman rose in unison. Agent Andrews closed the blinds, shut the solid oak door, and activated the lock.

"Mr. Cutler, my name is John Willis, Deputy Director of the Los Angeles branch of the FBI." He was a dapper African American with salt-and-pepper hair, the gritty look of a war-vet, glasses too large for his head. "To my left is Agent Martineau from our New York organized crime division." Martineau wore a shirt and tie. With shoulders a yard across, the tie seemed comically small. He had olive skin, a mustache perfect for 1970s pornography, and curly hair. He reached across the table, and swallowed Alex's hand in a powerful grip.

Alex's stomach turned as he remembered these people had created much of his current suffering. With every recent life-fork leading him down a wrong path, he couldn't bear to consider what Sophie's choice they had for him, or its eventual outcome.

"And Jodi Reister," Willis said, "chairperson of the committee on federal spending. Easily the most important person in this room." Alex put her in her mid-fifties, her blond hair cut short in the staggered fashion of many women in power.

They all sat. Andrews was left the chair at the end of the table, eight feet from the others.

Jodi Reister spoke. "Mr. Cutler, let me first say how sorry I am for your tragedies and losses over the past few weeks. I, like millions of others, enjoy an annual vacation with family inside the Lobby and am crushed by the latest developments." She interlaced her hands on the table and searched his face. "As I imagine you yourself must be."

"Well," Agent Andrews said before Alex could reply, "something was bound to happen."

Willis fixed him with a look of annoyance, and adjusted his glasses.

The others waited for Alex's response.

"A machine inside the brain and all," Andrews added.

"That'll be enough, Andrews," Jodi Reister said.

"Thank you for your condolences," Alex said. "I'm still processing everything. I'm really not sure what to make of it."

"None of us are," Willis said.

Alex saw Agent Andrews fidget in his peripheral, no doubt wanting to chime in with his complete comprehension of the universe.

"Mr. Cutler," Willis continued, "we appreciate you coming in today, and allow me to apologize for our part in adding to your discomfort. Henceforth, I fully expect we will be partners."

By threatening to toss me in prison for life? Alex wondered. He glanced at the locked door, and wondered if guards were stationed outside of it?

"Before I turn it over to Agent Martineau," Willis said. "I want you to know it's not the agency's intention to eradicate the Lobby. We do not see it, or you, as our enemy. The goal of this meeting is to make us allies."

Were they enemies? Alex still couldn't believe he sat on the opposite side of the law, that strangers held his fate in their hands, yet again.

"There are many serious domestic and international conflicts brewing as you know," Willis said. "What you don't know is a date will soon be set to bring countries with differing beliefs to one table, in hopes of settling those differences. The United States must enter those talks with the ability to control access to the Lobby."

That made sense to Alex. "Well, you have the manpower to control the Atriums."

Dour looks spread on the faces across from him, stealing the remainder of his reply, and proving that more drama existed. Racking his mind produced nothing as outrageous as the current problems, so he waited.

"Do you know who Rebecca Trevino is?" Willis pushed his glasses tighter to his face.

Alex leaned back, and cocked his head to the right. Was there anyone who didn't?

"Tonight, her program will ignite controversy. In this great nation, we allow the media free reign, regardless of its effect on society. We simply prepare to minimize the damage," Willis said.

"Will her program impact this upcoming international meeting?" Alex said.

"Not as much as our current dilemma," Willis looked beyond the big man beside him. "Ms. Reister and I have read the rough outline of the United States' proposal to maintain peace. The plan is only possible if we control access to the Lobby."

To avoid repeating his previous statement, Alex withheld the urge to comment, and wiped his clammy hands on his pants.

"The world is worse off than all the horrors you see on the news," Willis said. "Many countries do not believe in a free press, and during crises of this magnitude, we appreciate that. A chasm is rippling across the globe. The suppression of facts helps slow the tide of outrage, but it's coming."

Jodi Reister cut in, her short blond hair hardly moving as she leaned closer. "Mr. Cutler, we need your help. President Tanner personally sent me to meet with you. My presence is to inform you that any workable scenario you produce will receive funding. Do not allow cost to hinder your creativity."

Alex fidgeted. As long as his creativity happened outside of a cell, he wanted to help.

Jodi added a seriousness to her tone and said, "We need your cooperation by this meeting's end."

"If for some reason," Agent Andrews inserted, "Mr. Cutler is unable to help, I'm sure I'd do an equal, or better, job." After a look from Willis, Andrews shrugged. "If it's a programming issue, is all."

"Thank you, Agent," Willis said.

Andrews swallowed.

"Agent Martineau, will you apprise our friend of the current situation?" Willis continued.

"Certainly." The big man filled a glass with water, sipped, and rose, blocking some of the room's lighting from Alex.

"First off, my condolences for the losses a' your friends." His voice carried an East Coast accent, with a twinge of Southie, making Alex suspect he'd worked some undercover. "The world's a kicked beehive, little soldier bees is out stingin' normalcy in a hundred places." He frowned. "Our mission is to get life back to its former self.

"Many military leaders believe the singular threat we are about to discuss holds the key to avoiding war. You're the man best able to help."

Alex rolled his chair back a few inches as if to escape the thought. Who could he help? The program he poured his heart and soul into for the past seven years rushed in untold joy. With one alternate amendment, it was now being cited as a catalyst for destruction.

The media hinted at international tension at the opening of every program. He'd considered it ratings fodder. How could there be this much outrage over people killing themselves? The world endured thousands of suicides a day, for decades. It was a personal choice. Their loved ones suffered emotional stains, but the rest of us moved on, and no one protested.

Alex understood. Give the right person a Bible or a Quran, and you supercharged them with power. Nearly every monolithic preacher and doomsday blogger yelled about the current evil. The speeches resurrected attendance. Who could blame anyone for taking advantage of free speech and capitalism? God bless America.

Fights abounded at protests, whether for or against the Lobby. Since Glen's suicide, five Broumgard employees had been shot and killed, ambush style. With only one shooting officially linked to their employment, the trend avoided media coverage. And now war? Military action? America still worked to extricate itself from the last half-dozen battles.

The dangers surrounding Alex made him feel like he stood in the center of a dry field of waist-high grass, with a half-dozen lighter-wielding, meth-addicted pyromaniacs around him. Remembering where he sat, he focused on the now, to best offer his advice.

Apparently noticing his return to attentiveness, Martineau continued. "We believe if this summit is handled correctly, everyone, excluding some in the Middle East, will be happy. Japan and those in the East want to use the machine as a carrot on a stick, telling their citizens if they live honorable, useful lives, they may," he made

245

quotations, "'retire' in the Lobby. We, in the West, want to avoid that, but we can compromise. Perhaps beef up our screening, add a heavy tax. They could limit their permanent trips, impose age limits. Who knows?"

Alex considered the implications. How could the U.S. prevent suicides with an operational Lobby? Strip people naked and make them sit in a cell for twenty-four hours? Cavity searches? X-ray scans?

"You ever heard a' Paul Spagnelli?" Martineau asked.

Alex shook his head.

"Paul Spagnelli is boss a' the crime families operating along the East Coast. Their criminality has lessened over the last few decades as they enter more legitimate ventures, but there's still drugs, prostitution, gambling, murders.

"Yesterday, we executed a search warrant on the nephew a' the big man in connection to a double homicide. It was more a cage-rattling session, but we found some guns, a stockpile a' cash, and some very disturbing machinery."

Martineau paced from behind his chair. Each time he pivoted, one side of his broad shoulders dipped, reminding Alex of air brakes lifting on a 747.

"We didn't know what we had until our techies started digging. We assumed we were looking at some rig for cheatin' slot machines or skimmin' gas pumps. Possibly a bomb, which would a' been a little out a' character for these guys, but it's a crazy world." He shrugged, retrieved a briefcase from under the table, popped the dual locks, then tossed a binder on the table before Alex. "As it turns out, it's much scarier than a bomb, Mr. Cutler. This device could rock the world. That right there could derail the international peace talks by removing our leverage."

Alex opened the five-inch-thick three-ring binder. Inside, photographs of electrical equipment, each followed by a section with schematics, another with analysis.

Martineau pointed at the binder and said, "We're hoping you can verify our thoughts, and more importantly, that you can crush this."

246

Alex was a software guy, one of the rare computer geeks who avoided hardware. Back in Chicago, Sean did his changeouts, and since then, there had always been someone skilled and willing. Picturing his old friend, knowing he now lived among the deceased, dried his throat. He leaned forward, poured a glass of water, and drank.

Ten minutes passed in silence as he examined the collection of data. He looked at what should have been an impossibility. The content in section D represented a type of macroserver, but a model light-years more compact and sophisticated than Broumgard's next-gen diagrams. The photographs in section L sucked him in. It seemed this odd contraption of loose wires and welded sensors functioned like an access chair, allowing someone to hack into the Lobby. The processing speed had to be abysmally slow, but a macroserver capable of accessing the Lobby was ludicrous.

If he read the schematics correctly, the entirety of the Lobby existed in a case no larger than a shoebox. Built of a titanium alloy, it must have cost a hundred grand to assemble, a pittance of the necessary R&D to reach this model. He hefted the binder's contents and returned to the front page. Before reviewing it again in more detail, he looked at the three patient faces across from him and asked, "Is this… a pirated access point?"

Willis's head dropped, his glasses slipped down his nose.

Agent Martineau squeezed the back of his chair hard enough to make the plastic groan.

"That's our fear," Jodi Reister answered. "The last thing we need is organized crime getting into the business of Death Trips. The only positive here is that this group is usually ahead of the curve, but others will follow."

"When it comes to a planned suicide," Willis added, "people will pay any amount because, to them, money will soon lose its value. If citizens go around maxing out their credit with plans of defaulting, putting up homes, cars, and college funds, with plans to vanish, it would destroy the global economy overnight."

Agent Martineau cut in, saying, "On a criminal front, there'd be a wave a' insanity; guys willing to do *anything*, and instead a' money, they'd get everlasting life in a dream world."

Alex picked up on the syntax of it being *a* dream world, not *his* dream world. Realizing he wasn't a witch to burn eased a degree of worry.

"Judges, politicians, prosecutors—no one would be safe," Martineau said. "Society will crumble."

"If we lose the ability to control access to the Lobby," said Jodi Reister, "this upcoming summit will be a waste of everyone's time. If random thugs can offer Death Trips, we can't ask the East to shelve, or even limit, theirs. If they don't limit them, we have a hard right-wing military branch that might find a way to start a war over unfettered suicides. Control of access is our only diplomatic leverage."

"We are trying to avoid anarchy," Willis said. "Do you get that?"

"Americans believe we are the superpower of the world," Jodi Reister continued. "But we don't want to quarrel with Japan's navy and technology or China's numbers and training. Alex, if we can't contain this, if these pirated access points proliferate…" Rather than finish her sentence, she shook her head dramatically.

Alex examined the first photo: the many components of the pirated access point.

Agent Andrews cleared his throat, waited to be chastised, and when he wasn't, spoke. "From my initial review, this is a prototype." He pointed to the binder. "We confiscated the schematics and an engineer at the scene. Evidence suggests he designed that contraption."

So this seizure gave them a reprieve, but not a permanent one, Alex thought.

"Can you confirm this device's purpose?" Willis said. "Can it actually connect people to the Lobby?"

"I'd need more time with the equipment," Alex said, "but someone sunk a fortune into this."

"We have a more ambitious expectation," Willis said. "Can you circumvent its capability? From my understanding, it needs to jack into the system and copy the entire Lobby infrastructure before a person can load in."

"That is correct," Andrews said.

Alex looked at the photo then back at them. "When can I put my hands on the actual components?"

"We can get them here within the hour," Willis said.

Alex nodded absently. "I'll need Ike Wood, my networking guy from the L.A. Atrium."

"Done."

Alex glanced back down and then rocked in his seat to test its comfort.

"Privacy, a speakerphone for access to Victor, two packs of Oreos, and a two liter of Barq's root beer."

They all nodded with growing enthusiasm.

"I can't make any promises," Alex said, "except to give this my full attention."

Agent Martineau left the room without a word. The others stood.

"That's all we're asking for, Mr. Cutler," Willis said, extending his hand. "If there is anything you need, just poke your head out the door and ask."

"You have no financial constraints," Jodi Reister said as she walked around the table, patted his shoulder, and left.

"If you need my expertise," Agent Andrews said, "I'm available." Willis motioned for Andrews to exit. After another glance at Alex, Willis left as well, granting Alex his privacy. The rest, saving the world from madness, seemed up to him.

Chapter Thirty-Three

Tim Vanderhart only knew the word exodus from the Bible. He'd looked up the definition. Exodus—a mass departing, often with aims of arriving at a favored destination. That description often applied to stories from Scripture. It also fit very well with the soldiers vacating Northern Michigan.

There were some members of the newly formed Lord's Thorn that were too weak to make the journey. Some physically, but most mentally.

Most people lacked purpose, drive, or a belief in anything. Even some of the men around him used camouflage, shotguns, and training as a way to transform today into the next. Their rants about the government dictating their lives and the minorities diluting their race with inbreeding were only condiments to beer consumption. If born in California, they'd have their hair in dreadlocks, and smoke marijuana, talking about how everyone was stupider than them, that their way—despite having been tried millions of times over thousands of years—was the right way to govern, and how they needed to breed with minorities to unify humanity into a less intelligent, more aggressive race.

Tim believed what he believed. He entered life with a purposeful destiny, like everyone. The difference was that he had located, embraced, and was now acting on the signs that had unearth his path.

Whoever that short, confident Man in Gray had been, he sure knew his stuff. Specifically about the people he referred to NMCD. Of the two hundred eleven troops traveling to northern Nevada, eighty-four were walk-ons, singled out by the Man in Gray and encouraged to join the Lord's Thorn through emails, letters, and phone calls. These people knew their purpose. Their grit and determination validated the term exodus.

Two school buses held supplies. Members piled into an old Greyhound and more vans, trucks, and SUVs than an eye could take in.

Tim would go—no one could keep him away—he only hoped Alan would give him a fitting role, or would he try and assign him a role as janitor or errand boy?

Lacking an assigned vehicle, he leapt into the back of an F-250 filled with crates of ammunition and two drums of grease. The impulsive decision to cross the country in an open bed evolved into a bad one. Rather than complain about the painful jounces and radical shifts in the elements, he endured in silence.

When they got within four miles of their destination, a Nevada desert ranch, the discomfort vanished. He sat up and took in the scene.

The F-250 assumed its position in a near-static line. Hundreds of additional vehicles, with plates from all over the Midwest and East Coast, proved the NMCD were one feather in a wing of the exodus flight.

It was hot in the desert. The openness of the tan-colored horizon and blue sky in all direction but up, astounded him. He'd never seen so much space. Michigan's woods offered a more isolated beauty. Trees and rolling meadows always limited what the eyes could take in. Peeling off his shirt, he frowned at having neglected to pack sunblock. If he burned, Alan would razz him for lacking foresight.   At least he brought his army hat. He adjusted the brim and pulled the hat down, making his ears stand out more than

251

usual. As he looked around, intent on borrowing or trading for some sunscreen, a shadow darkened the bright morning.

Looking up revealed a unified cloud. It covered the sky above him, and was near perfectly square. How strange. The massive coagulation of dust and humidity hovered above the road they traveled and continued on in the distance they were heading. God had sent His own sunblock.

Up and down the traffic jam, car doors opened, and people exited their vehicles, stretching their limbs.

Tim tugged his Wolverine boot laces tight, put his hand on the bed rail, and in one fluid motion, threw himself over the side. Retrieving his SKS rifle and backpack, he enjoyed the familiarity of the weapon he'd fired for nearly ten years, and the weight of the pack. He curled the bag a few times to strain his thin bicep, scoffed at the minimal bulge. It didn't matter that he was skinny and easily winded. Muscles didn't make the soldier; intelligent and bravery did. He'd teach Alan that lesson.

One step and he paused. A large machine that resembled a blue post office drop box, except painted in desert colors, sat alongside the road. The closest one waited a hundred feet from him, so he reserved judgment as to its purpose.

Pacing alongside the asphalt, the crunch of sand under his feet made him feel like a gladiator ascending a gated tunnel.

He peeked in vehicles as he passed, shared nods, or if a window was rolled down, a terse greeting.

A gap in the vehicles showed an identical machine to the one Tim previously noticed sat on the opposite side of the road. Mist poured from its "mail receptor." Continuing to rack his mind, he reached one of the machines and stopped, his eyes following the stream upward.

Working collectively with other contraptions, positioned every hundred yards or so, the mist blended in the air, providing the exceptional coverage above them.

Holy smokes, he thought, *fake cloud machines*. Tim almost laughed. *I'm in with some real players.* Holding his hat with two hands, he searched the line of idling vehicles ahead of him. A security checkpoint waited two miles further on. Behind him, the trail of automobiles, of various makes and models, stretched into the horizon.

The white truck he'd been keeping an eye out for was fifty yards ahead of him. Picturing Alan all pissed off about something, Tim inhaled, adjusted his posture, and walked confidently toward the truck. The four-door, extended cab, dually one-ton, diesel V8, King Ranch edition's back door opened as he neared. Seeing Alan's abnormally hairy arm, which had reached back from the passenger seat to open the door produced grin, but Tim knew better.

Climbing in, he tossed the backpack on the seat, positioned his rifle on his lap, shut the door, and melted into the chill of air-conditioning.

"Careful which way you point that barrel," Alan said.

Tim double-checked its direction; safe, as always. Alan's hair, mostly gray, matched his beard, and was pulled into a ponytail. With a protruding belly and round limbs, Alan reminded Tim of a walrus, a really strong walrus without blubber. Tim had grown up jabbing the man's stone-hard thighs, core, and shoulders.

"Been wondering if you hitched a ride on this trip." Alan cracked the top to a Coca-Cola, passed it back. "Guess I can find a use for someone as scrawny as you."

"Thanks," Tim said as he took the soda. The can was bitingly cold. So much so, he kept swapping hands as if playing an Eskimo version of hot potato. He glanced over the aisle, looking for a cooler.

Alan tapped the middle console. "Built-in fridge. Men who've earned their stripes get these types of luxuries."

Tim raised his eyebrows, sat back, and sipped carefully. He'd earn more than stripes. *Just wait*, he thought. *I'll earn more than a set of stripes.*

"You got any idea what those machines do?"

Tim looked at the unknown driver. Part of his training included erring on the side of caution, so he stayed quiet.

"Don't think the little squirt trusts you," Alan said.

The driver forced air through his nostrils.

253

"Graham's a mechanic from Dayton," Alan said. "One of the Man in Gray's men. A firm believer in our Lord and the evils around the world that work to lead the weak astray."

Tim let that settle, and then replied, "I'm pretty sure those machines are making that big cloud to block our activity from whoever is up there watching."

"Kid ain't all dumb," Graham said.

"Ah, even a blind squirrel," Alan said. "Besides, he's only half right. There's a Man up there whose watchful eye can't be blocked."

Tim placed the Coke in a beverage holder. Alan would establish the hierarchy of the men under his command. He'd known Tim the longest, so Tim took his shot. "How about me for one of the leadership roles? A captain? Lieutenant, maybe?"

"Shit, son," Alan said. "Can you even do a hundred push-ups?"

Graham peeked at Tim's bare chest. No doubt he registered its hairless concavity.

"Given enough time," Tim said.

Alan chuckled. "I need hardened men for the days ahead."

"You need loyalty," Tim said. "Who's more dedicated than me? Who's more willing to follow any order?"

"Kid's got his head on right," Graham said.

"He hasn't reached manhood yet," Alan said. "His father sounded just as noble at that age. Then the booze and pills took over. There's weak blood in him."

"Not in me," Tim said. "I honor my temple. You could assign me as your second in command, and if, God forbid, you took a mortal wound, die confident things would move forward as you envisioned."

"That ex-colonel's already slotted as my number two. With a three hundred-man regiment, I've already picked out and notified my captains. You got the godly morals to be of use; I'll give you that. Get down to the sergeants—you might make the cut."

"Well," Tim said. "No one's more ready to kick ass."

"Ha!" Alan smacked his wide thighs. "Sometimes I think bluster is the only thing keeps you from blowing away."

"Honor to God, country, and family," Tim said. "That's my credo."

Alan pointed at the time on the dash: one fifteen. "We should be settled by four. There's a conference for the brass tonight at seventeen hundred. Find me there around then, and we'll see if there's a lieutenant willing to take you on."

"I'll be there."

Minutes ticked by as the truck slowly advanced. The cool air provided by the air-conditioning made Tim feel complacent. He needed to stay battle-ready. Big things awaited him. He'd show Alan.

"May I be dismissed, sir?"

"Yeah," Alan said. "Find yourself some deodorant, and sunscreen."

Tim returned to the heat. He'd be at that meeting, and get assigned a leadership role. His ascent to hero in the battle for humanity had been predestined since the beginning of time.

Being associated with Alan carried perks for Tim. One of the Man in Gray's men had towed a small trailer out West. Seeing Tim wandering amidst the ranks, he invited the young man to share it.

Inside the beat-up fifteen by eight, his roommate presented him with a most glorious gift: a leather vest with the Lord's Thorn emblem stitched onto the back. The word "Lord's" arced across the top with the word "Thorn" horizontal at its base. In the center, the *L* overlapped the *T* to form a cross of sorts. The letters were tinted gold and bronze and wrapped loosely in a thorny vine. The bottom of the *T* morphed into a menacing brown thorn with a drop of blood on its tip.

Slipping the vest off the cupboard handle, its weight surprised him. An empty mark waited above the chest pocket. He already envisioned "Vanderhart" stitched on the front left side.

Beneath that, another patch would read "Sergeant." On the right, the infamous underlined phalanx would signify his rank.

He slid one arm in, then the other, and felt anointed, protected.

255

He understood bullets passed through leather, but still, he imagined himself daring someone to shoot at him from twenty feet away and laughing at each errant shot.

This vest represented more than a token of brotherhood; it signified a responsibility. Rumors circulated that they might be deploying for their first mission as early as tomorrow. A mission to secure a permanent base with armaments and natural defenses.

Two weeks ago, he'd been hunting turkeys, daydreaming of future events. Now he stood among a thousand like-minded soldiers. A portion of whom would be looking to him for leadership and answers. He was determined to fill that need.

On the way to his trailer, he'd noticed that the impromptu base supported a diverse crowd.

Outlandish bikers walked alongside men with thick glasses, closed mouths, and darting eyes. He saw a group covered in tattoos that looked as if they'd recently been paroled, another dominated by polo shirts and sandals, casually standing as if waiting to tee off on the ninth green. He saw a surprising amount of Mexicans and blacks. Despite this contrast, everything remained orderly. This was a real band of brothers.

The vehicles were parked in a specific area about two hundred square yards. Those designated for transport were maneuvered to yet another site and emptied, with intentions of being reloaded. People bustled to their assigned tents and unpacked.

Originally, Tim assumed this would be their base. That would have suited him fine. Isolated in a desert, with a generous line of sight in all directions, the place offered advantages. Knowing they were moving to a more fortified location only bolstered his confidence.

Finding a mirror on the outside of a narrow door, he admired himself. The bare chest looked white trashy, so he'd wear a T-shirt under the vest. After changing, he smoothed down the vest and stepped outside, where he paused to take in the activity. The first person to see him—a bear of a man in his forties—glanced at the new vest and saluted. Tim swelled with pride and returned the gesture.

When the man walked on, Tim descended another step and, feeling lightheaded, realized he needed to let his endorphins cool down. The man who saluted him wore a plain white tee and carried a leather vest over his forearm. Testing his equilibrium with another step and feeling more in control, Tim trailed the man. They knifed through the tents and intersections of people until the burly man met with a group of guys with similar builds: middle-aged with bellies, beards, and tattoos.

A line of a dozen men and two women led to a burning barrel. His mark reached the front of the line and to Tim's horror, tossed in the leather vest he'd been carrying. Yet before Tim could scream, a peer passed the man a new vest. As it wrapped around the sturdy frame, Tim recognized the Lord's Thorn insignia.

Once adorned, brief hugs and hard congratulatory back slaps showered the man. As Tim watched, others tossed in their old cuts, some hesitantly, some with pride. Tim knew that for a militia member, even moreso a biker, their cut represented honor, and to burn one displayed a serious rite of passage.

Looking past the man, Tim considered his next step: arriving at a command tent for the biggest interview of his life.

The headquarters, a recently erected wooden roof on stilts, had canvas walls, able to be rolled up during the arid days to allow an airflow, and dropped down at night to ward off the chill.

With the majority of the pavilion open, Tim slowed his pace and surveyed the interior. Electronic devices topped tables. Men in vests already stitched with name and rank busied themselves.

He'd be there soon enough. For now, he had a second rumor to investigate.

A ranch house centered a forty-acre patch of desert land sectioned off by two-plank fencing. Behind the home, which should have been better guarded, sat a staggering sight. Seven well-spaced rows of mismatched helicopters stretched the length of a football field.

Due to the variety of shapes and colors and sheer numbers, it resembled a mega used-car lot of copters. Mechanics in jumpsuits leaned over open engine casings, others tweaked rotors, a few manipulated switches in cockpits. Two Ford Ranger pickups dispensed oil and other necessary fluids.

On the stroll back, he heard a half-dozen people speculating on the purpose of the aircraft. Most believed they would ferry in the soldiers' families after they reached the base. Tim thought that possible, but he thought it was more likely wishful thinking. Talk of reuniting with old ladies and kids annoyed him. He sympathized, but they had more pressing matters.

He actually listened when those in charge spoke. Those men had recently said that joining the Lord's Thorn meant risking your life. Tim understood that meant death, which meant killing. A machine currently threatened God's people. The group surrounding him had been assembled to stop it.

In an earlier speech, Alan indicated that their families and loved ones would arrive in Nevada one to three days after the first wave departed, and then follow the horde to its new base along the same time frame, yet questions persisted. After he wore those stripes, he'd listen for inquiries about wife and family and snap on the first man, help the private get his head on right. And if the man griped, or elevated backtalk to disrespect, Tim had never met anyone faster at applying an arm bar than himself. He'd break the first bone, earning him respect.

Checking his watch that doubled as a compass, and seeing he had twenty minutes, he thought it best to loiter around the main structure.

Remembering the field of choppers jacked his heart. With that volume of helicopters, the brass planned something much more spectacular than transporting women and children.

258

Chapter Thirty-Four

Staring at the written outline for his course of action, composed with scribbled notes on both sides of two pages, filled Alex with equal parts pride and dread. His solution to the pirated access points should prevent global war, but at what cost. He shook his head at the magnitude, necessary logistics, and moreover, the end result. He hoped Jodi Reister's use of "unlimited budget" applied; he'd written one of the most ambitious schemes in history.

Without his plan, he predicted an end to society as we know it.

He checked the time on the cellphone. Ninety minutes until *Inside Today* aired. Every outlet hyped tonight's edition as the most important of Rebecca Trevino's career. It promised to put facts to the whispers circulating the world. With regret at knowing he'd miss the episode, Alex summoned his hosts back into the office.

Saving the world from collapse was on Alex's agenda, and they'd need a miracle to pull it off. His plan would require immense effort, cooperation, and funding, along with the formation of a new governmental agency. The United States would jump at his proposal to form a new branch of monitoring, which left ten thousand hurdles to overcome.

Andrews entered, leaned over Alex's shoulder, and peered at his notes. "What's your idea to fix this? I have an excellent plan, if you're ready for it."

Alex flipped his notes face down. "Perhaps another time."

"Well, bounce what you have off me before the others arrive. Maybe my pointers will stop you from looking like a fool."

"I'm just going to wait until everyone's present." Alex felt uncomfortable about their close proximity, and said. "Do you mind backing up?"

"It's your funeral." Andrews plopped into the far chair and crossed his arms.

Alex's goal was to avoid millions of innocent people having to host early funerals.

When the final three members arrived and sat, Alex placed his hand on the closed binder. "I have good and... complicated news."

"Good news is a relief," Willis said as he adjusted his glasses on his face.

"I've identified avenues we can exploit," Alex said. His body tensed; the added density seemed to pull a billion molecules toward him.

"I'm sure you understand, every way we run this ends in disaster, unless we take drastic measures."

"Do you have a plan?" Willis asked.

"I have a plan. It's ambitious, but I think it's the only way."

The three agents shared looks. Each appeared ready to comment, yet withheld.

Alex breathed deeply. The work he'd have to do behind the scenes, without their approval, compounded his fear and uncertainty.

"After discussing the issue with Ike, I feel confident that whoever designed this had help from inside Broumgard. Someone either smuggled information out or assisted with hands-on. The good news is, the list of people with access should number fewer than fifty. I'm sure you'll be able to root out the betrayer."

"We'll punish 'em harshly," Agent Martineau said. Without his sport coat, the curly-haired man seemed even larger.

"When we started at Eridu," Alex continued, "we housed the Lobby's server in a twenty-thousand-square foot storage facility—an impressive feat for the amount of data being processed. Since globalization, we condensed the necessary hardware to ten cubic feet." Alex paused to allow that marvel to settle, then continued, "Our

R&D department has the sharpest minds in the field, and they believed we possessed top technology. What you've captured," he tapped the binder, "seems to house the entire Lobby in a macroserver the size of a shoe box. I looked over the schematics. It still doesn't make sense to me, but if it works, it's remarkable.

"The other good news, beyond catching the guilty party, is that with this device, the load-in process will be time-consuming. When someone jacks into the Lobby with the setup, it will take no less than four hours to mirror everything and establish a viable connection. Perhaps a three-minute load-in time after that, which I imagine would be disorienting and draining, like an anesthesiologist slowly administering a sedative."

Agent Martineau lifted his meaty paw. After Alex nodded to him, he said, "I'm eager to hear your plan a' action, Mr. Cutler. It'll commence the most important undertaking a' my career, but… I just wonder, since I have you sitting here, if perhaps a greater understanding a' how this whole thing works might help us out. I can't figure where a person's spirit is housed once they're dead. Like, if a guy off'd himself while connected to that contraption, would he be in that shoebox? And if we pulled the plug, we'd end his life? Or is he in a main server? Or is he copied a thousand times to each of those dump sites you referred to?"

"Those are questions I'm not sure I can answer," Alex said. He then exhaled, and leaned back. Who could know the truth for certain? It was like debating the genesis of life. The big bang sounded plausible, but every theory ran up against the beginning. Humans lack the ability to comprehend something with no start. Prior-to-time contemplation was reserved for gods. Having a theory he liked, he decided to share it.

"But I have an analogy in my head," Alex said.

"Please share," Jodi said.

"If you were to take a photograph of a man standing on the sidewalk," Alex said, "and tear it in half at the waist, half of the data that makes that man would reside in one section of the photo, and the second half in the other. So each half of the information would be needed to create the full picture. That's logical reality. Now, let's say you took that same image of a man standing and displayed it using hologram technology. A hologram is nothing but a three-dimensional photograph manufactured with the help of a laser. Starting with the same image of a man on the sidewalk. If you tear this image in half, or in ten pieces, or into millions of tiny shreds, and shine a laser through any shard, the full image would reanimate, using that morsel of information. That's reality also, just totally illogical. The same system seems to apply to a person's consciousness. If you tear it into a thousand pieces and spread it to a thousand sites, every section of code that delineates that person possesses all of their data. Making them everywhere at once, as if there's a genetic memory of self, stored in every atom.

"You have to understand, in an electronically molecular world, every byte of knowledge interpenetrates everything else, to where space is nothing but a wholly connected grid of energy."

Alex didn't fully comprehend the theory he'd pieced together after surfing Seventh Plane blogs and programmer chatrooms, but its grand understanding sometimes felt one thought away from comprehension, and each time he shared it, he detected this greater truth beneath the logic.

"That's a way to look at it," Agent Martineau said with hesitation, as if digesting all he heard.

Agent Andrews said, "I think for most of us, this answers one of the oldest questions in history, as to whether the soul is a separate entity from the body. If so, that would be the proof scientists need to accept God into their lives and back into our society. The Lobby separates the body and soul, proving this long-debated hypothesis, yet propaganda denies that fact to the masses."

Alex had considered that, and it held plausibility.

"All of this is very intriguing," Willis said. "No matter your belief, this energy could be named the soul. I'm agnostic, so to me the soul defies mortal concepts, but no doubt this has underpinnings."

"Basically," Agent Martineau began, "if you are you, and you are put in any situation with the exact same feelings and knowledge, you will always make the same choice. Meaning even a trillion a' you being separate would always be doing the same thing simultaneously.

In a nutshell, as long as one macroserver exists, the Lobby sustains its entire population."

Before Alex could nod or maybe shrug, Andrews interjected.

"The travesty here is by being trapped in this machine. These people are being denied entrance to the real heaven."

"Gentlemen," Jodi Reister said as she extended her hands to calm the table. "We are way off topic. Let's get back to how we stop the world we do understand from falling into complete disarray."

The sound of Martineau pouring water from the carafe into a glass filled the next few seconds.

Alex rocked in his seat. He knew the pirated access points represented imminent importance, but he wanted to talk this thing out like the rest of the world: ignore the implications and postulate, share in the common charge of energy that comes from a group of individuals discussing a profound notion. He didn't want to deal with the world's problems. He wanted to be back in his one-bedroom shack in Chicago, texting Sean about the insanity of it all, reading nutty blogs, trolling the esoteric chatrooms.

After a minute of controlled breathing, he accepted that duty ruled desire, and continued. "Well, as I was saying, whoever uses these pirated access points will need at least four hours to mirror the Lobby. With the proper software and equipment, we can create a system that will alert us when anyone attempts to jack in. Once identified, we'll have their GPS coordinates. From there, we send in the police, commandos, whoever. You foil their plans and make an example out of them." Alex permitted the room a minute to visualize this scenario before hitting them with the bad news. "For this to work, we'll need to build monitoring stations across the globe, leaving no zones unaccounted for."

The room remained silent. Monitoring stations covering every four-hour block of the planet presented a colossal feat.

"And you can design this software?" Willis said.

"With the right team I can."

"Great," Andrews said. "I will have no problem assembling that team."

Even though Alex preferred this controlled Andrews to the former one, working with him was out of the question. "I need my own people, my team from Eridu." He slid a list of names to Willis. "All of these people. Immediate passports. Easy travel. Give me a week with my team, and we'll program the software. Then ship us to different parts of the world, give us the authority to train a certain type of software engineer in its application, and we can have the pirated access points under control by month's end."

"My team could be helpful," Andrews said.

"We appreciate that, Agent," Willis said, reading Alex's body language. "But I think Mr. Cutler would rather use his own people. I'm not sure you'll be needed beyond today."

Alex exhaled.

"I think this teaming up is a great idea," Jodi said. "We give Agent Andrews and Mr. Cutler shared control, pairing a government employee and a private citizen—something you're suggesting with this monitoring system, if I'm reading you right." She stared Alex down.

Despite his wishes, he nodded. She read that part correctly. However, working with Andrews would jeopardize his sanity and destroy the full scope of his plans. Yet how could he refuse people who, with a word, could have him in fetters?

"Mr. Cutler," Willis said, "there is a logic to that. We will need the government and private sector to coordinate on a scale never before seen. You two could lead the field."

"It's really the only way it will work," Agent Andrews said. "We're both professionals. It'll be a friendly competition."

"Wonderful," Jodi ended the discussion with a brisk nod. "You guys give us the software and establish a training method. We supply funding, smooth global travel, and remove possible regulations."

Alex couldn't agree, but he couldn't go to prison either. He was too famous, too weak.

"Please keep in mind, things around the globe are changing at a rapid pace," Jodi said. "It would be nice to get in front of something for a change. And without control of Lobby access, chaos will reign."

"I'd rather be sent to prison," Alex blurted, stopping the room. He would. Besides, with Andrews over his shoulder, he couldn't accomplish all he needed for this to work.".

"Excuse me," Jodi Reister said. "Prison?"

"I cannot work with Agent Andrews, with anyone other than the people on my list." Alex stiffened his spine. "Jason Johnson is in London, Carl Wright is in Dallas; several others are here in California."

Willis snickered, looked at his peers. "No need to get dramatic, Mr. Cutler. If you feel that strongly about it, we're in no position to refuse."

"I want all of my things returned to my house as well," Alex said, as a surge of clarity coursed through him. He made the choices in his life, and he dictated his future. "Today."

"We haven't fully inventoried the seized items," Andrews said, "let alone inspected them."

Locking eyes with Jodi Reister, Alex said, "I just want my team, my things, and control of my life."

"I think we can accommodate that," Jodi said in a cautious tone.

"Send everybody on that list straight to my address," Alex said.

"You'll have your things this afternoon, Mr. Cutler," Willis said as he stood. "Good luck to you. If you'll excuse me, I'd like to get my calls in before the special edition of *Inside Today* begins."

Alex nodded. Tonight's episode no longer intrigued him. When he executed his plan, he'd make historic news of his own.

Chapter Thirty-Five

Inside the Lord's Thorn command post, an aisle split rows with six chairs on each side. Lieutenants, majors, and captains headed the room. Judging from the number of sergeants, Tim estimated sixteen hundred fighters occupied this ranch. That amount staggered him. Especially since vehicles continued to trickle in.

Sitting near the back, in the front of the sergeant's row, Tim waited for the meeting to commence. The men around him speculated on the possible missions, the origin of their funding, and the immensity of what two-thousand similar-minded soldiers could accomplish.

Tim knew at his age, he should listen. Intellect arrived through genetics (expanded with study), wisdom through observations (compounded by reflection), and commitment—something overflowing in him—increased with vigilance to immediate duty.

Until the day arrived when he'd lead men, he exercised mind, body, and soul, and obeyed orders. He adhered to a version of Aristotle's dictum that stated, "To become a great leader, you must first be the best follower."

A hush fell over the room as the thud of boots on compact earth sounded. Tim fought the urge to glance behind him and glimpse their new leader. An active one-star brigadier general had assumed command of their crusade. A crusade intent on establishing a forward base. What lay beyond that vague promise, no one knew. Tim believed the Lord's Thorn would adopt the mission of eradicating every Atrium on the planet.

Confidence struck Tim as the general passed. Tim didn't get into all that hippie nonsense about auras, but who would deny that certain people carried a presence? The general's started with wide shoulders, a gray buzz cut, and bronze skin. His arms swayed in precise arcs, striking the same spot on the upthrust as the back swing. Tim hoped to walk like that someday.

When the general executed his about-face, it surprised Tim to see the boyish features of a Vietnamese man. He had expected burns or at least one horrible scar. His letdown instantly changed to respect: the man knew how to avoid harm.

"Gentlemen, my name is General Trieu. It's an honor to be here." He took a position in front of a white marker board. "Some of you know me." He nodded to one of the lieutenant colonels in the front row. "Others have heard rumors, but I'll set them all straight. I've resigned my Air Force post for a promotion to general of the most important outfit in American history: the Lord's Thorn."

A few men barked their support.

He paced lightly and increased the volume. "That is exactly what we will be, gentlemen. We will be the thorn in Satan's backside. Now, if you don't believe in the everlasting benevolence of our Creator, or the evils of His nemesis, God help you. If you can't read the signs of impending doom around the world, I'd prefer you left this pavilion."

No one stirred.

"This is a fight for our very future. You must understand, and your men must know, that our efforts will be constitutionally illegal. If we fail, we will be branded terrorists. If caught, many in this room will receive death sentences.

"If you're unwilling to pay that price, I won't consider you less of a man for excusing yourself, but do it *now*. There is no shame in wanting to preserve your life. It's a God-given instinct, same as bravery, foresight, and conviction."

Tim didn't bother to look around. These men, like him, were committed.

"The second truth may be a little more jarring." He flipped the white marker board, exposing the opposite side, which displayed a map of sorts. A large square at one end, numerous squares at the other, a single "road" splitting the connection. From the legend, the location appeared to have an airport, a hotel, and an Atrium.

The complex was unfamiliar to Tim, but seeing an Atrium at one end instilled disgust.

"They named this city 'Eridu,' a name chosen by inflated egos. Tomorrow, we storm this compound, with violence—learn whether brains or brawn win skirmishes. We bring death, gentlemen, to their side and ours. You must know this. Your men must know this.

"Our intel puts forty-eight highly trained, extremely motivated men with state-of-the-art small arms on the compound. We have over fifteen hundred semi trained, fledgling mercenaries. Believe me when I tell you that forty-eight well-disciplined men can defeat a ragtag battalion. Normally, I'd request three months of intense training to prepare. We lack that luxury. Evil is blanketing the world. Many believe this man, Adisah Boomul, is not only the Devil incarnate, but also that he is untouchable, his palace impenetrable.

"Tomorrow, we will test those claims."

Chapter Thirty-Six

When a segment finished, and as the lights brightened, Rebecca Trevino liked to remain stationary and watch the newsroom's tumult, before moving to the lavatory. The scene reminded her of feeder fish seconds after a net dipped into the tank.

New York City represented efficient congestion. *Inside Today*'s studio mirrored that. Fifty-three employees intersecting across forty-two hundred square feet often made forging your way from one side to the other a game of red light/green light.

The central bathroom always teemed with activity, and throughout the years, people had unconsciously slotted their daily usage times. A far bathroom offered execs and on-screen personalities privacy. Rebecca stood there now, a hand on each side of the porcelain sink, head down, focused on the clean, white gully.

After tonight's episode, she would be allotted a larger studio. A neutral reward. More room, but in her quaint studio, she appreciated the camera's close proximity.

Insisting on a neurotic makeup specialist, her face never revealed its natural flaws. When the lens panned out to include her surgically enhanced cleavage, her breasts looked firm enough to be enjoyed, yet soft enough to be natural.

The sound of toilet paper spooling in a stall turned her around. What madness! The far bathroom was one hundred percent off-limits before taping or airing of her programs. Everyone knew that. The toilet flushed, and Rebecca turned back to the mirror, her scowl internalized.

"Knock 'em dead," a woman said as she rinsed her hands under the faucet two down from Rebecca.

Keeping her grip on the sink, Rebecca stared at her own reflection, saying nothing. She couldn't place the voice. This stunt earned whoever it was a transfer, possibly a termination. Thankfully, the interloper seemed to recognize her mistake and exited without drying her hands.

The woman was probably an intern. The regulars granted her the needed privacy before each episode. This episode was going to be epic. In the last few weeks, she'd ended the battle for most-watched primetime program. She now danced as queen atop the mountain. And she'd soon make Carl Bernstein and Bob Woodward's Watergate reporting seem as relevant as junior-high gossip.

Lifting herself on her toes, she moved her face close to the mirror, examined her skin, and then checked her teeth. It baffled her when people said the camera added ten pounds. Even if it did, it removed ten years, eradicated all blemishes, and caused people she was used to seeing on television to take on haggardly appearances when encountered in the real world. Particularly the makeup-less men.

Feeling centered, she exited the wooden door and found two women patiently waiting. They smiled and wished her luck. Those women she knew. Daynah produced the show following hers, and Allisa managed miles of audio cables.

As Rebecca made her way to the breakroom, everyone she passed nodded and shared encouragement, a way of ushering her to her throne.

The world had never experienced anything as compelling as the Lobby, and the discovery that the alternate-reality machine preserved life catapulted it into unimaginable levels of interest. The notion that millions of people longed to sign onto a machine and die gave her goosebumps, but she wasn't one of those people. This world held the action. Here, each day brought incalculable surprises. For proof, one only needed to recap the emergence of computers over the previous half-century.

They started as math aids, codebreakers. Small businesses soon utilized the technology, and eventually, computer nerds exploited them for simple games. Fast-forward a few decades, and we had more computers than homes to hold them. Cellphone applications existed that could monitor a person's heart rate and ensure they properly brushed their teeth. Then came the Lobby, which dwarfed those amenities, and then exceeded its own greatness by offering an amendable afterlife.

Nothing would ever surpass the awe of reality. Knowing a larger story loomed in the future allowed her to attack each day with an enthusiasm unknown to womankind.

Entering the densely packed breakroom initiated a light applause. Everyone greeted her with congratulations, gratitude, and lit-up faces. She made sure to return them all. These people were like family. They were the blood that flowed through the body of *Inside Today*. They made it function, while she acted as its heart, and its soul.

A eighty-inch OLED headed the room. Corner speakers bolstered the sound. She glanced at the clock. Three minutes until they aired.

Jack Fleeman, a field reporter she'd worked with for the past four years, offered to fill a cup of coffee for her. She politely declined. Any added stimulant could burst her heart. Someone shut off the lights as she nestled into her proffered seat in the front row between Casy Marvin, a studio executive, and Ryan Lambert, her boyfriend of ten years. She smiled at each, hugged one, kissed the other, and realized a fact she'd never voice: she no longer needed either of them.

The opening credits finished, and when *Inside Today* returned from commercial, the on-screen Rebecca sat inside the cockpit of a Maersk cargo liner—an expansive triple-decked ship—packed with cargo containers stacked eight high. In front of her waited the silhouette of a man sitting atop a stool, a well-placed shadow protected his identity. The horizontal-patterned, tan shirt that covered the man's bloated belly looked outdated by twenty years.

"Good evening," on-screen Rebecca said. "I'm here with a ship captain who wishes to remain anonymous. We are on a cargo liner we will not name, that started its journey in one of the numerous ports along the west coast of North America. For reasons that will soon become frighteningly obvious, all identifying images will be edited.

"Sir, tell me, how long have you been a captain, and what do those responsibilities consist of?"

The man's voice sounded deep and off-pitch, as if played through an old-style tape recorder set on too slow of a speed. "I've been on these waters for over thirty years. Been fortunate enough to stay alive, gain the notice of my employers, and have had the pleasure of piloting this same vessel for the better part of two decades.

"The job description varies, but mainly we pick up products from countries 'cross the Pacific, often China, but there're others. We ferry 'em back, unload, get paid. Some shore leave, and then hope to resupply with American products." He leaned forward. "Though I can tell ya, for a long time, we were forced to leave with empty bellies. In a nutshell, that's my job."

"Thank you. And I understand there have been recent changes in outbound cargo. Can you explain?"

"Oh, we're not empty no longer." He shifted on his stool.

"So you've found a shippable product from America?"

"Yes. People mainly."

A few viewers around Rebecca hitched their breaths. She pictured tens of millions of gasps around the world and had to squeeze her thighs together to control her excitement.

"Are you saying human beings are the outbound cargo?"

"Yes, ma'am."

"American citizens are paying you to smuggle them out of the United States?"

"Sure. Tho' some're Canadians, Mexicans… paying big bucks too."

"Wow," the on-camera Rebecca adjusted her sitting position. "I can tell you, that is quite a shock."

"Ain't no shock. Maybe to some rich gal like yourself. But people been talkin'. When you're down here with 'em, ya hear."

272

"Yes…well, can you tell us how this came about? How you located these passengers?"

"Now they find me. I gotta call from a skipper a few days back. He says he's already to sea, but he's got people he couldn't fit on his ship, lookin' to hitch a ride. Says the number of people and the amount they're willin' to pay would knock my socks clean off." The captain's shadowed form nodded as if in deep reflection. "That it did."

The camera panned around for a panoramic view of the surrounding ocean, while Rebecca posed a question. "How far out to sea are we now, Captain?"

"Hmmm… Lemme see. We're almost through day two. That'd be 'bout halfway. 'Bout eight hundred miles outta port, I reckon."

"And you have people onboard now?"

"Yes, ma'am," he said with pride. "Full hold."

"Do you have an estimate of how many travelers you have on this vessel, and what their reasons are for boarding?"

"Their reasons're for them Death Trips," he said matter-of-factly. "Open to anyone with a wad-o-cash and a desire to leave this pit-o-(censored word) called life." He scratched his face, and paused. "Well, that ain't 'tirely true. I s'pose some're travelin' to see that monk fella preachin' 'bout salvation, harmony, and all that nonsense." He fidgeted. "Wait a minute, let me take that back, too. It'd been nonsense a month ago, but when a man preaches 'bout somethin' specific, sayin' he had visions and whatnot, and those visions come true to the letter, there ain't no more second guessin' him, now is there? But still, most're here for that final ride. The Death Trip."

Rebecca watched herself cross her legs. To viewers it seemed inconsequential, but that two-second break created pacing and set her apart from her peers. "You said you had an idea as to how many people you have onboard?"

"Sure, sure. I can do ya one better. We got exactly fourteen hundred and ninety-two souls onboard this vessel."

More gasps from the audience around her. Rebecca knew this dialogue word for word, yet a bomb going off in the next room couldn't break her attention from the screen. Knowing that degree of

273

rapture must be amplified in others tenfold was the truest testament to the power of information in the real world.

"So you're saying, right now, below us are hundreds of people, riding with full intention of killing themselves?"

"Nah. They won't be dead, ya see? I'd call it freein' themselves. Free from pain, torment, bein' judged. I'm sure a pretty thang like yourself knows the deal. Betcha can't walk to the market without a hundred eyes checkin' ya out. The Lobby's a great option. 'Less ya think there's some old guy in the sky waitin' to pamper ya. If so, I won't say you're wrong, but that ain't nothin' I can sink my teeth into."

"Well, sir, I'm not sure if you're aware of this, but almost ninety percent of the world believes in a higher power. Are you saying you don't?"

"I'm not sayin' that, but most people're brain-dead sheep. Don't know what they believe, juss say what they think ya wanna hear. That much I know. And I do believe in a higher power. It's 'lectronic. I can touch it, feel it, hold proof of it."

"I see." On screen, Rebecca checked a pad of paper in her lap. "Can you tell me how difficult it was to reach that number?"

He snickered. "Wasn't. I coulda turned people away after few hours. I had some rules too. No kids under eight. Tho' I fear some mighta smudged the ages on me. I had one couple wanted to bring their newborn." He shook his head. "I wasn't sure if they was to see the monk or... ya know. But I can't see how loadin' up an infant is right. Shoot, I didn't even need this many people. Guess it shows I got a kind heart."

"Need? Can you elaborate?"

"They payin' whatever ya ask. Five thousand, fifty, a hundred per head out there. I had more than enough after the first two dozen, to be honest. "

"'More than enough' for what, Captain?"

"For my own Death Trip, 'a course." The shadowed figure checked his watch. "I'll be out of this bag a' fat and (censored word) in less than three days. I ain't never been so 'cited. If I was you, lady, I'd leave that 'copter parked on my deck, call that deep bank a' yers, and join the rest of us 'fore they find a way to lock us out." He added, "One thing I know: it's a great time to die."

The program faded to commercial.

The room stayed so quiet, a hair dropping would have sounded like a cannonade.

Coming into this, she'd anticipated applause, pats on the back. This shocked silence meant so much more.

Following the commercial, *Inside Today* panned a flowing shot below deck. People of all ages and sizes filled narrow hallways and every hold. Families huddled close, suspiciously watching the cameras pass. A New Year's Eve-type of party raged in one of the larger areas.

In voice-over commentary, Rebecca reinforced the thoughts of a nation. "All of these people have chosen to abandon faith, hope, and humanity for a one-way ticket to cyber prison." Rebecca didn't necessarily agree with that, but in modern journalism, it's not what you report—it's how portentous you make it. Fear sold ads, ads created revenue, and revenue led to recognition in the form of millions of fans tuning in to watch the greatest journalists cover the biggest stories.

Her lead segment did just that. It showed doomed people preparing for the inevitable. The misgivings on that cargo ship occurred five days ago, but they continued today, would expand tomorrow.

Her next segment focused on religions and their gurus, covering Buddhism conversion rates around the globe. Before this theory of life to death to everlasting existence on a machine hit the population, roughly twenty-four percent of the world had been Islamic, slightly more were Christian, twelve percent were Buddhists, and members of the other thirty-three thousand registered religions added up to another twelve percent. Agnostics and atheists claimed what remained.

Since Sung Yi's preaching became widespread, a full one-third of the world now considered themselves students of Buddhism—a more than three hundred percent spike in thirteen days.

Those same people now thanked Gaea, Creator of the World, for gifting the Lobby to her children. Sung Yi's YouTube videos had been translated into ninety-one languages. They converted people by the second.

For supporters of monotheism, the most frightening statistic came from the chart that showed the projected conversion from the two major religions to Buddhism. Even with a drop in the current rate, in twenty years, Christianity would be all but extinct and Islam nothing more than backwoods voodoo.

Another commercial. This time chatter erupted, but no one spoke to her. You can't run from facts. This was their new world, and her report would ignite a controversy and spark a struggle for the ages. Controversy, strife, death—the ingredients of good media.

Although Rebecca would never be knighted or anointed to sainthood, she was saving lives by creating conflict. Millions of people would forego an eternity inside the Lobby simply to catch that day's news.

Outrage would follow this program. Faith in Jesus and Allah strummed in billions of hearts. This would be like paddles jolting that passion to life. Her research didn't lie. Society strolled the path to a new world religion. The only way to avert its destination would be to derail the engine. People would try, and she'd report all the gory details.

The final segment touched on Tara Capaldi, Brad Finder, and Roy Guillen, presented a four-minute exposé on Alex Cutler, and ended with a six-minute finale on Adisah Boomul, the reclusive mastermind hiding in his futuristic fort.

What an amazing interview that would be. Maybe she'd reach out. The world had a right to know what was happening in those Montana mountains.

Chapter Thirty-Seven

Tim rode in a 1989 MD helicopter. Not a single cloud, created by man or God, populated that morning's expansive blue sky. Yet a roving shadow of rotating blades and visually amorphous shapes blanketed the land.

His particular ship spent almost twenty years in Hawaii, flying tourists over a specific, uninhabited island known for its lush vegetation, heavy boar population, and rumors of cannibals.

Somewhere along the way, the craft had lost its doors. Wind blasted through the interior. The noise was deafening, and the sight awe inspiring. The nearest helicopter was six feet longer than his and painted in faded yellow. A lime-green stripe ran along the side, as if its past life involved promoting Mellow Yellow soda.

Tim's helicopter soared on the armada's left, northern edge, close to the middle of the pack. The MD would touch down twenty-one minutes after the old steel tankers that led the fleet. Each would hit the ground, offload their troops, and return to the sky.

Standing in an aged helicopter, the craft's steady vibrations kept his body pulsing in time with his anxiety. Shooting people was in his immediate future. Landing twenty-one minutes after the first wave could spoil his chance for glory. Knowing hours of fighting awaited them, possibly days of random skirmishes, brought comfort.

Seven men—the full load under his command as a sergeant—along with a rookie pilot, caused the MD to be four passengers over capacity. A lenient figure. Other crafts of comparable size held ten men, crammed in like clowns in a circus car. However, his team transported two M107, fifty-caliber rifles. Four feet ten inches in length, the guns weighed twenty-eight and a half pounds when empty and had enormous ammunition, each bullet as big as a cigar. These weapons more than compensated for the lack of warm bodies.

Though they adhered to a near-silent radio status, a headset connected him with the pilots and other team leaders. Their tight flight formation allowed for eye contact with passengers of nearby helicopters, linking the army on a more personal front. He read the emotions on others' faces: nerves, anticipation, fear.

The rotating blades created a deep thwumping that blotted out other sounds and whipped every strand of prairie grass below and head of hair above.

At one point, they crossed over a herd of deer. The dark, encroaching shadow and heavenly roar made the animals bolt as one, but as the crafts centered over them, and the tumultuous cacophony worked into their bones, they abandoned ranks and scattered.

Tim imagined the men at Eridu would first hear a slight buzz, alerting them to something amiss, then mounting caution as the rumble reached a thunder. When the sky blackened with metal carriages, terror would set in. These metal carriages carried the end of life as those men knew it or, if Tim got his way, the end of their wickedness, period.

"Twenty miles to visual," a voice informed him through his headset. They traveled at sixty miles an hour—a little over half the MD's top speed. He estimated fifteen minutes until a true combat mission unfolded. Holding a strap with one hand and a loaded rifle in the other, Tim concentrated on slowing his heart rate.

Leaning out the side, he bathed in fresh air. After the ablution, he pulled himself back in and surveyed the men under his command.

Three sat shoulder to shoulder in the rear seat. One prayed, one chewed gum, another rocked to his headphones, and a crouched pair across from them tried to converse with shouts.

"Contact approaching, west end. Assume spread pattern," the voice in Tim's headset spoke with control, but confusion layered his tone.

Tim's helicopter yawed left, stumbling him and the two without seats. Securing his footing, he watched out the opposite opening, as over a hundred craft tilted in synchronization. He couldn't help but appreciate the sight. Thirty feet of distance had separated each. The recent command tripled that space. Even if equipped with binoculars and unobstructed vision, identifying the model of the farthest craft, from corner to corner, might be impossible. The memory of the words that started this shift interrupted his marveling. Contact approaching? What type of contact?

Their government source informed them that Eridu had a sophisticated airport. In the unlikely event someone manned the tower, and the pilots flew high enough to be detected, Eridu's radars would identify the inbound helicopter as far away as twenty miles out. Regardless, their ally assured them they'd sever Eridu's communications to stop them from calling for help.

With the pack flying over the only road in or out for the last few miles, the biggest worry involved the enemy ferrying Boomul to safety in a private plane. Again, the government man guaranteed them that Boomul would remain at his compound, and that his men would fight.

"Enemy bogey, eleven o'clock, stagger pattern." The voice in his ear held its command, but something else had crept into the pitch. Fear? Tim peered out of the main windshield for signs of danger.

The MD dropped fifty feet in altitude, taking his stomach with it. After the aircraft settled, he noticed the Mellow Yellow representative had risen out of sight, as if the rows alternated between climbing and dropping. Though spawned by a complication, the aerial acrobatics invigorated Tim. He hoped, decades from now, when he met his maker, he could revisit this event, live it from an omnipresent point of view, because he was participating in a glorious action.

"Oh, shit. Contact. Fire." A new voice piped across the headset, and ended the radio silence.   Dozens of voices yelled and cursed.

279

A pilot screamed for another to watch his three o'clock, followed by the crunch of an in-air collision in the distance, and the flash of an explosion.

Another, more portentous sound overtook the headphone chatter and rotor wash. A familiar sound. A noise similar to the spat of a buzz saw, a squeeze and release of a chainsaw: automatic gunfire. Distant, but of a large caliber, rapid, like no weapon Tim had ever fired. And he'd fired hundreds.

The men in the rear of the MD jockeyed and jostled in their attempt to view the outside commotion. The shifting weight rocked the overburdened aircraft. Using urgent hand signals, Tim commanded his men to stay seated. Their first-time pilot didn't need extra distractions. Sweat rimmed the pilot's scalp. His hands held the control stick so tight, Tim feared it would snap off. And then, from out of the main windshield, Tim witnessed the unimaginable.

Loud reports, and then a Lord's Thorn helicopter skipped backward in a series of jabs, and, like a stone loosened from a clasped hand, plummeted to earth. The burning fuselage dropped out of sight. Seconds later, he heard the boom of steel impacting earth.

Another rattle of the massive caliber gun in the distance. Another explosion so intense, he imagined a thousand men shuddered in unison.

Did the bastards at Eridu have an attack chopper? If so, what a grievous oversight. The Lord's Thorn had no defense against an attack chopper? Their plans involved a ground assault, using small arms.

The radio chatter reached pandemonium. A man ordered everyone to "break off," "use evasive maneuvers."

Wouldn't help. They'd be torn to shreds.

The silence between each rhythmic spat of gunfire, although never more than a few seconds, seemed an eternity. Buzz saw, break; buzz saw, break. A lifetime in between. Birth, aging, and slaughter. Buzz saw, break. Each silence brought a mourning for a downed helicopter, each brought his craft closer to the cross hairs.

The pilot climbed to a desired height, pitched the craft forward, and increased their speed. Tim bent into the cockpit. The pilot leaned toward him, and while keeping his eyes forward, shouted, "We're in one of the fastest machines. Someone's got to ram that mother. By my count, he's brought down nine of us. If we can't stop him…"

The pilot's words echoed in Tim. Become a martyr? A noble death, sure. Though it flew in the face of him leading society to a renewed time of faith, sacrifice, and discipline for the Lord.

The pilot shook his head, as if denying his intention. "This guy could wipe out our entire fleet."

Perhaps a dozen helicopters had elevated to this new height. With the MD in the middle, they all converged on a single source.

The assault chopper appeared smaller than he imagined. Compact, painted in a tiger-stripe pattern of brown and mustard. Thick with armor, near invisible when plastered against the mountain backdrop.

The attack helicopter fluttered, skipped, rose and fell like a hummingbird. Two gun barrels near its nose flashed, followed by the clattering buzz saw, then silence. Tim pursed his lips.

The enemy craft climbed with the grace of a ballerina, ripped off another burst of fire, and turned healthy craft into confetti.

The smell of burning fuel suffused with unsullied mountain air. The nearest Lord's Thorn helicopter was a hundred feet from their target. Tim focused on it, willed success into his comrade. If the tan, tiger-striped craft stayed distracted a few more seconds…

Right before a guaranteed kamikaze strike, the bumblebee reversed its angle, tilted its nose at the ramming helicopter, and activated the buzz saw.

Tim grimaced at the effect huge bullets had on the commercial crafts. It lurched to the side as if hit with a three-punch combo, and, as if slugged in the gut by a titan, dropped down and to the side.

Tim jumped at the next buzz saw. Damn, he was close now.

Six hundred yards out. Fourth in line. He and his men would soon be dead, in a vain sacrifice.

He slipped into a quiet acquiescence. He envisioned the enemy pilot relaxed in that cockpit, listening to Mozart, sniffing an aged cognac before finding a target and depressing the trigger.

The kamikaze pilots were adding difficulty. Longer breaks between kills, but it seemed the entire mission was lost, unless this guy ran out of bullets.

Another destroyed craft. This close, Tim spotted the softball-size holes left by the ammunition.

He secretly hoped one of those massive rounds took him in the chest. That seemed preferable to screaming in a freefall.

Tim's eyes grew wide with an idea: The fifty cals in the back. His false hope ended before it began. He didn't have the time to dig out the guns, let alone load, aim, and fire.

Giving his life for his cause, his Lord, and his men was no problem, but knowing that service would be as human fodder depressed him.

Three crafts back. The preceding duo before him went high and low.

Tim rubbed the patches on his vest. "God, grant them success. Thank You for all of Your blessings, for the gift of life. Accept me and my men into Your heavenly embrace."

Before he decided to join his men in the rear—and pass along his peace—an object entered his peripheral. A small, two-person reconnaissance helicopter, painted all black, hovered over the eastern mountain ridge, as if a spectator to the abattoir of steel.

Buzz saw, break. The lead Lord's Thorn helicopter exploded. Tim was now second in line.

A beach-ball-size periscope hung from the spectator's bottom. It was an Army XL42 spotter. The craft looked new, waxed, but what was it doing here?

It dipped behind the mountain, leaving Tim to wonder if he had hallucinated the image. Before he processed it all, a craft he'd saw a thousand time popped up from behind that ridge line. He'd had a poster of an Apache AH-64 on his wall since the age of twelve. A rub of his eyes proved it was really there.

The Apache floated in the bumblebee's blind spot. It casually faced the dancing copter of death.

A cough of smoke erupted from under the Apache's right wing, headed straight for their enemy.

Tim slapped the pilot's shoulder, squeezed, and pointed. The pilot yanked on the stick, throwing everyone off-balance as the MD climbed and banked. Thankfully, Tim saw the heat-guided rocket meet their nemesis, transform metal into fire, heavy fragments, and an explosion loud enough to ripple the valley.

The cheers of a thousand men overtook the whooping of rotor blades.

Tim shook the pilot in triumph.

"Afternoon, gentlemen," a new voice came over the radio—clear, crisp—silencing the celebration. "Captain Riley Parker, United States Army, at your service. Hoo-rah!"

Tim had never wanted to be an American soldier. He often envisioned them as his enemy. Those feelings vanished as he joined a hundred other men by yelling, "Hoo-rah."

"You gentlemen have a pleasant and safe afternoon. Captain Riley Parker, signing off."

Voices shouted. The men in the back pumped their fists, cheered, clamped onto one another.   Tim didn't bother asking them to watch their movements. They'd been tested, and they'd thwarted evil. He closed his eyes, thanked God, and asked Him to help preserve these emotions. Today would always be his first time cheating death.

As the helicopters settled and regrouped, Tim estimated eighty percent of their fleet had survived. His craft assumed a spot on the pack's outer edge, closest to the approaching city.

Hot waves of anger washed over Tim. This defenseless murder might backfire on the folks at Eridu.

Patting each man on the shoulder, he stared into their eyes until they shared his focus. This had become personal. For all he knew, Alan was dead.

The radio chatter dimmed to words of encouragement, prayers for those fallen.

With a bit more determination, the fleet continued toward the sinister home of Adisah Boomul.

"Approaching target," said the voice in his headset. Clear. Distinct. With no fear.

Tim could see the tip of the Hotel La Berce in the distance, like a spear thrust in the ground as a challenge.

A red bulb illuminated inside the fuselage, signifying the front of the formation had reached the range of small arms fire.

How many of the steel titans initially leading the pack remained? They had anticipated their outer shell to draw the majority of the rifle rounds. The floorboards and cockpit had been lined with Kevlar to provide extra safety.   Kevlar and inch-thick steel would be like toilet paper against ten millimeter cannon fire.

The buildings were clearly in view now. Tim saw movement on rooftops. He heard the familiar pop-pop-pop of small arms fire. Originally, he'd thought that sound would jack his nerves—knowing people fired at him and his—but after the earlier terror, recognizing the caliber brought relief.

"Contact," came through the radio.

Contact? A surge of adrenaline. A survey out the windshield. No flighty choppers. Tim eased back, rubbed the patches on his vest, and prayed for the safety of the lead men.

Continual patters of rifle reports echoed off the canyon. He gripped the strap and leaned out. Each rooftop held armed Eridu staff. These were the leftovers, shooting in hopes of a lucky hit. The majority of their forces would protect the Atrium, where they housed the equipment, and most likely Adisah Boomul.

After the earlier battle, Tim now disliked flying on the outermost edge, closest to the buildings, basically defenseless.

The increased sound of gunfire alerted him that someone targeted his MD. They passed within a hundred yards of the nearest building. Plenty close enough to take a round. Using an inner calm, he visualized the landing. It would be chaotic, men screaming, wounds gaping, explosions all around. He would spot Adisah Boomul in the distance. The man would be rotating his arms in wide circles, chanting some satanic prayer to summon some hideous demon from the pits of hell. The earth would start to rumble as the beast woke. Some men would panic, a few others would run. Not Tim. He'd aim down his rifle sight, and from two hundred yards, score a head shot, splattering brain mist and matter. No more warlock. Hero born.

Tink. A bullet punched through the floorboard in between his men, bringing him back to the present. Judging from the relieved grins on the surrounding faces, no one had been hit.

Through the headset he heard someone say, "Wave one down."

Tim glanced outside, knowing that the Lord's Thorn had boots on the ground. The two-way battle had commenced.

A trio of Eridu soldiers ran across a roof three hundred yards ahead. They lumbered with a tilt, as if weighted, drawing Tim's attention. The three men worked as a unit. As he recognized their maneuvers, his blood froze.

The men lugged an A-98 LAW rocket launcher. It was rectangular, the length of a pool stick, and as square as a small microwave. It was also a weapon capable of firing four heat-seeking stinger missiles.

The man in the center hefted the metal onto his shoulders. His spotter selected Tim's approaching MD.

Tim snatched at the pilot's shoulder, tugged, and pointed to the trio, now engulfed in a cloud of smoke.

The pilot yanked the stick right.

Tim stumbled to the back for a better view. The missile traveled leisurely toward them in a looping patter that if followed with the eyes alone would cause vertigo.

The pilot would either raise them high enough to avoid impact, or they'd explode. Deciding to increase his survival odds, he moved from his shoulder to a shooter's grip, clicked off the safety, aimed, and fired a three-round burst at the missile. Dat-dat-dat.

He fired again. Dat-dat-dat.

On it came.

Another short burst.

285

Tingling heat he identified as horror filled him as the rocket tilted up, keeping pace with their climb. With his few remaining seconds, he looked off in the distance, at the previous location of the Apache and its spotter. Something would save him. This wasn't his destiny.

The scream of the missile's propulsion system overtook the thump of the rotors.

Closing his eyes, he rubbed the patch on his chest.

One of his men screamed.

In the middle of thanking God for all He had bestowed, a thirty-eight-pound rocket, traveling at a hundred and twenty miles per hour, slammed into Tim's chest, drove him into the ceiling, and exploded with the force of three hundred sticks of dynamite.

Chapter Thirty-Eight

Growing up in Gisenyi, a war-torn village outside the capital of Rwanda, Adisah Boomul understood tumult, suffering, and ignorance. Violence acted as a daily occurrence long before mayhem brought his nation fame. Being born in a corrupt land motivated Adisah to work harder, study more, and focus on getting out. Being Tutsi, it could be said the effort saved his life.

He'd been living in America when the Botswana refugees rebelled against their government.

Men had gathered to chant, march, protest their limited food, porous shelters, and inhumane treatment. They were gunned down with rifle fire, sparking a revolution. For years to follow, the entire population lived at risk of militant bombings and the equally volatile military sweeps.

The insurgency ended in 1993, when President Juvénal Habyarimana, a Hutu, and the Rwandan Patriotic Front signed a power-sharing agreement. Months later, rebels shot down an airplane carrying President Habyarimana and Burundian President Ntaryamira. This instigated the greatest genocide in the continent's history.

The Hutu, a majority underclass distinguished by darker skin and short stature, attempted to eradicate their Tutsi neighbors using door-to-door sweeps, mob raids, and military assistance.

In 1994, during a largely ignored, three-month stampede of murder, mutilation, and rape, the Hutus killed, overwhelming with machete, more than eight hundred thousand of their fellow citizens. Eight hundred thousand. He thanked God, near daily, that he had avoided that mayhem.

His father's position on the counsel and his mother having full-time employment as a nurse allowed him to be homeschooled. On the three days a week when both his mother and father worked, Adisah accompanied her during each twelve-hour shift.

The awe of the hospice ward sent him into the field of electronics. He still remembered his amazement at learning that the wheezing, buzzing, and chiming machines all around him kept people alive. The reality that small boxes of electricity sustained organic life sent shockwaves of possibilities through his young mind.

A lifetime later, he opened the Lobby to the infirmed the world over, and created a haven for those who suffered.

The current gunfire outside the Atrium, and the people hustling and fretting around him, transported the elderly Adisah back to the walks with his mother along dirt streets. Back then, it seemed the simple act of holding her hand blotted out all horrors.

A new-age Christian, she believed everything men created, or would create, came as a gift from God. Adisah wondered how she'd view a machine that trapped souls, instigated mass suicides, and generated social outrage. He assumed her initial frown would curl into a grin. She identified positives in everything; always predicted beneficial side effects, and considered each morning progress.

"What should we do?" Dalton's deep voice pulled Adisah from thoughts of his mother.

He squinted and looked up at his loyal friend. He knew Dalton, along with most of the staff, viewed him as invincible, but he felt his age. Discomfort accompanied the simplest movements. Sleep either eluded him, or took hold at inappropriate times. His sight was dwindling, incontinence was on the horizon.

Currently, he rested on a maroon sofa in the center of a serenely decorated room. Seven years ago, this section of the Atrium bustled with clients eager to enter the secretive Lobby.

Gone were the glossy tiles and company walls. Now, the same stinkwood flooring he had in his La Berce condo decorated the

288

floor. A koi pond and a cascading waterfall created the main attraction to the community center.

Kids of all ages huddled around that pond. Many tossed food to the fish. When a gun cracked especially close, drawing a scream and everyone's attention, one of the mothers pointed out a certain fish, another oohed at a splash. The distraction worked for the young, but the anxiety level climbed with the person's age, climaxing with wide-eyed adults, who suspected that despite the immense security, Eridu had been overrun.

Dalton positioned himself in front of his employer. "Some of the people are sneaking up to the access rooms. I don't have to tell you their objectives." He sought out the pond. "People want to know your thoughts."

Thwack! Glass shards tinkled upon the stinkwood. A bullet had punched through the protective glass on the front wall.

Adisah glanced at where the projectile had entered. The aim had either been errant, or meant as a warning.

The invaders had fully surrounded the old Atrium an hour ago. Demands from a bullhorn started thirty minutes after that.

The bullhorn squawked, "We ain't gonna wait all day."

"Let those who want to enter the Lobby go," Adisah said as he kept his gaze on the ray of sunlight passing through the bullet hole. It epitomized the view of life he'd adopted from his mother. Every act, no matter how horrible, forwarded humanity toward a more positive future. Evil never prevailed. Everything, to differentiating degrees, ushered goodness. This pattern long ago revealed God's existence to him.

Though nowhere near the cost of the pain and suffering, even the Holocaust created a light. It unified a fractured people, alerted the world to the detriments of apathy, and defeating the Nazis filled the Allies with a generational pride. A pride that led to world-changing advancements in all fields.

On the opposite end, guilt reshaped the next generation of German social philosophy. They learned to stand up against injustice, regardless of personal consequences.

Adisah knew, when the next human atrocity that edged toward the magnitude of the Holocaust arose, the German people would oppose it to their last citizen.

Dalton leaned closer, and spoke in a whisper. "Some parents are taking their children up there."

"That's their right," Adisah said. He then searched Dalton's distraught face. "Are you seeking my permission to join them?"

Dalton bolted upright. "Of course not. I don't leave your side—you know that."

The firearm at Dalton's hip smelled of cordite. Second-degree burns charred his left hand. Adisah heard men talking about how Dalton emptied a rifle, expended two of the pistol clips, and killed several of the intruders as he guided a small group from La Berce, first in a convoy, then on foot.

Another member of his security team approached, pulled Dalton aside, and whispered in his ear.

"Go in peace, brother," Dalton said. "He understands your worry. He wishes you well."

The dark-skinned man who had whispered to Dalton stared at Adisah, sorrow evident on his features. Then he moved to a crowd, spread a message that drew many glances, then the group hurried to the elevators.

Adisah would pray for them. Evidence abounded that the invaders lacked an interest in prisoners. They arrived for a duck hunt.

A squawk. The bullhorn. "Come out with your hands up, slowly, and no one will be hurt."

Adisah wanted to believe them, yet he always trusted his eyes over another person's mouth.

That saying had applied to judging people as individuals, based on their merits, regardless of their past. He imagined it applied to this situation, but saw few alternate options.

An argument existed that Adisah, through his dream to help those suffering had instigated this round of horror. Imagining the wonder that would follow a global strife of this depth kept him from wallowing in shame.

"We have an active phone line," a man yelled from behind Adisah, near the desk.

"Get us some damn help," Dalton barked. "The contact numbers are next to the phone."

"I can't get an outside line." The man shook his head in frustration. "But we have an incoming call."

"Answer it," Adisah said. To Dalton, he motioned to the front door. "Tell them to stay calm. We have women and children inside. I will speak with them, if that is their wish."

Dalton pointed to a tall, wiry man with cornrows and pantomimed to his undershirt. "Go wave that in the doorway."

The man removed both of his shirts, placed the outer one back on and held the white undershirt above his head as he crept toward the front door.

Adisah extended his arm in a plea for Dalton's assistance in standing. Once given, he shuffled to the phone.

The man with the cornrows opened the door, exited with the white shirt held high.

Adisah waited for a rifle report. Hearing none was a good sign. The man yelled their impending concession.

The bullhorn reminded, "We ain't got all day."

Everyone's eyes stayed glued on Adisah. Many considered him an icon, the most accomplished African American in recent history, easily the wealthiest.

Behind the desk, he stared at the blinking phone line, and then at the people around him. "I am sorry to have placed you all in harm's way," he said. "I cannot promise to know the intentions of the men outside. But I enter negotiations seeking your fair treatment. If you wish to join those who went upstairs, I will not find fault in your decision. We all walk our own path. Each one leads to a brighter future."

A few of his staff gathered their loved ones into small huddles, and chatted privately. A few more shuffled down the main hall toward the elevator, flashing terse smiles or keeping their heads down and feet moving as they passed. Many more stayed, and for reasons Adisah wouldn't attempt to articulate, he considered that a

291

good thing.   Examining the faces of the remaining people, he lifted the receiver.

He listened and then agreed. Listened, agreed. Listened, and agreed. He then disconnected.

Adisah spoke softly to Dalton. "You must understand, any mercy bestowed upon us is a blessing. Our only option is to trust their word."

"We do have options," Dalton said. "We send the women and children to the rear of the building and we make a stand. There are twelve highly trained—"

"Yes, I understand your thinking. However, they have assured me that if I surrender, they will harm no one. And I have agreed. Doing this ends this part, and allows us to begin another, bringing us closer to a return of harmony for the young ones."

"Don't go." Dalton dropped his head. "I'd rather die than see you mistreated."

"We must think of the others." Adisah gestured toward the frightened crowd. "Our actions will decide their fate."

Dalton surveyed the group, and swallowed. "How can you trust them?"

Adisah edged around the corner of the desk. "I am a wealthy man. They will demand things, I will give them, and all of this will blow over." He rested a hand on Dalton's enormous triceps. "I am to come out alone."

"I'm going with you."

"Now, now, my big friend. Your size will scare off the lot of them."

Dalton lowered his head and spoke deliberately. "It would be my life's honor to accompany you."

Taking in the man's stone features, Adisah sighed. "Very well, Dalton Lewis. Let us become captives."

Dalton shared their intentions with the room.

The remaining people formed a procession of sorts toward the door. Each gave thanks, shared encouragement, and tried to hide their concerns.

Adisah placated them with smiles and brief nods. With the door halfway open, Dalton paused. Adisah took a final look at the people he'd shared utopia with for nearly a decade. Sadness entwined his spirits, but even Eden had its downfall, and look at all the wonderful things that followed. With a final smile, he stepped into the daylight.

The afternoon sun floated at the perfect spot to blind, and hide the majority of the parking lot.

What he discerned beneath the golden rays shocked. Armed men pointed weapons at them from various positions: prone, kneeling, and standing. A concert crowd worth of killers.

The squawk. "Very carefully throw down your weapon."

Using two fingers, Dalton extracted his sidearm, and placed it on the ground. He then raised his arms and kicked the pistol well out of lunging range.

Adisah felt centered, but his legs wobbled. The exertion from holding his arms above his head threatened to collapse him.

Glancing at Dalton, he wondered what they would do to the man afterward.

A force collapsed Adisah's chest as a boom reached his ears. He crumpled to the ground as if he'd been a robot whose power source had suddenly been severed.

Like many of the stories he'd heard, time slowed and movement stopped, but the key detail omitted from descriptions of being shot in the chest with a high-powered rifle was the overall calm. His form decorated the concrete, but he, Adisah Boomul, spiraled up toward a point, gaining strength and clarity as he twirled. Whether to an end that culminated in blackness, or a warp to a new essence, he couldn't be sure. As if in answer to his question, a woman's hand stretched to him from the darkness. He smelled menthol gel, heard the whine and hiss of a distant nebulizer, the beep of a cardiograph. And though his face and body didn't react, he beamed as he reached for the offered hand.

That the fingers he extended were those of a young boy didn't surprise him.

A distant knowledge of someone hollering, reached his senses. Adisah felt the energy of Dalton's shocked rage, but knew the man would overcome this loss. God was good, and every action, no matter how misguided, made the future a better place.

Chapter Thirty-Nine

"This like no smart plan, Alex," Song said as he admired a row of hardcover books in Alex's library, featuring Darwin, Lewis and Clark, and other tales of exploration.

Alex wondered when Song had abandoned his signature orange hair. Today's natural black streaked with blue patina presented a more chic look. The familiar sound of his voice, along with his continued enthusiasm for life, comforted Alex.

Over the past two days, as he'd welcomed his old team from Eridu, that sentiment struck again and again, begging the question: why hadn't he done this sooner? These were the true friends his life lacked—Kole, Denise. Carl. Jason.

They'd spent the previous evenings dabbling in Alex's new plan—the program he'd mentioned in the L.A. Federal Building, the one designed to keep the world functioning.

The more controversial details—one's he'd been too scared to share with members of the government—bubbled out of him. Having finally revealed his next-level, affect-every-person-on-the-planet code, he awaited a response from any of the reeling attendants.

Because those present owned healthy shares in Broumgard's, he worried about misjudging their inner character. His plan would negatively affect their net worths

The possibility of offending his previous underlings' fundamental beliefs brought equal concern. If one of them left indignant, they could end his ambitions, and jump-start a global catastrophe.

Song's initial statement lacked confidence. Knowing Song, Alex hoped the words were sarcastic.

Each ticking second frayed another nerve.

Looking from face to face, he tried to gauge at least one reaction.

"Don't listen to Song, dear," Denise said as she leaned forward in one of the over-size leather chairs. The woman had lost over a hundred pounds since her Eridu days and openly wore her new found wealth: big-faced Rolex, diamond broach, gaudy rings on each finger. "I, for one, lloovvee the idea."

"You have something to drink in here?" Kole asked as he rose from an ottoman and opened a nearby cabinet, then another. Judging by the broader shoulders and wider thighs, he'd been spending more time in the gym. His teeth looked whiter, too. Other than that, Kole hadn't changed much, except that he now dated actresses, models, and ballerinas.

Alex almost told him which cabinet to check, but Kole was only two doors away from figuring it out.

"Anyone else have a thought?" Kole asked as he found the liquor and filled a glass halfway with Jameson. "I mean, this is heavy stuff. The end of cash, lawlessness."

"Been there, did those," Song said with a dismissive wave.

"Open them pretty brown eyes, sugar," Denise said to Kole. "The world is changing. Broumgard did us good and I'm as loyal as anyone in this room, but they in trouble no matter what we do. This shit going down is bigger than one company. I see what you want to do, Alex. Hand some countries the glass slippers, and others the big F.U. I'm with you though, one hundred percent."

"Way crazy idea, but I way crazy," Song echoed as he stood behind Kole, awaiting a drink.

Kole handed him the one he held then poured another. "We know the big man's in," he said, jutting his head toward Jason Johnson, who read from a Kindle while resting in a chaise lounge.

Alex laughed at how Jason hadn't bothered to lose any weight or change to any perceptible degree. His faded New England Patriot's T-shirt seemed to be a pre-globalization hold over.

296

Jason completed the line he was reading and looked up. "Of course I'm down. I have yet to visit Cosmic Conflict, and my guys and I are waiting to launch a mermaid world that's going to restructure our physiology, create a massive... splash." A blank stare. "I need this pissing match to be over."

"How 'bout you, Sticks?" Kole said before sipping from the aged whiskey.

Carl Wright's white hair sported the same bowl cut. Perhaps the top had thinned. His freckles looked less prominent. He waited a tick, looked about nervously, and then replied, "Alex always has the best ideas."

"That leaves me, and hopefully you all know I'd never miss being a part of this." Kole lifted his drink. "To old times and monumental reunions." He upended the Jameson.

"Live long and prosper," Jason said before returning his eyes to the Kindle.

"Well, I guess it's settled," Alex said. "I know it's a wild idea, and it'll take all of our effort and resources to saturate the globe in the given time frame, but it can be done. And because of the people in this room, it will be."

"I'm actually getting excited," Kole said. "I feel the old juices flowing. It's world changing time for us, yet again."

With his team reassembled, Alex's leadership juices flowed as well. "We've all agreed to commit, and I expect everyone to honor that. Forget our past accomplishments or our current lives. We need to go back to working like impoverished interns."

"So, you want me to smoke hella weed?" Kole said. "And play video games when no one's watching?"

"Show lots of cleavage to increase my odds of sticking around?" asked Denise.

Alex laughed. "I was thinking more like dedicate every minute. Embrace our deadline and exceed it. Things like that."

"Gotcha, boss man," Song said.

"Tomorrow we meet down here at six-thirty, breakfast, then head downtown to the Atrium, where those we trust will be waiting for us. For everything to work smoothly, we need our own people.

Remember—keep the end goal as need-to-know only. I don't want to sound cliché, but the world is counting on us."

In less than a week, his team would be criss-crossing the globe. Song spoke Mandarin and Korean, giving him that part of the world. Jason headed the London Atrium, putting Europe under his domain. Denise could choose between Australia and India, leaving the other English speaking country for Carl. Kole staked a claim on all of South America.

Every nation had talented programmers more than eager to comply with a well-respected Broumgard employee trying to assist the Lobby.

Alex patted Kole's back, shook Song's hand, and left Jason to his book before heading upstairs to his room. As he trekked the glass halls, he thought about his upcoming tour through America—no longer the most divided nation in the world, just one divided country among many. If things went well, he might be able to stop the growing chasm. Perhaps his plan could even stitch the United States, and the globe, back together.

Rosa waited on the sofa, watching the news. Upon seeing him, she smiled, and patted the seat next to her. "How did everything go?"

"Excellent. It's nice to have the old faces in one room again. To see them embrace my plan, despite its controversy, was special."

"Well, you're doing a good thing," she said. "I'm proud and relieved. The world is losing its way. Technology has been luring us away from God or, in softer terms, away from truth, and our humanity for decades. The Lobby amplified that to the millionth power. You stopping the illegal entries, allowing our government to get a grasp on things, to pull in the reins—that's important. I've wanted to have this talk, ask how you really feel about all this. It's comforting to see, by your actions, that you value a position I can support."

Perhaps, but he wondered if she really considered all the possible endings, knew all the details, and some of his selfish thoughts, would she react differently. He wanted to share his true values. And he would share them, when they stopped fluctuating.

"Half of me agrees," he said. "Our government needs control for it to have leverage. Criminals controlling access frightens me. I'm unsure about technology stealing our humanity. Perhaps technology worst attribute is the digital lynchings, but it offers many conveniences."

"Alex, before Roy's death, you'd promised to seek help for an addiction. I want you to consider the possibility that your addiction skews your opinion. I'm positive you're incapable of thinking clearly on this subject. I'm equally positive that smart phones, texting, selfies, and creating the perfect profile pic are a sickness eating away at reality, at God's world, at *our* ability to experience."

"That could be true, Rosa. But who's to tell people what's right; what's healthy?"

Rosa studied him. He read concern on her features, waited for her to say, "The Bible." Instead, she smiled in that sad way that caused him to reflect on his position. Perhaps he *was* cracking up, making poor decisions, and being driven by an unseen force. Rosa squeezed his knee, leaned in and touched her forehead to his.

He exhaled and admitted. "Sometimes I know, am dead certain, that no matter how I approach this Lobby situation, I'm betraying something or someone I love."

"Alex, you're doing the right thing. When it's under wraps, I'll fight to get you into rehab. Once you're clear-headed, you'll see what I'm saying. Just hold on—trust in me—until then."

"You're probably right." *But just as likely, you're wrong.*

"I can't shake this image of mobsters controlling the world with violence and brute force. You'll be stopping that."

Internally, he reflected that his task involved transferring power from Peter to Paul. In a perfect world, power would stay in the people's hands. Could his plan really produce that end?

On the wall converted to a television, President Tanner orated to a crowd. Something he, and every other leader, had been doing daily. Alex pushed aside the magnitude of everything. The idea that his actions might impact the worlds both digital and constructed of matter, frightened him to the point of inactivity. He couldn't stop a percentage of people from hating him. It felt like every decision he made brought a greater viscosity to the atmosphere around him, making it harder and harder to proceed.

He paddled on, hoping for a rescue.

In a light voice, Rosa said, "Anyway, did you have any luck contacting Adisah?"

An undertow pulled on his lower body. Where was Adisah? "No, I have Victor trying hourly. There's a problem with the connection at Eridu. Some message plays when you call, asking to respect his privacy." He licked his lips, closed his eyes, and inhaled deeply.

Alex needed Adisah's counsel. Perhaps he'd expound something enlightening enough to lead Alex down an alternate path? Yet Alex understood the desire for privacy. News vans lined Alex's neighborhood streets for a quarter mile. He couldn't imagine the types of people trying to access the Montana facility.

"Peter stopped by and brought you some papers," Rosa said. "He asked me to make sure you look at them ASAP." She walked to the night stand near their bed.

Alex watched President Tanner wave his enthusiastic end-of-speech wave as he exited the stage.

A montage of tanks, soldiers, and riots led viewers to commercial. He fantasized about what the world would be like a year from now. Traveling down each of his two possible forks brought vastly different endings, neither ideal. One ended in global destruction, the other in a collapse of *his* world.

"Here we go." Rosa handed him an 8x11 envelope.

Accepting the packet from over his shoulder, he held it at arm's length, and stared at the presidential seal emblazoned on the front.

Tension floated away as Rosa sat next to him. Her love kept him sane. Wondering whether that would be enough to see him through this stole hours of his sleep each night.

Tearing off the top of the presidential seal, he pulled out a half-inch-thick stack of paper.

A letter in business format sat on top. A scan of the bottom revealed Tara's signature. He knew she'd been as busy as him over the past few weeks. Eager to learn what consumed her days, he read.

Alex,

I am aware of your current responsibilities in building monitoring stations to insure we control access to the Lobby.

Thank you for what you are doing. Your task may be the most important in a line of monumental assignments. My team has worked closely with our nation's legal representatives, trying to improve our position for the upcoming summit. I write this with President Tanner's consent: the rumors are true—conflict is escalating. Not some tit-for-tat posturing, but a global strife that could escalate to the use of nuclear weapons. It appears that interpretating ethics and morality provides the deadliest game of all.

This letter is to invite you to that global summit, on August 6th.

This meeting will involve leaders and representatives of twenty-seven nations.

The summit will take place inside the Lobby's Honest Meeting Room. We will discuss the future use of the Lobby. Our goal is to remain there until we reach an agreement that staves off military action.

This is only possible if *we* control Lobby access. You must excel at your duty.

You should know that numerous world leaders have requested your presence. They will want to hear your opinion. Stay focused. Stay vigilant. Do not fail.

Sincerely,
Tara Capaldi

He passed the letter to Rosa and scoffed. Meeting in the very machine they delegated over must be the height of irony. But Honest Meeting Room provided immense advantages for something of this magnitude. It guaranteed ease of travel, it negated the debates over who would host.

Honest Meeting Room hovered near the top of the Lobby's most popular worlds. Business transactions consumed the majority of its use, but also custody hearings, negotiations, and discussions of all types, because every statement made passed through a lie detector.

Real-world polygraphs gauged physiological indicators like sweating palms, erratic heartbeats, and/or irregular breathing. All of which could be manipulated with training or because of mental illness, such as adopting false memories. The detector in Honest Meeting Room monitored the brain's electrical signals. Human thoughts sprouted near the center of the mind in the temporal lobe. When a person recalled a fact from memory, they retrieved it from the hippocampus in the bottom middle of the temporal lobe which also stored memory.

When a person fabricated a tale, the brain processed information through circuits in the cerebellum, located in the frontal lobe, where imagination and abstract thinking occur.

This made the deception detector in Honest Meeting Room unbeatable, regardless of training or mental illness. You're either recalling a memory, or creating your own. Follow the current, and know the truth.

Alex perused the remaining documents: other personal letters of support, the probable proposals from various countries, the Health and Wellness outline that Tara had presented to him after Roy's death.

When he reached the end of the attendants list and found Agent Andrew's name absent, a twinge of joy curled the corners of his lips.

Picturing the strange man reading the list two dozen times, fuming to greater degrees each moment he reached the end; each time he read Alex's name and not his, made Alex laugh.

"What is it?" Rosa said.

He dropped the rest of the packet on the table. "I was just laughing at one of Adisah's life maxims: No matter what, the world finds a way to continue down an ever-improving path."

Chapter Forty

Live news challenged the most seasoned anchor person, but the concept intrigued audiences, which boosted viewership. Gimmicks meant little to Rebecca Trevino. She boasted a massive following. Next to Alex Cutler, she might be the most recognizable person on the planet.

Adjusting her posture atop her new chair—one that still smelled of treated leather, on her new set, which covered twice the area of her old one—she scanned the list of off-limit topics for tonight's enigmatic guest, and found it surprisingly short.

"Quiet on the set," someone yelled. She passed the tablet over her shoulder.

Pressing her beige, knee-length skirt flat against her thighs, she looked over at the producer as he counted down. "Five, four, three…" He pantomimed the final two numbers.

When he made a fist and pointed, Rebecca mentally counted one-one thousand, then began, "Hello. Welcome to a special episode of *Inside Today*. My guest tonight is none other than Iranian President, Reza Shah." She faced him, knowing the camera would pan out to encompass both of them in the shot before zooming in on his face as he responded to her first question.

"Thank you for having me," he said in clear English. "It is my pleasure to be with you."

"With fourteen days until the global summit that will decide the future of the Lobby—and many speculate, society as we know it as well—I imagine your administration must be very busy."

"Yes. Very busy."

"I understand you have declined your invitation to attend the summit. Can you tell me about that decision, and where the Iranian people stand on this divisive topic?"

"I can tell you, first, that the Iranian people are not divided. We are united as a people, and as a nation, in direct opposition to that device.

"I, and other noble leaders, will not attend, for there is nothing to discuss. We have formed our own thirteen nation coalition, one that your media neglects. We are focusing on our salat prayers, asking Allah the Benevolent for guidance, pleading with him to impart wisdom into the hearts, and sensibilities into the minds, of these New Age Axis and Allies.

"They must understand: God's world has no place for an invention devised to tempt man into the gravest of all sins."

Rebecca nodded somberly, as if she didn't experience a tingle with each rise in the death trip total. "There is much speculation that the nations you labeled the New Age Axis and Allies will reach a compromise. A deal that could include the Eastern nations promising their citizens that if they live honorable, beneficial lives, they'll receive eternal retirement as their reward. And that the West will not interfere with this practice as long as strict procedures are in place, including the denial of Lobby access to citizens from specific nations. Some even suggest that Atriums will reopen throughout the United States and its Western allies."

A frown creased the president's face. "That would be most unfortunate."

Rebecca appreciated the twinkle of conviction in his eye. "However, ample evidence exists that both sides have increased their military readiness, should a compromise become unachievable." Pausing, she prepared to lob her bombshell. "Would you say the Middle Eastern coalition, like the coalitions in the East and West, is willing to compromise to avoid war?"

The president adjusted himself. Her arm hairs reached for the skies. If her research proved correct, this would be the mega answer—the one that the estimated two hundred and forty million viewers had tuned in to see.

Pursing his lips as he shook his head slowly, he answered, "There can be no compromise with Satan."

Internally, Rebecca screamed for joy. Outwardly, she remained stoic. That line would air on every station for the next two weeks.

"You're saying these thirteen military powers are united and ready to use force if the Lobby is allowed to operate?"

"I am saying that we are praying for a peaceful resolution. We have yet to identify any nation as an enemy of God. Any actions in the near future will reflect the true views of the two billion outraged Muslims around the world who, along with our Christian brothers, want to eradicate a machine that lures souls, which are otherwise destined for paradise, into a false platform of devilish design."

The camera stayed on him for a full six seconds, then panned out.

"Thank you for your candor, President Shah, but to be clear, you are saying that the Middle Eastern coalition, comprised of thirteen powerful countries, will target buildings—even if they sit on the sovereign soil of peaceful nations—in pursuit of eradicating the Lobby?"

He folded his hands in his lap, straightened his spine, and said, "We shall do everything in our power to assist in the destruction of each wire and every bolt that threatens the world Allah the Righteous has bestowed upon his children."

With that, they went to a commercial, during which time Rebecca Trevino envisioned herself going onstage to claim her Pulitzer in journalism.

Chapter Forty-One

The United States military's enlistment number hovered around one point four million. Only seven individuals, out of that vast number of soldiers were four-star army generals. Having such an important figure visit you and your organization should have brought the highest honors to Colonel Alan Cox of the Lord's Thorn. Instead, he felt defeated.

After securing Eridu, Alan asked after his protégé, Tim Vanderhart. Thirty hours passed until they confirmed his death. Alan had known within ten minutes. Had Tim survived, he'd have been at Alan's heel, hollering about the thrill of conquest. Alan had intended to boost that excitement with a bump in rank, which would have granted Tim access to the meeting just wrapping up. Witnessing two generals shake hands could have crossed off a goal on Tim's bucket list, if he'd have lived to age twenty.

Alan exhaled as he watched US Army General Koster enter the elevator and exit the gargantuan condo occupying La Berce's top floors.

General Trieu of the Lord's Thorn had dismissed the other colonels and asked Alan to stay behind. As their honored guest descended, Trieu strutted back, beaming.

"Can you believe all that?" He passed over one of the dark-stained wooden bridges throughout the home. The water that used to run underneath had been drained long ago, leaving a dry bed. Each step over the bridge echoed, amplifying the emptiness.

Alan had spent his life in Northern Michigan, where home prices hovered around seventy thousand dollars. Much better than Detroit's ghettos, where a once-loved brick home could be purchased for two-thousand bucks. Where five grand got you the best home on the block. Where sometimes the city paid you a hundred dollars to take a home, if you promised to make it livable.

He imagined this cavernous marvel of earth-smelling wood carried a value triple that of entire Detroit neighborhoods, and probably cost more than entire square miles of property around the NMCD old clubhouse property.

"You're a smart man, Alan," Trieu said as he passed him and peered out the window, no doubt to savor every glimpse of the four-star general's departure. "You tell me—why did I ask you of all people to stay behind?"

Alan snorted. He thought he'd dread this. Instead, relief accompanied his expected termination. He'd been insubordinate, bordering on mutinous, since their landing, but as the saying went, "life off the farm wasn't all song, dance, and long legs."

"To relieve me of my duty?" he said.

Trieu's eyes' glimmered. "No, sir. I want to promote you. Hand us each a new star, courtesy of General Koster."

A military Humvee drove beneath them. From this height, it resembled a crab scurrying across a beach. Their army friend had choppered in various military equipment: high-density receivers to allow excellent satellite relays; crates with M4A1s and AR-15s and one with rocket-propelled grenades; containers of leisure items for the officers; low-temperature clothing; night-vision goggles; climbing gear diverse enough to allow multiple teams to operate in any region—a bountiful reward for a successful mission.

Eridu teemed with activity. The women and children had arrived two days ago. The vehicles that brought them filled the Atrium parking lot and desert beyond the airport. And though most of the helicopters had survived the assault, most of them had been returned to their original owners.

Due to the volume of new arrivals, families were still locating loved ones. Once done, they were assigned lodging at the compound's east end.

It disturbed Alan that none of them asked where the previous residents—whose photos decorated the walls and whose clothes filled the dressers—had gone.

Alan didn't want a promotion but assumed if he refused, he'd die. Trieu's first order after touching down at Eridu—to shoot anyone who moved—revealed the man's heart.

Each night since the takeaway Alan feared waking to a blade slitting open his throat. Without Tim to mold, and with having ingested a lifetime worth of nightmares over the past week, Alan hardly gave a shit.

"You still with me?" Trieu asked. "No ideas as to why I'd want that?"

Alan shook his head.

"You've opposed nearly every decision we've made here."

Easiest thing I've ever done, Alan thought. Instead of replying, he worked his jaw to one side, dug his tongue into an upper molar.

"Yet you don't vocalize your disapproval. You haven't tried to organize a revolt."

"Perhaps I don't disapprove," he said with causticity.

"Ah, but you do, Alan. We both know it. But you have impeccable respect for the chain of command."

"Unfortunately."

General Trieu swiveled his body, taking in his burly guest. "You broke Verhultst's nose. Fractured his eye orbital." He looked back out the mega window. "What was he doing? Harassing one of the female captives?"

"Raping."

"I guess that's applicable." Trieu inspected Alan's reflection in the window. "Despite you being one against three, you helped that woman because you're a good man. It earned you major respect around here."

"Lot of good it did her."

Trieu shrugged. "War's a nasty business. In this situation, we can't let anyone go. Can't afford to take care of them, risk someone slipping off. Poisoning their food was a mercy."

309

Alan inhaled through his nose. The general might be better trained, but Alan was twenty years his junior and sixty pounds heavier. Alan experienced a flash of clutching the back of the man's neck, and bashing his face into the glass before them, to see if he found death by severe head trauma a mercy.

"You remember walking into that room on the first day?" Trieu said.

Alan flinched. They'd entered the upper-level access room together on the first day. He'd never forget the sights, or the smell. Slumped bodies occupied dozens of chairs. Three times that number were strewn on the floor, like discarded garbage. Enough piss pooled on the floor to constitute a pond.

"That's what we're fighting here, Alan. It's uglier than my tough decisions. It's the Devil's work."

Alan nodded. He'd led the volunteers who had hauled away the corpses.

Those twenty-four hours passed in a haze. Fill the elevator with human bodies, and send it down. After each return, they'd wash it out, get that floor spotless, then dirty it again. For what?

Unconsciously, they'd saved removing the children for last. Thirty-two of them. Twelve no older than nine. The youngest, a toddler, died with a look of absolute horror on his face. A single gunshot wound punctuated his chest.

"You a New Testament guy, or an Old?" Trieu asked.

Alan had dyslexia, so had never read either. He knew God existed. He knew that more and more of the world was being cast under some spell of MTV stupidity, short skirts, and society as a hive-mind. He knew big-name pharmaceuticals were drugging a generation to make them dependent, so those in control could attain dominance.

Trieu continued, "The Old Testament is all that matters. Ain't no substance to the New. It's passive bullshit about turning cheeks. Ain't no mention of God. How crazy is that? Just some guy going around talking to people, tempting them to go against everything said in the first half of the Bible."

In the distance, the Humvee stopped near a helicopter, and specks boarded the awaiting transport.

310

"If you love Jesus, I'm not going to knock it, but he ain't God. It don't say that on 'nan one of them pages. God tells us the Devil'll strike, and it's up to us to douse his fire." He paused, then said, "Do you have any doubts this machine is Satan's minion?"

The memory of lifting that young boy off the cold floor remained fresh. The kid had been chucked aside with such disregard that he'd landed on his face, smashing his nose almost flat to one side. The boy's tight, well-kept afro showed his pride in appearance, which meant pride in self, and often in others. He might have been a good-looking kid, had rigor mortis not molded that final look of death into place.

He pictured Tim's face battered and distorted like that and inhaled. The one solace of Tim's death: he could move on, avoid being siphoned into a godless machine.

"No, I have no doubts. It's a soulless evil devised to destroy everything good and pure in our world."

"That's right. Yet you think many of my decisions have been... harsh."

Alan scoffed. "They could have been handled with more compassion, yes."

"That's why you have to be our second in command."

Alan focused on his own haggard reflection, as the helicopter blades in the distance started to spin. With a heavy beard, a mustache grown to cover both lips, and thick hair, he looked like the last survivor of a lost clan.

"Between you and me, we have unwavering loyalty from every man on this compound. This thing's just beginning. We have a short time to train until this international summit decides the fate of every breathing body on this planet.

"If what General Koster just said is true, America is willing to compromise her values. They'll discard God's laws. Thankfully, some in the military will protect our future. They intend to take the fight to foreign soil, and start a war, regardless of commands. As they lay waste to the enemy, the Lord's Thorn must cleanse our homeland.

"We have our targets, their addresses, and the men. We have technical support, the explosives, and the financing. What we need is

311

leadership." Turning to face Alan, he extended his hand as if to shake. "I know you're still ready to lay down your life in the pursuit of destroying this great evil. Be the check that balances me."

Alan looked at the hand. He couldn't support General Trieu's actions, but they lived in a fallen world. Alan's only certainty was that the Lobby brought wickedness. "As long as in that process, we don't become the monsters we intend to defeat."

"Fair enough. But you accept that our hands must get bloody."

Alan clasped and squeezed his general's hand. "Absolutely."

Chapter Forty-Two

Examining himself in a section of his bedroom wall that was temporarily converted to a mirror, Alex admired his look: well-groomed hair styled with Rosa's supervision, a coal-black suit. Respectable. His true opposite.

When thinking of the acts he'd put in motion over the past three weeks, Alex was eighty-twenty. Eighty percent crippled with depression, twenty percent filled with exhilaration; both pertained to his future. The disproportionate, fluctuating emotions left him feeling woozy, like a hypnotized man standing on an automated walkway that would transport him through the next four hours, regardless of his desire to step off or turn around.

Attending the summit as a representation of knowledge and confidence, his suit presented a side of him he was unsure existed. Embracing that he had been, *was* a decent person, dragged the eighty-twenty skew toward a complete meltdown. Having once read that a smile blocked melancholy, he forced his mouth to upturn. It somewhat helped.

Rosa spent most of the morning at her preferred salon. For the past hour she'd been in the bathroom, with the occasional dart to the closet for this or that.

The inner him might dislike what his appearance portrayed, but as he rotated for peripheral views, he could see this Alex being photographed on the red carpet and plastered in major magazines. He sniffled and thought about his first magazine cover, *Computer World*. He was just as uncertain today as then.

By this time tomorrow, Alex would cover thousands of magazines, newspapers, and webpages. He hoped the captions would read *Alex Cutler, Catalyst of Peace*. But he feared many would be labeled *Alex Cutler, Assistant to Tyranny*.

This big-ticket event lacked the glitz of a red-carpet gala. However, the global summit would provide more drama than anything the most talented fiction writer in Hollywood could sensationalize.

Everyone with access to media would be transfixed by their screens until the summit concluded. Everyone would soon learn if their nation, and by proxy, their loved ones, would be plunged into war.

Throughout the previous weeks, Alex had traversed the United States. In each major city, he employed his resources to gather the desired network. His station gained him access to any office, his presence garnered attention, and the belief he showed for his current work instilled dedication.

Through these meetings—often with well-connected individuals—and encrypted updates from Luke Dean, Alex learned of many nefarious plans in incubation. Each one compelled him to go a little further.

In spite of receiving continued silence from every attempt to contact his mentor, the rumors of Adisah's murder and Eridu being hijacked by an American-born terror organization threatened to stunt him with despair. Like with his youth, the heavy workload buried the pain.

Additional verified information said a US Army general planned terrorist acts against Atriums on foreign soil.
Alex believed that he, and his team, presented the only scenario for thwarting those plots and avoiding World War III, a conflict to dwarf all prior.

His strategy disturbed him and conflicted on inner, outer, and social levels. He typically avoided actions on such a grand scale. Lying to people hurt, he kept doing it, and the wheels kept turning. With his network growing exponentially, momentum reached an avalanche—and that force would soon meet an immovable object.

Stepping out of the bathroom, Rosa commanded an overhead light to shine on her. "How do I look?"

314

Taking her in, his eyebrows raised of their own volition. Despite the worry regarding his finale's implication, he swelled with affection toward Rosa. If he deserved to cover a magazine, she should wallpaper newsstands. She wore a hip-hugging black dress that showed off the hours she dedicated daily to her fitness. A diamond necklace glittered around her neck, and a matching bracelet cast flecks of light on the wall and floor. But neither of those accessories outshined the beauty of her face—the softness of her skin, the fullness of her lips. Her brown eyes beamed as if polished. Her satiny, dark hair had a slight curl and bounced against her shoulder.

A lump caught in his throat when he thought of all she might endure because of his actions. She deserved a life free from strife. Knowing such a life didn't exist pained him.

"That good, huh?" she said.

"You are the most beautiful woman in the world," he said honestly. He strode over, and kissed her passionately.

After a half-minute of mutual enjoyment, she nudged him away. Her smile threatened to pull him in for more, but she laid her palms on his chest and shook her head.

"Did you know there's a presidential motorcade waiting for us?"

"You deserve nothing less."

"Look at the big charmer." She blushed, and reexamined herself in the mirror. "If only all the death threats didn't necessitate my chariot being bomb-proof."

Turning her, he wrapped his arms around her waist. With their stomachs pressed together, his weight gain was emphasized. He'd been knocking out two to four Oreo package a day.

"Everyone of those threats are directed at me. Without me in the picture, you're perfectly safe."

She put her hands on his forearms. "They want a piece of you, they're going to have to go through me." Another grin, and she pried his hands off, smoothed the wrinkles from her dress.

The thought that some psycho might agree with her constantly troubled him. He kissed her neck and stepped away, dabbing a tear from his eye.

"It is ten minutes to four," Victor announced, per Rosa's instructions.

Along with three military officials from the West Coast, Alex would log into the Lobby at five-thirty from the Los Angeles Atrium and rendezvous with the rest of their delegation by using President Tanner as a reference.

Alex knew that America's committee members had been cramming all day, every day, for the past few weeks on what to say to who, on the cultural differences for displaying respect, but he'd been on his own mission, to save humanity.

Last night was his first night home in nearly a month, leaving him no time to do the one thing he'd hoped to do: update Rosa on his plan's intricate details and the reasoning behind them, and attempt to convince her of the plan's benefits.

On the flight home, he'd penned a letter, figuring he could revise it a time or two and then read it aloud to her.

That opportunity never presented itself.

Swallowing his regret, he focused on the task at hand. In an hour and a half, she'd have her explanation.   Hopefully, he'd be viewed as the genius who averted what analysts predicted as a guaranteed global conflict, in every nation and city.

Alex stared at the back wall, viewing the rolling surf of a private Caribbean beach: a large sun in the distance, crystal blue waters, white sand. Illusion or not, it provided the soothing effect Rosa intended.

"We'll get there," she said, sidling up to him in hers, taking his hand, and staring at the twelve-by-ninety-foot screen.

Dabbing another tear, he thought, *We're in so much danger, and she has no idea.*

Adisah had been, at best, incommunicado for a month, and the possibility of his murder, however unpleasant, loomed. If he'd been killed in spite of the cult-like following of ex-military security forces around him, what chance did Alex and Rosa stand?

As Alex thought about the approaching events, Rosa squeezed his hand. After another minute or two, they separated and walked to the elevator.

As soon as the doors opened to Legion's main floor, he saw the security presence. Professional types, wearing suits, earpieces—crack shots who emptied clips into center mass.

Six men occupied the space from the elevator to the front door. As the couple passed them, they fell in behind.

Outside, the real weather appeared: a light drizzle, clouds, suffocating humidity. More than unusual for Los Angeles in the summer. But these times were more than unusual.

A pair of helicopters hovered overhead. Men with dark sunglasses and rain slickers scanned everything in sight. Thanks to Luke, Alex knew that military vehicles filled with soldiers waited nearby, that snipers manned roofs, and that a dedicated satellite would monitor the entire trip.

They passed by foot-thick, reinforced steel doors to enter the limousine. Alex had learned the doors could withstand a direct hit from a rocket-propelled grenade.

Inside, the small, muted television flickered with activity. The news broadcasted a crowd of Lobby protestors, accentuating their emotion with a constant jostling. Judging from the surrounding architecture and vehicles, Europe was hosting this particular skirmish.

Retrieving the remote, Rosa turned off the monitor. "Seeing that doesn't help."

Staring at the blank screen, Alex wondered if his plan and all the extreme work it involved would have the positive outcome he imagined, or if he'd just doomed humankind.

"Mr. Cutler?" Luke's voice sounded through an intercom in the vehicle. Alex pressed the button to reply to his head of security, who was riding in the passenger seat.

"Yes?"

"You might want to watch channel seventeen, a local station with coverage around the Los Angeles Atrium."

Rosa picked up the remote, held it away from Alex, then turned on the TV.

Though interested, he continued to stare out his window.

317

They had chosen a route through a residential neighborhood. Two police motorcycles led and trailed the motorcade. Their blue-and-red lights swirled, but no siren sounded. The nine-vehicle convoy must have presented quite a spectacle when viewed from a living room couch.

Rosa sucked in breath between her teeth, drawing his attention to the television.

The amount of people packed in close made Alex think an angry mob was storming a warehouse that held the depleting cure of a killer virus.

Aerial shots showed heavy rain. Thousands of people littered the light-industrial area surrounding the Los Angeles Atrium, a place he'd grown so familiar with. The picket signs were split between support and calls for the Lobby's annihilation.

The parking lot remained empty, yet seeing it without vehicles seemed nearly as strange as the demonstrators. Police and military officers in full riot gear manned wooden barriers along the parking lot's exterior, shoving back the swell of bodies.

More sophisticated barriers were erected fifty yards in. The officers protecting that area held rifles. Hopefully, they'd be loaded with tear gas and rubber pellets, but the live stuff—ammunition for killing—would be close at hand.

The armored limousine slowed in the middle of a side street and halted. Alex surveyed each window view. Wondering why they had stopped?

Behind him, two SUVs formed a *V* by parking their noses together to block the road.

"Mr. Cutler?" Luke said over the intercom.

Alex attempted to peer out the windshield, but the car's length prevented him.

"Do you see something?" Rosa asked.

"Mr. Cutler," Luke said, "they've decided to bring you and Mrs. Cutler in by air. The upcoming roadways are congested and unsafe."

A final glance at the news broadcast ended any thoughts of opposing the suggestion. The camera panned out, granting an expanded view. Tents, barrel fires, booths—the scene reminded Alex of a Third World refugee camp. Except outrage, anger, and defiance, not necessity, bound those present.

Turning off the television, Rosa stated, "I hope this helicopter has a closed cabin. I spent four hours on my hair." Her smile faded before it fully formed.

A squadron of men rushed to the limousine and stood sentry around it, waiting for the black helicopter, which had a sealed cabin, to touch down.

The limousine doors on both sides opened simultaneously. One team attended to Alex, the other to Rosa. With force just short of a yank, they pulled him out, bent him forward at the waist, and huddled around him as if snipers lurked behind the windows of the surrounding suburban homes.

During liftoff, he noticed that many of the neighborhood residents had exited their homes, stood in driveways or on front lawns. Alex couldn't shake the scary truth. According to the math, at least one of those people hated him.

The thought of being that paranoid—and the danger threatened Rosa—again reminded him of past invitations from Dr. Brad Finder, who lived on his own island off the coast of Argentina. But Alex knew that wouldn't work. If insurgents could root out Adisah, relocating was only a temporary fix.

Seeing Rosa patting her hair, Alex gave her a thumbs up as to its perfection, and with the exception of one side puffed out two inches, and fifty strands seemingly zapped with electricity, he was telling the truth.

Approaching the mob revealed it stretched ten times farther than the news had shown. A half-mile separated Alex from the edge of the bedlam, yet even directly beneath them, in a residential area, groups of people camped out.

The passing helicopters magnetized faces, drawing people from smoking grills, car windows, and huddles. Umbrellas tipped like dominoes. Arms waved, and plastic-wrapped signs shook up and down and from side to side. Driving through that would have been impossible.

319

A *tink* sounded against the craft's underbelly. The helicopter jerked upward, climbing at a steep angle.

A security officer across from Alex held his finger to his ear, then leaned forward. "Someone took a potshot at us. Small arms can't penetrate our armored hull, but we're increasing altitude as a precaution."

The new elevation exposed more of the crowd, and the downpour. Judging by the amount of rain, the Los Angeles Atrium was its epicenter. Once they centered over the parking lot near the main door, they eased onto the pavement. The helicopter landing on the asphalt elevated his anxiety. It made today and his actions real.

Alex and Rosa had spent enough time with security details that they knew to remain seated until instructed otherwise. Two groups of soldiers rushed from the Atrium. A few carried bulletproof shields. They formed a horseshoe on both sides of the craft, and whether by design or bad luck, they'd landed where Rosa had to climb out on the far side, closest to the protestors.

Indoors, Alex rose to his full height and found himself in a sea of suits and military uniforms.

Rosa led him by the hand to a nearby bench.

Before he gathered the strength to reach for her letter and read the important words, she said, "Big day, huh?"

He hesitated.

"You're going to be okay, Alex. It's all so awful. But you know what? You might end up being a man historians talk about for generations?"

Over the past few weeks, that idea had increasingly crept into his thoughts. If the world survived, would his actions be considered noble or heinous? Would he be a liberator or an enslaver? In his unrecognized arrogance, he'd never thought about how the world would view his loyal, supportive wife. Perhaps because that one was easy: "I'm not sure what future historians will say about me," he said, "but all mentions of you will start with benevolence, and philanthropy."

Her face lightened, but her lips frowned, as if anchored by inner sorrow. She'd seen his restlessness, weight gain, and irritability.

"I know this has been a whirlwind," she said. "I just hope when it's done, we can get away for a while."

He reached for the envelope.

"Mr. Cutler?" a man in a navy blue uniform said. The many medals on his chest clanked with each movement, like a tambourine of pride. A man in a designer suit waited behind him. Alex first thought of the envelope. He should shove the envelope into Rosa's hand, but he wanted to read it aloud.

"Excuse me, ma'am." The officer said to Rosa. Then, to Alex, "Mr. Cutler?"

"Yes."

"I'm Colonel Emelander. A room full of people is waiting for you. If you'll excuse us, ma'am, it's urgent that we brief your husband."

"I understand," she stood, and looked Alex over.

He wasn't ready. He had so much to say—to her, about her, about him, about the world and the Lobby, and his work these past weeks.

Leaning over, she kissed him, and despite his plan's uncertainty, the soft touch of her lips scattered his worry—he'd always have her love.

He exhaled, forced the letter back into his pocket. At least he'd written it all down. He appreciated that, because after this meeting, no matter how it went, the world would be a different place.

Chapter Forty-Three

The men in suits had requested Alex's presence, but his summons lacked pragmatism; it was simply a display of power. Thank you for your great contribution. Thank you for allowing me to help. Did everything go as you planned?   Yes. Were there any problems we should know about? Umm…no.

To these bureaucratic men of prominence, Alex was a computer nerd, like thousands of others. He received a job, and had completed it. He held no official title, knew nothing of politics, and should have no part in the negotiations. To many, his involvement was just them coddling an arrogant, rich man.

This situation was a story as ancient as time. These men were the old hats, unable to accept how fast the world shifted. In 1966, Gordon Moore, who later went on to found Intel, proposed Moore's law, which stated that, in the modern era, technology doubled every eighteen months. That law itself had become outdated. Today's technology doubled in bursts. Crackling explosions of progress detonating simultaneously from multiple launch points. Science, medicine, space, nanites—the world was constantly swelling with advancements. One day, perhaps soon, that tension would burst and precipitate a reset.

Alex believed that society must be governed with limited oversight, particularly the Lobby. Don't take from others. That could be the lone law. Searching for criminals in every unfortunate act, needing to terminate after lost profits, war—all were ridiculous.

Any war fought over the Lobby involved controlling it. That understanding motivated Alex.

Ten minutes into his summons, he learned his attendance at the summit hadn't been a request by the so-called New Age Allies—his team—but rather a demand from the other side. The Eastern world valued his input. Alex knew Sung Yi, the monk, had been expounding Alex's greatness for weeks. Despite the absurdity of the monk's sermons, Alex felt proud that his unexpected contribution offered the best chance for a peaceful resolution.

At the appropriate time, the group moved to the elevators and waited for transport to the access rooms. He stood in the back, allowed the others to board first—some of whom had probably forgotten he was with them.

Standing with a group of analysts, he listened to them explain that if the East and West reached a compromise, the Middle East would bow out with nothing more than threats. That, or it would be destroyed. The Middle East nations maintained impressive armies, when compared to one another, but the powerhouses of the world were still Japan, Great Britain, China, Russia, and the United States. Any one of them could battle, and possibly defeat, a Middle Eastern coalition. The analysts trivialized the seeming inevitability of mass casualties, which turned Alex's stomach.

Upstairs, the smile of a young woman acted as a beacon. Gravitating toward her, he allowed himself to be guided to an access room. Once inside, the closed door sealed off the chatter.

"What's your take on all of this?" he asked.

"Me?" She glanced away from the control panel, looked him up and down as he sat. "I think... what you have built is a wonderful escape." She honed in on the timer and initiated its thirty-second countdown with an extravagant push of the button. "But it has become... uncontrollable. You people will figure it out, but give me all the power...and I would shut it down. Destroy it all." She shrugged.

Her candor surprised him into silence. He had hoped for a reply that aligned with his actions.

"Sorry." She gave a half-smile. "But you asked."

That I did, he thought as the timer hit five, four, three...

Popping into the Lobby decompressed his chest, and lightened his entire aura. *Had I actually harbored that much tension?* The expulsion of stress was like being pulled from a tar pit. He kicked a leg, rotated an arm, and smirked at the notion that people wanted to destroy this.

Taking a deep breath, he surveyed his white surrounding. Instead of the calming tranquility he expected, his yelped in fright. The remaining CO_2 leaked out of him in a slow stream. His vision blurred, then returned. He'd never seen anything like this, in the Lobby.

People—strangers not invited to the summit—were clustered close. They stretched for miles, talking in low tones.

Alex couldn't help but wonder if he was seeing an optical illusion? Turning to face the opposite side, he found the same sight. Innumerable people of all races, but heavily Asian in appearance, stretched into infinity. *Have I entered the mirror room in a loony-bin funhouse?*

A message sprung to life before him. President Tanner sought Alex's permission to come to his location.   Absentmindedly, he okayed the request.

The president appeared a few feet away. After locating Alex, he stared beyond him with wide eyes and a craning neck. Three inches taller than Alex, the president's view probably encompassed even more people.

The hushed voices of the crowd carried an ominous feel. With a population a ten-thousandth of the visitor present, the Lobby echoed with boisterous talks and jeers, vacationer excited about their upcoming experience. The loudest sounds in this populated room were the nervous queries coming from the New Age Allies, as they appeared near him. One voice, considerably louder than the rest, attempted to gain control by starting a roll call.

Each barked name drew more of the crowd's attention. People whispered, as they studied the continuing manifestation of politicians and officers around the president.

Alex heard his name mumbled more than once in the crowd and felt a fright so deep, pertaining to his global work, that it threatened to morph into madness. He could have avoided this moment, these people's presence, a dozen times over. Standing here, with his deed done, he worried that a malevolent force had guided him to this fate.

The endless crowd formed rows and focused on the congregation. They padded silently toward him.

"Alex Cutler."

He turned toward the President of the United States, who wore an impeccable suit with a red and white tie. The president's voice remained steady, but with an undercurrent of concern. "Do you have any idea who all these people are, and what they want?"

At the mention of Alex's name, the crowd zeroed in on him, and the chatter expanded. The mass shuffled closer, like an army of dazed zombies.

"That's him."

"Alex Cutler is here."

"He's arrived."

"Thank you, Alex."

"Thank you, Mr. Cutler."

Similar sentiments created a ripple effect in both directions. The hairs on Alex's neck stood on end.

As people ventured into his personal space, Alex reacted. "Employee command, Alex Cutler. Space, thirty feet, forward direction, full width." Upon completion of his order, the wall of people slid backward as if they stood on a patch of ice and were pushed by an invisible plow.

The shouts of gratitude and praise increased, all directed at Alex. The voices reached a roar.

"Employee command, Alex Cutler. Volume decrease, fifty percent."

The sounds muted.

"A little help, please, Mr. Cutler."

Turning, he found the mob engulfing the president and his men. A few of the entourage who were familiar with Lobby commands had evoked their ten feet of personal space, but lacking Broumgard managerial status, that limited their capabilities.

At the opposite edge, Alex stretched out his arms, repeated his space command, and granted the group thirty feet of space on that side. Once done, he overrode the personal space commands, so their party members could rejoin as a group.

Having sufficient area between them and the surrounding mob allowed everyone to catch their breath, and compose themselves.

"Well done, Mr. Cutler," the president said, speaking loud enough to be heard above the polite chaos. "Now, do you have any idea who these people are, or why they're here?"

"These are the sick freaks," a man in military accoutrements said as he strode closer. "The suicidal nutjobs from around the globe."

"No, it can't be," a man with gray hair, who looked somewhat familiar to Alex, said. "There's way too many for that. This is like an entire city."

"Why are they here?" asked another.

"It's a sad world we inhabit. Wouldn't you say, Mr. Cutler?" President Tanner said.

Alex surveyed the crowd. Thousands, tens of thousands, possibly more?

Had this many people dedicated their future to the Lobby?

Since he hadn't included the word "personal" in his command of thirty feet, the space started from where he'd previously stood, creating a flat wall of bodies. He crept over to an Asian woman in khaki pants and a teal blouse.

Noticing Alex, she slowly dropped to her knees, bowed her head, and stretched out her hand.

A wave of euphoria paused Alex.

"Please stand," he reached down to assist her.

She rose bashfully, glancing left and right. A man next to her sunk to his knees and placed his head on the white.

"What are you doing here?" Alex asked the woman. To the man, he said, "No, please stand."

The man ignored him. People to both sides of the man followed suit, setting off a chain reaction—a wave of people dropping in supplication.

326

"What is this horseshit?" The military man blurred by and forcefully lifted the first kneeling man.

The man allowed himself to be pulled up, but hung loosely. As soon as the military man released him, he dropped back down.

"Stop this nonsense, you demented freaks."

"It's okay, Don," the president said.

"No, it is not, Mr. President," the military man said as he yanked a petite woman up. She kept her head bowed and dropped back down when released. "Make these freaks stand up," he yelled at Alex.

"Don, leave it alone," the president said. He scanned the miles of people falling like dominoes. "Let's…let's get on with this. Mr. Cutler, are you ready? Our Japanese counterparts are excited about your participation."

Enthralled by the woman's fascination with him, the trust and love on her face, Alex barely heard the man. Releasing her hand, he insisted that she stay standing, and bent to lift the man next to her, the one next to him, then another one beyond. Four uplifted people later, the process of people kneeling reversed. The people in the front rose on their own, the people behind followed suit.

"I'm sure you've heard of their prophet, Sung Yi," the president said a little louder.

Alex didn't reply. Instead, he looked past the president, guestimating how many miles the hall would extend if a hundred thousand people populated it.

"He'll be in attendance today," the president continued. "He's basically the opposition leader. And despite the misconception, they view you as ours. I pray we can use that to our advantage, persuade them to agree to our fair terms."

"Mr. President, we should get going," a short woman said.

"Sung Yi has been preaching all month that on this day, you'll provide answers to solve our differences," the president said. "What do you think, Mr. Cutler? Are you going to push our agenda, or are you keeping an alternate answer up your sleeve?"

Alex smiled as wonder mixed with shame, as a lifetime of uncertainty and self-conscious thoughts floated from his person. He pushed aside regret, and replaced it with hope. "I do, Mr. President."

"Sir, we need to go."

The president turned to the woman, but he seemed to ponder Alex's words.

"It should be you who opens the door, Mr. President," the woman added.

The president nodded. "World select, Honest Meeting Room, Seventeen Seventy-Six."

A door appeared twenty-five feet from where the president stood.

He looked expectantly at Alex. "Well, are you going to share this plan of yours before we head in, or just spring it on us?"

This was Alex's moment, a resetting of his life. He affirmed his resolve and spoke, "I won't be attending your meeting."

A million fears fluttered off of him. The universe seemed to brighten. He smote his anxiety and uncertainty.

The president furrowed his brow.

"Whatever game you think you're playing," the military official said, "You can bet—"

"Silence aggressor," Alex said. A green halo displayed above the military man, and when Alex confirmed him as the intended target, the man's voice cut off mid-gripe.

The president looked at the man and then back at Alex. "What do you think you're doing?"

"I'm bowing out, my friend. Relinquishing your, and everyone else's, authority over me."

"That's not possible," the president said in his most commanding tone, but he swallowed twice before adding. "You will attend this summit as our ally or face imprisonment."

"I'm afraid not," Alex smirked. "I'm out of your world. The truth is, you're standing in mine."

The president shook his head. "You couldn't have harmed yourself after entering. We've had eyes on you since you exited Legion, so whatever you were planning, it's not going to happen."

Perhaps the president believed himself to sound authoritative, but his words rang hollow to Alex. He pitied the man. In the Lobby, President Tanner was just another visitor. Alex's life of being threatened and labeled, being told what was right and what was wrong and what he should believe, had ended.

"Time-release cyanide," Alex said. "It won't kick in for another ten minutes or so, but there's no stopping it. I'm free, Mr. Tanner."

The man in the military uniform looked ready to burst. The veins in his neck bulged.

Alex resisted an urge to laugh. He was finished with cruelty—receiving or giving. With a conciliatory frown to the president, he shrugged.

"We don't need him, Mr. President," the woman said. She eyed Alex, and he detected something in her gaze. Envy? "We must go," she added.

He ignored the comments of him being a traitor, or worse. This was his rise to power. His resurrection. Alex's inner child wondered how these complainers would like his other surprises.

"I still must insist that you accompany us," the president said.

Alex nodded sympathetically. "Employee command, Alex Cutler. Corral participants of Honest Meeting Room Seventeen Seventy-Six, exclude self, move to entrance."

At once, and from all angles, the congregation of summit attendants slid along the white toward the awaiting portal, ending as a huddle near the world entrance.

He wouldn't be attending their conference, living their rules, or swallowing their lies. For the first time, he considered Sung Yi a true prophet, and felt remorse that they had never met.

Someday, he thought as he smiled. After all, he had eternity.

Using one final command, he silenced the grumbling crew, knowing that once they entered their world, his restrictions on their speech and movement would fall away.

They would get over what Alex had done.

He faced the swell of people who, having risen, had watched everything in awe.

Taking the closest woman by the hand, and wanting to converse a while before deciding how to spend his first lifetime, he led her through the parting crowd.

People summoned worlds and vanished. Others followed Alex Cutler, the defacto creator of the Lobby.

Chapter Forty-Four

Sitting on the bench where Alex had left her an hour prior, Rosa watched the busy people pass her by as if she were a shade. Having grown accustomed to the indifference, it surprised her when a man, whom she'd pegged as working for the secret service, approached her.

"Rosa Cutler?"

"Yes." She adjusted her posture.

"This is for you." He handed her an envelope, and once it was in her grip, he disappeared into the wash of activity.

She examined the envelope from all sides. Sealed. Normal white. Her name written in ink. Alex's handwriting.

Her hands trembled as she tore open the envelope.

Quickly unfolding the letter, she made it through the first sentence before she released the paper, covered her face, and sobbed.

Chapter Forty-Five

From the office of his Victorian home, General Koster stared through the rain at his well-manicured lawn. The faded wooden playset and sandbox always caused him to question his parenting—ask why he counted himself lucky to see his grandchildren twice per year. Behind the play area, a patch of Indian laurels and a lone queen palm created a natural blockade, granting privacy. Rain dived at a forty-five degree angle, and pelted the pane of glass, as if each drop were piloted by an enemy determined to reach him.

His hands had been clasped behind his back for an hour, separating only to pour and slam shots of scotch from the bottle atop his desk.

With the world summit underway, and the United States intent on dealing with heathens, Koster waited for a miraculous outcome. Otherwise, he'd commit treason. It'd be done in the name of righteousness, to save humanity, and ensure civility. That didn't soothe the friction in his chest, which increased by the minute.

Tomorrow morning he would initiate airstrikes on Moscow, Hong Kong, Tokyo, and Ho Chi Minh City.

His fabricated orders would be traced back to him. He'd be executed for high treason, or if he were lucky, he'd die in prison.

A rap sounded on his office door, startling him. Linda knew not to disturb him in here. When she poked her head in, his anger diminished. They'd been a great unit for more than four decades, and guilt for what his actions would mean for her weighted him the most.

"This just came for you," she displayed a white 8x11 Tyvek envelope. He often used them when mailing important documents, since they were waterproof and nearly impossible to tear.

"Just put it on the desk."

She did.

As she neared the door, he added, "I'll be out in a little while. Maybe we can watch a movie tonight?"

"That'd be nice." She closed the door.

She'd left the envelope face up, displaying the cursive handwriting on the front. He'd thought the use of ink pens to be a lost art. Curiosity about who still penned addresses intrigued him.

The package felt light, as if empty. No doubt it contained some parable about loyalty to country sent to him by a bitter, but cowardly, colleague.

Using his gold-plated letter opener, he slit the envelope bottom and extracted a single sheet of lined paper.

Scanning to the end, he identified the sender: Alex Cutler.

What in God's name does that bastard want?

With his temperature spiking, he poured, then gulped, a shot of scotch, and read the letter:

General Koster,

You know who I am, but you may not be aware that I know you, and the majority of your recent activities. I simply lacked the evidence and time to convince authorities of your plots. Also, I was preoccupied with my own agenda.

My recent tasks have absorbed over six billion dollars from the US treasury. I have completed my goal of saturating the globe with outposts, in an attempt to introduce state-of-the-art software and implement new training—both involving pirated access points and their macro servers.

I write this letter to notify you that your hopes of destroying the Lobby have no chance of success.

For the past three weeks, I have *not* trained a single person on how to detect pirated access points and macro servers. In actuality, I have trained thousands of the Lobby faithful on how to construct more efficient pirated access points and macro servers. These individuals are in turn sharing these techniques with the people they trust, creating an irreversible proliferation of free access to the Lobby.

I realize this is unwelcome news for you. My purpose is to give you the proper information, so you can make the best decision as to your next move. I no longer have a personal interest in your game, but there is a new fact, one you must accept: the Lobby is here to stay. It cannot be eradicated. So any criminal acts you commit now will be motivated by your own spite, with zero justification beyond cruelty and terrorism.

Again, I am sorry things happened as they did. My advice is to accept the changes and find a way to adapt.

Whether the Lobby is a gift from some deity, a machine created by the intellect of man, or the Devil's ultimate temptation will be for each of us to decide.

I have made my choice.

The world has changed. Are you mature enough to deal with it?

Sincerely,
Alex Cutler

General Koster stared at the page for what could have been a minute, maybe ten. He felt light, as if his surroundings didn't exist. He lacked thought. With a ferocity that had been building for days, he snatched the bottle of scotch by its neck and pitched it through his office window.

The crash of shattering glass and the ensuing tattering of shards on the wooden floor echoed as if in slow motion. The liquid pilots commenced their assault, wetting his front and the office around him.

Immobilized, he labored heavy breaths.

334

His office door flew open. "What's going on?" Linda asked.

Just the end of the world, dear, General Koster thought. *Just the end of the world.*

Chapter Forty-Six

Rebecca Trevino had always known that Alex Cutler would contact her. She layered *Inside Today* with verbiage directed at him. She never revealed her subliminal techniques to anyone, mainly because she didn't fully understand what worked and what didn't. She'd always acted on instinct. She would research a target and tailor programs to align with that target's past.

Since the onset of the death trips, every journalist had sought an interview with Alex Cutler. No one had succeeded. In her many fantasies of interviewing him, she'd never concocted any revelations as grand as the powder-keg story he shared with her from the grave.

The newsroom around her swarmed. In moments, she'd interrupt her network's coverage, which continued to speculate about the results of the biggest summit in world history. Intoxicating programming, but her bombshell would eradicate speculation with facts. Perhaps cause a few weak hearts to fail.

Along with a letter Alex asked her to read on air, he included multiple thumb-drives, and a three-inch stack of documentation. Alex Cutler might be dead to the world, but Rebecca appreciated his efforts to shape its future.

Her people were fact-checking the array of claims: proliferation of improved pirated access points, the assassination of Adisah Boomul, government involvement, backdoor conspiracies. All of which compiled a mountain of stories that she would be covering for the next two years, and discussing her entire life.

The majority of the lights around her dimmed, leaving her illuminated.

She saw the open hand, fingers counting down—five, four, three...

"Good evening, ladies and gentlemen. I am Rebecca Trevino, bringing you an exclusive report. The international summit taking place is set to continue for another six hours, but I have obtained the first bit of credible information as to its outcome. First, allow me to read you a letter from a man you all know, Alex Cutler, partner of the Broumgard Group, pioneer in the Lobby's design, a citizen for the modern era."

She allowed two seconds to pass, then continued.

"Hello, world. My name is Alex Cutler. For those who have heard of me, you may see me as a rich man or the face of a product or company. But I am a person, like any other. I try to live well, be decent, and make sense out of the life I was given.

"For me, making sense out of existence has been a difficult task. I've lived haunted by my brother's premature death, dealt with anxiety, and worried that life had no meaning.

"I'm oppressed by my own mortality and have spent my life avoiding inactivity, in hopes of thwarting reminders of its eventuality.

"I've come to believe that madness is the illusion of danger, pushed on us by those who govern.   Overwhelming fear has us living on a razor's edge. We spend each day so worried, we lack the separation needed to understand our own motivations or desires. We wake and fill our hours with anything to distract us from the existence we hold dear. Hypocrisy, apathy, and ignorance. Humans seem imbedded with a near disdain for other living creatures, for different ways of life, for granting forgiveness.

"It is mainly for these reasons that I ingested a time-release cyanide capsule before entering the Lobby today, and have added my name to the multitudes who have chosen a proven eternity over a hopeful one.

"I do not endorse any philosophy. I have made my choice. You will make yours. A great man once told me, 'We all walk our own path, and each one of them leads to a brighter future.' I believe that is true.

"Someday, technology may allow me to step back into your world. But for now, I'm going to wish you well, and enjoy my virtual heaven."

Author Notes

Wow. Well, thank you for taking this journey with me. Virtual Heaven was a long time coming. It's said we all have stories inside of us and VH has been in me since about 1994. I penned roughly twenty-five pages of it back then, but then let the story marinate for nearly twenty years. An accident had me limited in movement for a few weeks and I tackled VH for real.

It took five to seven years and much coaching until I felt comfortable putting the story on paper. It turned out darker than I had envisioned but I decided to leave it as it came out and hope to be merrier in my next book. In a perfect world, I would have waited another twenty years until I was a master at storytelling, but that's not how writing works. You have to make something quality and get it out there, mistakes and all.

The outlines to my next two novels, Live Like a God, and Dream Riders are written. I'm working through Live Like a God next. Mainly because it will be a lighter touch and had a more linear and easily defined conflict and story arc. Then it's onto Dream Riders, which will be another "ambitious" type of story, which is how I would categorize Virtual Heaven.

Over a ten year period, I received so much help with Virtual Heaven, I could never list them all. The first professional I sent VH to for critique gave me some harsh, but helpful advice. I knew VH was rough when I sent it to her. I knew my writing was even worse (at the time), and I told her not to worry about hurting my feelings. I asked her to tell me whatever would benefit me the most, in a step by step fashion, if possible.

She wrote me back and told me she and her husband had seventy years of experience in story craft and they had spent many hours discussing the themes and potential of Virtual Heaven. She told me I was an absolute genius at subtext.

Then I asked her what subtext was.

She really earned my respect when I reached her step by step instructions. Step One: take the next five years and learn how to write.

Ouch. But that is what I did. I hope the end result was something that entertained you. That's my goal with writing, to instill wonder and hope, in some cases, force personal inspections. If you enjoyed Virtual Heaven, please take a moment and leave me an Amazon review.

Other than that, I hope to meet you again, at the back of my next book. Since you made it here, we're closer as people, and that makes me happy.

www.ingramcontent.com/pod-product-compliance
Lightning Source LLC
Chambersburg PA
CBHW051223050326
40689CB00007B/776